Family Systems and Global Humanitarian
Mental Health

Laurie L. Charlés • Gameela Samarasinghe

Editors

Family Systems and Global Humanitarian Mental Health

Approaches in the Field

 Springer

Editors
Laurie L. Charlés
Family Therapist
Independent Researcher
Boston, MA, USA

Gameela Samarasinghe
Department of Sociology
University of Colombo
Colombo, Sri Lanka

ISBN 978-3-030-03215-9   ISBN 978-3-030-03216-6   (eBook)
https://doi.org/10.1007/978-3-030-03216-6

Library of Congress Control Number: 2018967260

This Springer imprint is published by the registered company Springer Nature Switzerland AG
The registered company address is: Gewerbestrasse 11, 6330 Cham, Switzerland

Contents

1   Introduction...   1
    Laurie L. Charlés and Gameela Samarasinghe

2   Through the Storm: How a Master's Degree Program
    in Marriage and Family Therapy Came to New Understandings
    After Surviving Both a Natural and a Human Disaster
    Within 6 Months 11
    Anne Rambo, Kara Erolin, Christine Beliard, and Flavia Almonte

3   Disasters Are Never Natural: Emerging Media to Map Lives
    and Territories at Risk 23
    Gonzalo Bacigalupe

4   Paved with Good Intentions? The Road of the Humanitarian
    Project of DNA Identification of the Missing in Post-Conflict
    Cyprus 35
    Anna M. Agathangelou and Kyle D. Killian

5   Undocumented and Unafraid: Resilience Under Forced
    Separation and Threat of Deportation 53
    Catalina Perdomo and Tiffany Adeigbe

6   "Do You Know the Tale of Cinderella?": Case Study of the Use of
    Metaphor and Proverbs with a Newlywed Syrian Couple
    in a Refugee Camp in Sidon, Lebanon 69
    Rima Zeid Nehmé

7   Between Family and Foreign Policy: A Gendered Approach
    to Understanding the Impact of Foreign Policy Failure on Human
    Security in the SIDS of the Caribbean 77
    Simone Young

8   Drawing in or Ruling Out "Family?" The Evolution of the Family
    Systems Approach in Sri Lanka 99
    Evangeline S. Ekanayake and Nilanga Abeysinghe

9   **Transvision: Unknotting Double Binds in the Fog of War** 123
    Douglas Flemons and Laurie L. Charlés

10 **The Role of Family and Culture in Extreme Adversity:
    Psychosocial Response to the Ebola Virus Disease (EVD)
    Epidemic in Guinea, West Africa** 143
    Neda Faregh, Alexis Tounkara, and Kemo Soumaoro

Index.. 165

Contributors

Nilanga Abeysinghe Faculty of Graduate Studies, University of Colombo, Colombo, Sri Lanka

Tiffany Adeigbe Our Lady of the Lake University, San Antonio, TX, USA

Anna M. Agathangelou York University, Toronto, ON, Canada

Flavia Almonte Nova Southeastern University, Fort Lauderdale, FL, USA

Gonzalo Bacigalupe Department of Counseling and School Psychology, College of Education, University of Massachusetts Boston, Boston, MA, USA

National Research Center for Integrated Natural Disaster Management (CIGIDEN), Santiago, Chile

Christine Beliard Nova Southeastern University, Fort Lauderdale, FL, USA

Laurie L. Charlés Family Therapist, Independent Researcher, Boston, MA, USA

Evangeline S. Ekanayake Faculty of Graduate Studies, University of Colombo, Colombo, Sri Lanka

Kara Erolin Nova Southeastern University, Fort Lauderdale, FL, USA

Neda Faregh Carleton University, Montreal, QC, Canada

Douglas Flemons Nova Southeastern University, Fort Lauderdale, FL, USA

Kyle D. Killian Capella University, Minneapolis, MN, USA

Rima Zeid Nehmé Clinical Psychologist, Beirut, Lebanon

Catalina Perdomo Our Lady of the Lake University, San Antonio, TX, USA

Anne Rambo Nova Southeastern University, Fort Lauderdale, FL, USA

Gameela Samarasinghe Department of Sociology, University of Colombo, Colombo, Sri Lanka

Kemo Soumaoro Universite Gamal Abdel Nasser de Conakry, Conakry, Guinea

Alexis Tounkara Independent Consultant, Conakry, Guinea

Simone Young Trinidad and Tobago Fulbright Humphrey Fellow 2016, Washington, D.C., USA

About the Editors

Laurie L. Charlés, PhD is a licensed marriage and family therapist and qualitative researcher based in Boston, Massachusetts (USA). She is a former faculty instructor and former director of the MFT Program at Our Lady of the Lake University, San Antonio, Texas, USA, and recent subject matter expert in family therapy with two psychotherapeutic interventions courses sponsored by the World Health Organization (WHO) and as a WHO Mental Health Officer during the Ebola virus disease (EVD) outbreak in West Africa in 2015, and with the UNODC in Vienna. Focused on scaling up family therapy practices for host country nationals in fragile states, Dr. Charlés' work as a scholar and practitioner includes the performance of qualitative rapid needs assessments and the supervision and training of psychiatrists, psychosocial workers, and family therapists for family therapy and psychosocial support programs in low- and middle-income countries. Dr. Charlés has both a PhD in family therapy from Nova Southeastern University and an MA in international relations from the Fletcher School of Law and Diplomacy at Tufts University. Her publications have appeared in *Family Process*, the *Journal of Marital and Family Therapy*, the *Journal of Family Therapy*, *Qualitative Inquiry*, and *Boston Globe Magazine*. She is a 2017–2018 Fulbright Global Scholar.

Gameela Samarasinghe, PhD is a clinical psychologist by training and is an associate professor of psychology in the Department of Sociology, University of Colombo, Sri Lanka. She initiated the design of and introduced the postgraduate diploma and master's in counseling and psychosocial support at the Faculty of Graduate Studies, University of Colombo. These postgraduate programs try to provoke thinking on alternative visions of what support to individuals and communities might look like while at the same time providing training on conventional counseling skills. She has been a member of various advisory groups developing strategies for post-conflict trauma in Sri Lanka and internationally. These include her role as a technical advisor to the Asia Foundation's Reducing the Effects and Incidents of Trauma (RESIST) Program and to the Victims of Trauma Treatment Program (VTTP), which are programs designed to support and treat torture survivors. She was a member of the international research team on "Trauma, Peacebuilding and

Development," run from the University of Ulster. She has written extensively on mental health and psychosocial wellbeing in Sri Lanka. She has been awarded many fellowships and has been the recipient of research grants including the Fulbright-Hays Senior Research Scholar Award (2004–2005) at Boston University and the Fulbright Advanced Research Award (2013–2014) at Columbia University's Mailman School of Public Health.

Chapter 1
Introduction

Laurie L. Charlés and Gameela Samarasinghe

The Transportability of Family Systems Approaches

In our first volume, our contributors shared their work and ideas about the philosophical and practice dilemmas brought when taking family therapy concepts and techniques to work in global mental health in humanitarian settings. Here, we build on those foundations, pushing them yet forward, with contributors who discuss methods and approaches that reach across a spectrum of family systems work. Ranging in locations across several continents, and from inter-, trans-, and cross-disciplinary traditions and educational backgrounds, our contributors' collective set of chapters bring to light the nature and utility of family systems approaches (FSAs) in the humanitarian space. A common theme in their work is the illustration of the transportability of family systems approaches, as applied to a clinical case, a community intervention, a supervisory dilemma, a training adaptation, or a foreign policy perspective.

Humanitarian situations are complex emergencies no matter where they occur, and distress and fragmentation of family systems are part of the landscape. Relationships are at risk of becoming fractured in emergency situations, and it is not unusual for that to result in, or further, psychosocial suffering. Nevertheless, family systems approaches can find unexpected utility in such chaos, as their form and substance can be designed to uniquely fit the conditions common in the humanitarian space.

As in the years of family therapy's origins, systems ideas have had wide, far-reaching applications. However, at its heart, the center of its sensibility, is the

L. L. Charlés (✉)
Family Therapist, Independent Researcher, Boston, MA, USA

G. Samarasinghe
Department of Sociology, University of Colombo, Colombo, Sri Lanka

© Springer Nature Switzerland AG 2019
L. L. Charlés, G. Samarasinghe (eds.), *Family Systems and Global Humanitarian Mental Health*, https://doi.org/10.1007/978-3-030-03216-6_1

powerful idea that people live and thrive in a network of relationships with others and that this sensibility is worth incorporating robustly in any effort at intervention. A further, compounded benefit to the transportability of the family systems approach is the unwavering declaration across communities that "family," as an idea and a collective unit, is worth our time and investment in terms of mental health and psychosocial support and in the promotion of community and societal resilience. This, too, is an ecological sensibility that defined the early years of the field.

Highlighting Family Systems as an Approach for Psychotherapeutic Intervention

Family, of course, among family therapy scholars and practitioners is understood as a critical buffer against stress and a protective factor in emergencies (Walsh, 2012). In this book, however, we do not focus specifically on the systemic family therapy clinical session, the professional who identifies herself or himself as a "family therapist," or the established interventions common to family therapy as it exists in a high-income country (HIC). Outside HICs and regions, there is typically no state regulation of family therapy as a profession and no routine existence of it as a choice of study in doctoral or masters' level graduate training nor a vast set of easily available resources such as books, articles, or manuals in a language other than English. Nevertheless, there is generous use of family systems ideas' application across low- and middle-income countries' (LMIC) context-, and in fragile-, conflict-, and violence-affected states (FCVs) and humanitarian settings (Charlés & Samarasinghe, 2016). This widespread relevance and utility is the point of our collection and the focus of the work that is illustrated by our contributors. It is *their* systemic methods and approaches in the humanitarian setting, whomever and wherever they are, that is at the heart of this book.

   This value of focusing so keenly on family and family systems, despite the challenges in doing so, is a theme that runs across each of our contributors' chapters. Family systems are important in Trinidad and Tobago. In Syria they are important; in refugee camps in Lebanon; in communities faced with the DNA identification of their missing loved one's remains in Cyprus; in vulnerable shantytowns in Chile; in marginalized communities in San Antonio, Texas; and in the midst of the 2014 Ebola virus disease outbreak in Guinea, West Africa, among graduate students in the midst of a hurricane in Fort Lauderdale or in a class role play in postwar Sri Lanka; in each case, family systems ideas are important. We can't name a place nor space that the idea of family, as a protective factor in complex emergencies, is contested. Rather, our attention here is to another question, a more critical and challenging one: *How* is a family systems approach useful in the humanitarian setting? How is that particular approach negotiated in practice? How is its stability and promotion, in terms of psychosocial health, a spark toward something useful for that community?

   In this book, our contributors address such questions, but not necessarily through the modality of the clinical session, although Nehmé (Chap. 6, this volume) and

Perdomo and Adeigbe (Chap. 5, this volume) do share their clinical work. However, the situations of migration in each country where their clinical work takes place (for Nehme, with Syrian refugees in Lebanon; for Perdomo and Adeigbe, with undocumented immigrants along the Texas-Mexico border) are quite different. Their chapters reflect the different ways that the fate of refugees across the globe is a topic of intense politicization in high-income countries and in LMICs. For example, "Low-income and middle-income countries [who] receive the largest number of asylum seekers and 80% of the world's refugees, yet these countries have few resources to address the substantial health, legal, educational, water, and food requirements of displaced populations" (Fazel, Karunakara, & Newnham, 2014), while "[s]ome high-income countries use immigration detention as a stepping-stone to forced repatriation" (Fazel et al., 2014).

What drives global mental health practice is not a focus on a particular population or geopolitical spot in the world, however, even though it often may seem that way. Global mental health practice is driven by "data about the disparities in mental health and its subsequent access by people across the globe, including disparities between and within states (countries), and between vulnerable groups within states" (Charlés & Bava, in press). In humanitarian settings, those disparities take on a different meaning, where communities are at risk of further fragmentation due to an ongoing or recent crisis. This pattern is well represented in some of our authors' work, illustrating both the highly contextualized nature of global mental health and also, how states and state behavior contribute to vulnerability.

Further, in this volume, our common focus is on the particular method and approach of a family systems intervention. However, that intervention is not necessarily a clinical, psychotherapeutic one. Systemic intervention in the context of global mental health and the humanitarian setting demands a hybrid approach, be it a training exercise or adaptation (Ekanayake & Abeysinghe, Chap. 8; Rambo et al., Chap. 2, this volume), a problem/solution set of cases particular to the humanitarian space (Bacigalupe, Chap. 3; Agathangelou & Killian, Chap. 4; Faregh, Tounkara & Soumaoro, Chap. 10; Flemons & Charlés, Chap. 4, this volume), or a historical injustice at the intersection of family psychosocial health and state policy, which is typically exacerbated in a humanitarian crisis (Young, Chap. 7; Bacigalupe, Chap. 3; Faregh, Tounkara & Soumaoro, Chap. 10, this volume).

In fact, it is the *approach*, not necessarily the identity of the professional (or his/her education or degree or license), which we want to highlight. This focus on process pays heed to the origins of the field of family therapy, which, of course, was constructed from and informed by global cross-, trans-, and interdisciplinary collaboration. What mattered back then, as now, is the *process* one engages in to understand a context, knowing the place, or space, and the situation from the inside. For those professionals not yet exposed to humanitarian settings or conditions in LMICs, immersing meaningfully in this "inside" may require both substantial unlearning and relearning. Many seasoned family therapy practitioners trained and operating primarily in HICs may find themselves encumbered by their traditional knowledge base when having to adapt to the everyday issues and factors specific to LMICS or FCVs. These factors change everything – not about the substance of systemic family therapy approaches, but, rather, about their form.

A Portfolio of Evidence: Intervention and Family Systems Approaches

In global mental health and humanitarian contexts, the conditions that threaten family psychosocial health and well-being are often uncontrollable, assiduous, and, sometimes, dangerous. Such conditions make experimental research on psychotherapeutic intervention challenging, though not impossible. For systemic family scholars and practitioners, who thrive in the "messy lived experience" of work with families, this is familiar territory. While perhaps not always so vivid as to be dangerous and unruly, family therapy is, as Lebow (2018) put it, "typically conducted under conditions far afield from those in the typical random controlled study" (p. 2). In global, humanitarian settings, such conditions are not only further afield – they are in a separate field altogether. What, then, is the role of evidence in family therapy approaches in a humanitarian context? How can critical matters of meaningful impact and sustainable scalability be addressed in such settings?

Whether it is through the efficacy of couple and family interventions (Pinsof & Wynne, 1995); addressing questions of outcomes with specific applications, populations, and settings (Liddle, 2016; Sexton, Datchi, Evans, LaFollette, & Wright, 2013; Sprenkle, 2002, 2012; Szapocznik, Schwartz, Muir, & Brown, 2012); or meta-analyses across large data sets or individual process-oriented case studies (Chenail et al., 2012), systemic family therapy interventions have been shown to be effective for a range of clinical issues. According to the World Health Organization, "Mental health strategies and interventions for treatment, prevention and promotion need to be based on scientific evidence and/or best practice, taking cultural considerations into account" (WHO Mental Health Action Plan, 2013–2020). The extant evidence base in family therapy is replete with such strategies and interventions, which are both "change mechanisms that underlie positive clinical outcomes" and "across methods and specific to certain approaches" (Stratton, 2016, p. 417).

The theoretical origins and ongoing development of systemic approaches illustrate a robust history of exploration with clients about whether the intervention they are part of is actually meeting their needs (Stratton, 2016). This history suggests, in addition to the extant evidence base, a particular appeal of systemic approaches, making them unique among a host of psychotherapeutic interventions. Essentially, research shows how much clients value it. For example, Chenail et al. (2012) conducted a qualitative meta-synthesis of 49 articles and from this created an "inductive grounded formal theory of CFT (couple and family therapy) client experience/evaluation/preferences" (as cited in Stratton, 2016, p. 259). Chenail et al. (2012) provided a rich, descriptive account that told in detail clients' reactions to their experience with systemic therapy. Of note is the client's appreciation for the therapeutic alliance in systemic therapy, how they felt they were fairly engaged in the therapy process, and how much they valued having the opportunity to hear what other family members contributed to the therapy (Chenail et al., 2012).

Such qualitative evidence that Chenail et al. (2012) contributed can be very useful beyond the clinic, as Langlois, Tunçalp, Norris, Askew, and Ghaffar (2018) recently pointed out:

> qualitative evidence is invaluable for national and local decision-makers and practitioners to understand factors influencing the implementation and scale-up of health policies and programmes. Qualitative data have proven essential in planning, developing and implementing health policies and interventions, including in low- and middle-income countries. Qualitative evidence also helps policy-makers and programme managers to make decisions about how to adapt a given WHO guideline and how to prioritize this guidance ... [It] is also aligned with a global movement towards the generation and use of a wide array of evidence in policy-making. (Langlois et al., 2018, p. 79)

Applying an evidence-based approach to policy-making, however, be it family systems intervention or another psychotherapeutic intervention may not be sufficiently meaningful to address the needs that are brought by the context in LMICs and FCVs. Nevertheless, critical questions must *always* be asked about how impactful treatments actually are and also how meaningful (Lebow, 2018). As Lebow (2018) noted, there are several reasons family therapy approaches are not easily captured in conventional experimental research. For example, clients may have more than one clinical condition alongside the presenting problem. We find this point particularly relevant with regard to conditions in LMICs and FCVs – although Lebow (2018) was not speaking of them. Of further interest, Lebow (2018) also pointed out that when therapists are likely to practice more than one "pure brand version" of therapy (p. 2), experimental research methods are unlikely to fit. We also find such conditions – practitioners who adhere to more than one brand or approach – pervasive, common, and actually quite amenable to practitioners working in LMICs and FCVs or in a humanitarian setting.

Evidence-based approaches to psychotherapeutic intervention, if done meaningfully, add to the credibility of all mental health and psychosocial support social science and can offer an important ethical and moral voice. However, our experience in global mental health and humanitarian settings suggests they are rarely sufficient on their own. Rather, such settings reflect the demand overall for a greater, more diverse "portfolio of approaches" (Schindler, Fisher, & Shonkoff, 2017).

Indeed, systemic approaches for families and communities in global mental health and humanitarian settings should include an expansive and generous definition of evidence. It should include approaches informed by evidence as well as multi-, trans-, and interdisciplinary innovation informed by best practice. It should include a broad set of systemic family clinicians and researchers, development and governance professionals proficient in foreign policy, and the international system in its application. Most significantly, it should include and engage client families and communities originating in the places where clinical research and projects are conducted. For us, this is the minimum requirement for a "portfolio of approaches" to global mental health and MHPSS in humanitarian settings. At the very least, it is what we can and should expect of our future discourse in the arena of global mental health – particularly when family systems approaches are the intervention. It is our belief that such a proposal is more typically suited to the circumstances on the ground of LMICS and FCVs, which demands a constantly inductive, sometimes unconventional sensibility to problem-solving, which may start with, but not necessarily end, with a randomized, controlled trial. The sensibility should be driven by circumstances on the ground and the people in the field who know them best. We offer this collection of chapters in that spirit.

Our Contributors and Their Methods and Approaches

Our contributors range in their professional backgrounds, and their work mirrors the interdisciplinary origins of systemic therapy. What is unique about their work, and a key focus of our book, are the authors' geopolitical locations on the globe, the set of conditions that define that setting as a humanitarian context of intervention, and how they address those conditions through the application of a family systems approach. As these authors illustrate, practitioners living and working in LMICs or FCVs are expert at managing the shifting dynamics or circumstances inside humanitarian corridors or state conditions. However, the questions they bring to the family therapy world are different, unlike the settings in HICs, where the humanitarian space may be a new character, the protagonist, and the unexpected arrival with whom one must learn to work in order for their FSA to be sustainable. Among all, it is the humanitarian space that is the common factor; all work must incorporate those conditions in the design if the approach is to be sustainable. When the systemic approach is brought forward by transdisciplinary professionals, it brings a new flavor to the method that challenges the status quo. Further, the challenges demand the attention of professionals beyond the clinical realm, as Simone Young, a foreign policy expert, demonstrates in her chapter.

Anne Rambo, Kara Erolin, Christine Beliard, and Flavia Almonte, in a chapter that is an approach to training and practice, discuss earnestly and with smart diligence how they had to review and revise very unexpectedly the contents of their master's degree program in marriage and family therapy. In Florida, where Rambo and her co-authors are based, the group found that they and their clients were faced with two emergencies, a hurricane and a shooting in a school, which made them question their own understanding of the relevance and appropriateness of the program they offered in their university to address the consequences of such tragedies.

Unlike in the USA where family systems therapy is an accepted and a used method to support individuals within family, Sri Lanka is beginning to discover its usefulness and potential with families in crisis situations. Evangeline Ekanayake and Nilanga Abeysinghe creatively and vividly present the challenges that proponents of family systems approaches are facing in Sri Lanka including their questions, doubts, and successful outcomes through the discussion of two cases. Most interestingly, and with aplomb and in robust detail, the authors point to how they gradually develop an approach more suitable to the Sri Lankan context, with the collaboration of trainees in a master's program and also, in a training program for counsellors in the hill country.

Cases are used in two other chapters as well. Rima Nehmé, and Catalina Perdomo and Tiffany Adeigbe, each share clinical examples of their use of family systems approaches with displaced families whose members are separated from each other: in Nehmé's case, with a newlywed family in a Syrian refugee camp in Lebanon, and in Perdomo and Adeigbe's case, with undocumented immigrants and their families near the Texas-Mexico border. Each of these two chapters present their approaches' differences, situated by the locality and the complexities it brings for each family. The case in Nehmé's chapter takes place in a camp in South Lebanon and demonstrates the challenges faced by the therapist to engage with a Syrian family. She eventually resorts, with the eye and ear of a seasoned clinician, to metaphors to get through to them and to help them think of ways of addressing their issues. In her chapter, the resentment to engage in therapy is felt in the way the family members or the client interacts with the therapist. This is in a sense not surprising given that therapy is not easily acceptable or an intervention that is sought in those parts of the world. The stigma associated with seeing a therapist is clearly evident. In Perdomo and Adeigbe's chapter, the objective is to argue that the work they are engaged in with immigrant clients in the USA is relevant to the wider global context. They also firmly emphasize the importance and effectiveness of brief or even a single therapy session in the case of a family member who has been deported or not living with the rest of the family.

The clinical examples share a connection, in spite of their geopolitical differences. In a humanitarian situation, families are not always together in spatial real time; further, in humanitarian contexts family members may not know where other family members are or if they are alive or dead, missing, or have forcibly disappeared. Nehmé's case, describing a session taking place inside a refugee camp, illustrates another spatial migratory issue commonly overlooked: forcibly displaced families living shoulder to shoulder in a refugee camp.

The chapter by Douglas Flemons and Laurie Charlés explores the challenges of the key role of expatriates who support host country nationals in LMICs and FCVs as supervisory consultants, and in this case, in Syria. One of the key roles for foreign expats in such settings is to provide continuing support via distance (Tol et al., 2011); many of the trainers who train in humanitarian settings such as ongoing, armed conflict are Western, foreign expats. Flemons and Charlés' chapter reflects how extraordinarily difficult such work can be, vicariously and in ways that defy the ease with which seasoned professionals are accustomed. Even if the technical preparation to do the work is present, it is not all that is required in the humanitarian setting. Being a skilled supervisor or "Approved" is not, in and of itself, enough (Green, Shilts, & Bacigalupe, 2001). Experiencing these difficulties shifts the implications of the effort to another dimension, disrupting established methods.

As in Rambo et al.'s chapter, Neda Faregh's, Alexis Tounkara's, and Kemo Soumaoro's chapter discusses a crisis situation of a different nature. The fast-spreading 2014 West African Ebola Virus Disease epidemic required quick thinking about how to treat the victims' illness and at the same time support their families. Programs therefore needed to address the needs of all in the form of psychosocial interventions considering the sociocultural, political, and historical factors that impacted on the survivors. These authors describe in vivid detail and with sensitive knowing, how all stakeholders operate "in reciprocal spheres of influence as they, individually and collectively, undertake the process of meaning-making along a continuum of shared values and the moral impetus, at home and abroad, that drive the humanitarian response to the needs and demands of those affected."

Gonzalo Bacigalupe's chapter addresses the use of technology in disasters in Chile. Bacigalupe vehemently proposes in his chapter that disasters are never natural as "they reflect and sustain social inequality." He very strongly points to the fact that invariably the most affected people are those who are the most vulnerable in terms of their access to basic goods for survival and security. He states that the "dominant approach to intervention is militaristic" as interventions tend to respond to the extreme immediate after effects of the disaster without being concerned about addressing the longer-term survival needs following the disaster. Bacigalupe, in his chapter, explores the use of media in Chile to develop more long-lasting, sustainable intervention through continued conversations on risk and resilience.

Anna Agathangelou and Kyle Killian's chapter focuses cogently and robustly on the professionals working on the DNA identification of missing persons in Cyprus. It points to the knowledge from DNA testing and to the consequences of this knowledge – not always positive – on the families of the missing. Closure is not necessarily reached. This reminds the editors of the challenges Sri Lanka is currently facing upon the establishment of the Office of Missing Persons where DNA testing is yet to be undertaken and there is no evidence of a plan to address the findings of DNA testing and certainly support a family systems approach when working with such families. The consequences of a disappearance have terrible impacts on the family and its functioning. Very often it is the main income earner who is missing. The roles and responsibilities of the family members change all of a sudden compounded by the emotions associated with the loss and living with uncertainty and insecurities.

Simone Young, on the other hand, discusses insecurities at a policy level, looking at conditions that are specific to the Small Island Developing States (SIDS) of the English-speaking Caribbean. Among the various insecurities in Caribbean SIDS, she focuses her discussion and skillful analysis on health care and particularly of women who are most important within family and community. She argues, with wisdom and a keen intellect, that "understanding the repercussions of policy failure on human security can facilitate earlier interventions to secure healthier futures, ensuring each person realises their full potential."

Family Therapy Disruptors: Mirroring the Beginning Story of Systemic Therapy

Systemic family therapy, as a practice, is typically framed in the literature in a way that befits a Western, Euro-American psychotherapeutic approach. However, the theoretical origins and underpinnings of systemic theory as a set of ideas are quite open and adaptable in nature in the literal sense and not so state-specific. Its beginnings were forged through a process of fits and starts, characterized by multi- and transdisciplinary professionals from across the globe, only some of them focused specifically on clinical work, yet all of them committed to work within the nature of mental process and how it was manifested in societies, in families, and in the nature of their communication with each other.

Fittingly, our collection of chapters is presented in a key moment of mental health and psychosocial support and collaboration in the globalized world. Global mental health and the role family systems approaches play brings something of a return to the origins of the field. The ideas presented here represent what we see as a fortuitous transformation of family therapy practice, through its application in ways that are familiar, yet also unexpected, new, and innovative – a disruption to the status quo in every sense of the word.

In the best way, the use of systemic approaches in global mental health and humanitarian settings, the process by which they find relevance, is a disruption to and innovation for the established traditions of family therapy practice. That is, the approaches bring a new category of information to the field, requiring further empirical examination including continued observation, direct experience, and thoughtful discussion. We have strived to produce a book that takes a closer look at that information, focusing on the application of systems ideas to family psychosocial health across the types of settings where humanitarian intervention is a recent or ongoing intervention. Circling back to the origins of the field of family therapy and its underpinnings, in this book our contributors' work brings forward a new set of questions about what it means to be practicing family systems approaches in the world today.

References

Charlés, L., & Bava, S. (in press). Systemic family therapy and global mental health: Reflections on professional development and training. In M. Rastogi & R. Singhe (Eds.) (K. Wampler Series Editor), *Handbook of systemic family therapy* (Vol. IV). New York, NY: Wiley.

Charlés, L., & Samarasinghe, G. (2016). *Family therapy in global humanitarian contexts: Voices and issues from the field.* New York, NY: Springer.

Chenail, R. J., St. George, S., Wulff, D., Duffy, M., Wilson Scott, K., & Tomm, K. (2012). Clients' relational conceptions of conjoint couple and family therapy quality: A grounded formal theory. *Journal of Marital and Family Therapy, 38*(1), 241–264.

Fazel, M., Karunakara, U., & Newnham, E. A. (2014). Comment: Detention, denial, and death: Migration hazards for refugee children. *Lancet Global Health, 2*(6), PE313–PE314.

Green, S., Shilts, L., & Bacigalupe, G. (2001). When approved is not enough. *Journal of Marital and Family Therapy, 27*(4), 515–525.

Langlois, E., Tunçalp, O., Norris, S., Askew, I., & Ghaffar, A. (2018). Qualitative evidence to improve guidelines and health decision-making. *Bulletin of the World Health Organization, 96*(2), 79–79A.

Lebow, J. (2018). Editorial: Effectiveness in couple and family therapy research. *Family Process, 57*(2), 271–227.

Liddle, H. A. (2016). Multidimensional family therapy: Evidence base for transdiagnostic treatment outcomes, change mechanisms and implementation in community settings. *Family Process, 55*, 558–576. https://doi.org/10.1111/famp.12243

Pinsof, W. M., & Wynne, L. C. (1995). Toward progress research: Closing the gap between family therapy practice and research. *Journal of Marital & Family Therapy, 26*, 1–8.

Schindler, H. S., Fisher, P. A., & Shonkoff, J. P. (2017). From innovation to impact at scale: Lessons learned from a cluster of research-community partnerships. *Child Development, 88*(5), 1435–1446.

Sexton, T. L., Datchi, C., Evans, L., LaFollette, J., & Wright, L. (2013). The effectiveness of couple and family based clinical interventions. In M. Lambert (Ed.), *Bergin and Garfield's handbook of psychotherapy and behavior change* (pp. 587–639). Hoboken, NJ: Wiley.

Sprenkle, D. (2002). *Effectiveness research in marital and family therapy*. Alexandria, VA: American Association for Marital and Family Therapy.

Sprenkle, D. H. (2012). Intervention research in couple and family therapy: A methodological and substantive review and an introduction to the special issue. *Journal of Marital and Family Therapy, 38*, 3–29.

Stratton, P. (2016). *The evidence base of family therapy and systemic practice*. Warrington, UK: Association for Family Therapy.

Szapocznik, J., Schwartz, S. J., Muir, J. A., & Brown, C. H. (2012). Brief strategic family therapy: An intervention to reduce adolescent risk behavior. *Couple and Family Psychology: Research and Practice, 1*(2), 134–145.

Tol, W. A., Patel, V., Tomlinson, M., Baingana, F., Galappatti, A., Panter-Brick, C., … van Ommeren, M. (2011). Research priorities for mental health and psychosocial support in humanitarian settings. *PLoS Medicine, 8*(9), e1001096.

Walsh, F. (2012). Family resilience: Strengths forged through adversity. In F. Walsh (Ed.), Normal family processes: Growing diversity and complexity (pp. 399-427). New York, NY, US: Guilford Press.

Chapter 2
Through the Storm: How a Master's Degree Program in Marriage and Family Therapy Came to New Understandings After Surviving Both a Natural and a Human Disaster Within 6 Months

Anne Rambo, Kara Erolin, Christine Beliard, and Flavia Almonte

On September 11, 2018, a massive hurricane predicted to be a category 5 hit Florida – greatly affecting our MS in MFT program then in the beginnings of the fall semester and touching the lives of both students and faculty. Our program faculty were called upon to respond in unprecedented ways, and our students responded in ways we did not expect. There was intense national media coverage and long-term recovery which did not receive so much media attention. Our students were all affected, to varying degrees, and some experienced more trauma than others.

Almost exactly 6 months later, on February 14, 2018, a tragic school shooting affected many of our students and graduates just as directly. The resulting whirlwind of community outrage and response challenged our program to respond in new and different ways again. Once again there was intense national media coverage and, to varying extents, direct personal trauma experienced by our students.

Our program has a preexisting commitment to community involvement and social justice, which was both reinforced and altered by these double disasters. We came to new understandings of the importance of shared community, strengthened by an understanding of privilege and position. We have always worked together as a program for social justice, but now we work together in expanded and at times more overtly political ways. We have learned that the political and the personal are intertwined and that therapy is inevitably a political activity as well as an interpersonal one.

A. Rambo (✉) · K. Erolin · C. Beliard · F. Almonte
Nova Southeastern University, Fort Lauderdale, FL, USA
e-mail: rambo@nova.edu

© Springer Nature Switzerland AG 2019
L. L. Charlés, G. Samarasinghe (eds.), *Family Systems and Global Humanitarian Mental Health*, https://doi.org/10.1007/978-3-030-03216-6_2

Voices in this Chapter

This chapter represents the combined, but also individual and different, experiences of three faculty and one student. In order of our appearance in this chapter, Dr. Anne Rambo is the faculty director of the Nova Southeastern University (NSU) master's in marriage and family therapy program (MS in MFT), and the onsite clinical supervisor for the PROMISE program, a program designed to interrupt the school to prison pipeline. She identifies as what McGoldrick et al. (2005) describes as Anglo-American. Dr. Christine Beliard is the faculty director of the doctoral program but also teaches in the master's program and is a mentor to many master's students. Her areas of interest include diversity training and racial trauma. She identifies as African-American. Dr. Kara Erolin teaches in the master's program as well and identifies as Korean-American raised mostly in the United States. She is certified in psychological first aid and critical incident stress management. She has primarily trained therapists and first responders to provide trauma-based services to survivors, a skill the program needed this year. Flavia Almonte is a master's student graduating in 2018. She is a AAMFT Minority Fellow, who identifies as Afro-Latina and Muslim-American. She is an active member of the MFT Club, Omicron Delta Kappa honor society, and the second-year WhatsApp community. Together we will share our experiences and reactions to two back-to-back catastrophes, one from natural and the second from human causes, which affected us all.

Before the Storms

The stated mission of our COAMFTE-accredited Master's in Marriage and Family Therapy program is to train family therapists to work in agencies, private practice, schools, and other settings. Our program has historically been focused on clinical skills training. Yet it is also a part of our mission to train family therapists to work in culturally sensitive ways and to work for social justice in both our local and national community. This dual mission, along with our location in South Florida, has attracted to our program a very diverse student body, from many geographic locations in the United States and from other countries as well.

We partner with the Broward County Schools district, the sixth largest school district in the United States, and one which serves 271,500 students from 204 different countries, speaking 191 different languages (www.browardschools.com). Our master's interns are an integral part of the PROMISE program, an innovative school district project which has interrupted the school to prison pipeline, reducing schoolhouse arrests by 63% (www.browardintervention.org), reducing overall suspensions by 25% (www.browardintervention.org), and reducing recidivism (defined as the student being suspended twice in the same school year) from 38% to 9% at the high school level (Mendel, 2018). We have an ongoing equine family therapy program, which provides services to children in foster care, women in shelters who are recovering from domestic violence, and other survivors of trauma. Our master's level graduate interns work in agencies, schools, hospitals, and residential treatment centers, in addition to Stable Place, our equine family therapy training center.

Our work at the PROMISE program is based on culturally informed solution-focused brief therapy as defined by McDowell, Knudson-Martin, and Bermudez (2017), which bridges the relationship between culture, societal context, and meaning. In this model, therapists enter the client's world by exploring their experiences and the way that they create meaning. Therapists invite clients to examine their societal context and its relationship to the presenting problems, as well as the ways in which these systems impact their lives (McDowell et al., 2017). This allows clients to give new meaning to their situation and to expand the search for solutions to the wider societal context (McDowell et al., 2017). At the PROMISE program, therapists take on the role of cultural brokers in order to include the wider societal context. Kelly (2016) describes this role as a sort of negotiator, who bridges cultural gaps between worldviews and values, experiences and contexts, power differences, and perceived distance. They do this by connecting students and their families to school district resources and information, assisting them in finding allies while learning how to advocate for themselves, helping parents navigate the larger system of the school district, and building relationships between the students, their families, and school officials. Most of our students rotate through the PROMISE program at one point or another during their training, and these ideas are infused throughout the curriculum. Every syllabus in every class reflects attention to diversity and a strength-based focus.

In addition, our students join together through the Marriage and Family Therapy Club, a social organization to which all students belong, and Omicron Delta Kappa, our branch of the international honor society for marriage and family therapists. These organizations sponsor toy drives for low-income schools during the holiday season and the annual College Brides Walk to raise awareness of domestic violence, as well as other community-building workshops and social events. The master's and doctoral program coordinators (Rambo and Beliard), together with students, host a monthly meeting, Courageous Conversations, to discuss issues of the day such as immigration and police shootings which affect both our students and our clients.

We would have said, before the dual crises happened, that the Master's in Marriage and Family Therapy students had a strong sense of community. This was shortly to be tested in ways we would not have imagined.

Category 5 Hurricane: Separation and Community

On August 21, 2018, we began our fall semester. By August 30, the National Weather Service was reporting Hurricane Irma approaching Florida. We were initially reassuring with students; our location is well inland, and most reported hurricanes cause us a few rainy days, if that. But by September 4, Irma was upgraded to a category 5 hurricane. Hurricanes are coded on a scale of 1–5, with 5 being the most severe and dangerous (www.weather.gov). To allow students, faculty, and staff to make storm preparations, Nova Southeastern University closed effective September 6. Thereafter, our communications with students were primarily through Facebook, email, and text, until the storm was over. By September 8, 5.6 million people had been ordered to evacuate, a quarter of the state's population, and the rest were encouraged to either evacuate or shelter in place in a secure location. All our MS in MFT students had either find secure shelter or relocate, many out of state and some out of the country, until the storm was over. Many of our first-year MS students had only moved to Florida a couple of weeks before and knew no one except those faculty and other students they had met at the orientation.

We were all in this storm together – except we weren't, because different levels of privilege and different positions affected how the hurricane was experienced. Most faculty were able to stay in their own homes, although some living near the ocean evacuated. This was however an individual decision. Students living in university housing were not allowed to make the decision; out of an abundance of caution, they were evacuated to shelters. International students faced the dilemma of either returning to their home countries and then possibly facing difficulties getting back into this country or ignoring the pleas of frightened family members back home. Rambo remembers and students confirm that every time we turned on a television set, we heard predictions that Florida would be destroyed (Rambo, 2018).

In this emergency, students banded together through social media. Even when the power was out, most students could get texts on their phones. The first- and second-year MS in MFT students had set up WhatsApp chat groups, and this became a lifeline for students sitting in the dark in shelters. Students could and did receive these texts not only locally but also in other states and other countries to which they had evacuated. As faculty, we (Rambo, Beliard, and Erolin) were not part of these groups, but we (especially Rambo as MS in MFT program director) constantly texted to individual students who would then repeat the information we shared to the whole group though the WhatsApp program. For the faculty, it was an education in the importance of social media in building community; for the students, it was a lifeline and a firsthand experience of increased cohesion. The information shared ranged from the very practical (which stores had not yet run out of bottled water; what to tell the international students' office about going home to another country for the duration) to the philosophical (how the wealthier were still treated differently in shelters and how privilege affects the ability to evacuate) (Rambo, 2018). Rambo remembers sitting in the dark with her husband, in the closet (a safe place during a hurricane), texting students for hours, with messages sent to individuals and also conveyed to the WhatsApp group. Her husband commented it felt like the entire MS in MFT program was in the closet too. Beliard remembers how only the week before, her students had been concerned about how to help survivors of Hurricane Hugo in Texas; now they were the ones in danger, not the helpers. Erolin remembers evacuating to Atlanta, with her partner and young child, and being on the road thinking the line of stranded cars looked like a disaster movie, while texting her cell phone number to students in need. Almonte remembers the WhatsApp group changing from a way for students to keep in touch about assignments, to a caring community which helped students find places to stay and to find support when alone. An example forwarded to Rambo went like this:

Student 1: I am an international student, and I don't know where to go and what should I do; I don't want to go into a shelter.
Student 2: Are you okay with cats? You can come stay with me – I have hurricane shutters.
Student 1: You would let me do that really? But you don't even know me that well! P.S. I love cats.
Student 2: Hey, we're in the same human development class. And the same program. Bring a bedroll.

The South Florida area largely escaped the worst of Hurricane Irma. We had a few days to a week of loss of power, but nothing compared to the devastation experienced by Puerto Rico, the Virgin Islands, St. Martin, and St. Barthelemy (Keneally, 2017). The community we built through the experience became a force for activism, and our students rallied to raise money for the affected areas and to be a voice for hurricane survivors at our national conference (Rambo, 2018). Still, our students were affected by the mandatory absence from campus and the repair work necessary to houses and apartments after such a storm. None of our students dropped out due to the hurricane, to our amazement, and only a couple took advantage of the university's offer to withdraw from a class without penalty to reduce course load during the reconstruction process. The most immediate effects were perhaps the increased sense of community, especially for the first-year MS in MFT group (Rambo, 2018) and increased faculty respect for the communal voice of students. There was also frustration, in particular, that we could not do more to help those in Puerto Rico who suffered from back-to-back hurricanes. Hurricane Maria hit Puerto Rico 10 days after Hurricane Irma; an estimated 300,000 left Puerto Rico to go to Florida between or after the 2 hurricanes (Dixon, 2018). This exodus was certainly reflected in our client case load and in the community around us. Almonte remembers how every class began to begin with a "check-in" – Is everyone okay? How is everyone doing? – and how this created a more personal relationship between faculty and students. Faculty worked with students to decide how work would be made up and how to adjust to the new schedule; the program director lobbied to get students extra financial aid to cover hurricane expenses. We were dealing with the aftermath together. But we were shortly to be tested again.

A Hail of Bullets: The Parkland School Shooting

On Valentine's Day 2018, a 19-year-old who had been expelled entered Marjory Stoneman Douglas High School with an assault rifle and opened fire. As the shooting unfolded, Beliard was teaching a couple therapy class for master's students; suddenly a master's student screamed out loud. The student had received a text from her younger brother, telling her that he was hiding in a classroom and expected to be shot any minute. He was texting to say he loved her and to say goodbye. Students and faculty alike rushed to news media to follow the unfolding events. This student's brother survived unhurt, though traumatized; 17 at Marjory Stoneman Douglas High School were killed, however, and 16 injured.

The resulting outcry galvanized national attention, resulting in extensive media coverage, a CNN Town Hall media event featuring surviving students, and nationwide school walkouts by high school students. Marjory Stoneman Douglas High School is about 25 min away from our campus; one of our recent MS in MFT graduates is the family counselor there (and is a direct survivor of the shooting), a number of our students and graduates live in the immediate area, and as we learned over the next few days, some of our students had family members at the school during the shooting (all survived). Two of our recent graduates are very involved in faith-based work (with the Latter Day Saints (Mormon) and Jewish communities, respectively) and they were directly affected when members of their communities were killed. In addition, all of our students working in our school-based PROMISE program were directly affected by fear, mandatory "code black" drills (drills where those in a school practice hiding from a school shooter), and increased responsibility to assess for risk when seeing troubled teens.

Students and faculty alike were motivated to immediately reach out to the school district and the community. We offered free services for families, students, teachers, and staff, both at Stable Place (our equine family therapy location) and at our campus-based family therapy clinic, sent response teams to assist at the school district's request the day after the shooting, provided longer-term support services to school bus drivers and other affected personnel, and, through PROMISE, stepped up our efforts to screen children suspended for threats or for violent behavior. We reached out to personally support our graduates, the family counselor, and the faith-based family therapists in their work.

Almonte remembers the frustration students felt about not being able to do more. In the immediate aftermath, the school district had so many volunteers; many of our students were sent home, as there was an abundance of licensed professionals who volunteered as well. Erolin remembers students expressing a strong desire to help, but not knowing how that might be possible or how much they could bear. In such a crisis, there is both the immediate desire to help and the simultaneous experience of vicarious trauma. Shortly after the shooting, one of our graduates worked with an understandably distraught mother to help the mother be able to calmly wash her child's head, to see if her child was injured or, as it turned out, "merely" spattered with the blood and brains of her classmates. The graduate was able to talk the parent through the experience but afterward came to talk with a faculty member (Rambo) to process her own shock and horror. Rambo was able to help the graduate in a calm way but afterward had to privately cry before being able to drive home. At every level there is trauma as well as compassion.

In response, given her background and training, Erolin agreed to present a training in the area of psychological first aid (PFA) and responses to emergency. The training was so well received it was repeated, and the second time school district personnel and area mental health professionals attended as well.

PFA is a crisis intervention for individuals who have been exposed to a traumatic event to promote healing. It assumes that people will experience a range of reactions immediately following a traumatic event, some causing enough distress to interfere with adaptive coping (The National Child Traumatic Stress Network, 2006). PFA is considered by disaster mental health experts to be the "acute intervention of choice" and meets four basic standards: (a) it is consistent with research evidence on risk and resilience following trauma, (b) it is applicable and practical in field settings, (c) it is appropriate across developmental levels, and (d) it is culturally informed (National Child Traumatic Stress Network, 2006, p. 5). It can be delivered by professionals and nonprofessionals, and first responders provide a calm, caring, and supportive environment to set the stage for recovery. PFA is utilized globally but was less familiar to our US faculty and students than it may be in other global contexts.

The goal of PFA is to provide an environment of safety, calm, connectedness, self-efficacy/empowerment, and hope, which have been identified as core principles for any intervention following disaster and mass violence (Hobfoll et al., 2007). Promoting safety first involves making sure individuals are physically safe and helping them find ways to meet basic needs. First responders also facilitate psychological functioning through calming and comforting, by being a compassionate presence, and through active listening while not pushing for information, normalizing, being flexible and supportive, and offering stress management techniques (Substance Abuse and Mental Health Services Administration, 2005). Connectedness is promoted by helping survivors contact friends and loved ones and keeping families together. First responders help individuals help themselves, by engaging survivors toward meeting their own needs. Instilling a sense of hope is achieved by providing services to help people get their lives back in place, helping them work through red tape, and highlighting and building upon peoples' strengths (Hobfoll et al., 2007).

Thus, PFA is a good fit with the strength-based models with which our students are already familiar. Yet the trainings provided an important reminder that family therapists are there to assist and support, not magically fix the situation, which in such a tragic case can only be ameliorated, not rectified. Students and faculty who attended the trainings reported a better appreciation of the importance of pacing, offering the opportunity to talk but not pressing, and understanding the long-term resolution of trauma over time. Students were reassured that if their help was not needed at this time, there would be plenty for us all to do over the months and years to come. This helped both our graduate students and the affected teachers and counselors compose themselves in patience for a long trajectory of healing.

That healing was not to be uninterrupted by political turmoil, however. The school shooting immediately attracted national attention, in part through the political activism of the Stoneman Douglas survivor students, who channeled their trauma into a crusade for gun control (Grinberg & Yan, 2018). Many of our students and faculty marched with the Stoneman Douglas students; both students and graduates attended the CNN Town Hall on the topic. The National Rifle Association and other political organizations which oppose gun control almost immediately attacked the

PROMISE program, and statements were made that the reduction in schoolhouse arrests brought about by the PROMISE program had prevented the school shooter from being arrested before the shooting (French, 2018). These allegations were based on misconceptions – the school shooter had actually been arrested several times, the school district had expelled the school shooter, and the school shooter was at no point a client of the PROMISE program (Travis, 2018). PROMISE was primarily designed to reduce the schoolhouse arrests of students of color (www. browardintervention.org), and the school shooter, like all school shooters to date, was a White male.

Yet the allegations persisted. Some of our students became involved in arguments about this online, on Facebook in particular, and program directors (Rambo and Beliard) had to caution students not to attempt to speak for the school district, even in fervent defense. Seeing firsthand how facts do not always affect people's responses was a political education for our students, many of whom found themselves galvanized into increased political action.

Through these difficult times, the WhatsApp group for students continued to be an online support group. Students shared information about the shootings, ways to help, and concern for those affected. Almonte remembers a student posting about attending the funeral of a beloved high school teacher, who had been killed trying to protect students. Faculty continued to take time in class for "check-ins," expressing personal concern and inviting students to share.

Multiple Levels of Trauma

Everyone experiences the storms of life, and all of our students and faculty experienced these calamitous events. Yet all did not experience them equally. Almonte remembers during the hurricane how issues of privilege were very apparent and were openly discussed among the student body, as some students had the financial and family resources to easily evacuate the hurricane, and others did not have such resources.

After the school shootings, racial issues became an increased topic of conversation. Beliard, Cunningham, Fontus, and Moye (2018) has written about the daily microaggression therapists of color experience. Students of color in South Florida also deal daily with the national and local experience of racial violence, in particular the Trayvon Martin and Charles Kinsey shootings, which took place here in Florida (www.circleoffathers.org). Based on incidents between 2014 and 2017, you are eight times more likely to be shot by police in Florida if you are Black (Montgomery, 2017). Charles Kinsey was himself a therapist, working with a client at the time he was shot, and Rambo remembers the alarm this triggered for students working in the community. Rambo also noted students of color were for the most part less surprised about the unfairness of post Stoneman Douglas allegations against PROMISE. They had not had the luxury of ignoring past misinformation campaigns and acute fear reactions. Beliard reports in a dissertation group she runs for women of color that students expressed pain about the national attention paid to the Parkland shootings, as opposed to other shootings which affected people of color. The experience of feeling hopeless to help was also not new. Conversations in class and in our Courageous Conversations increased, specifically about the "multilayered" (p. ix) nature of trauma (Kolayjian & Paloutzian, 2009) and the way in which trauma affects us all individually, but also affects our communities, our social networks, and our historical kinship frameworks.

Aftermath of Both Disasters

These experiences of trauma changed faculty and students alike. As a community, we experienced a renewed dedication to our field. The need for culturally sensitive family therapists to work with survivors of trauma could not be more apparent to us. We saw intensified commitment to the PROMISE program, to Stable Place equine therapy with trauma survivors, and to community service in general. Almonte describes a new sense of pride in being a family therapist, as she now sees the profession as incorporating a response to the whole system and to the entire communities in need.

Faculty came away with increased respect for the cohesive community which students have developed on their own and for the power of social media. Recently, the MS program director (Rambo) was told by several students of a student unhappy with a grade, who was posting negative comments about an instructor on the first-year students' WhatsApp group chat. Previously, she might have intervened with the student and discussed professional guidelines for appropriate use of social media. Now, remembering how the students were there in the dark for each other in a way faculty alone could not be, she chose instead to simply counsel the concerned students on how to support their colleague through these struggles. It all worked out. We were all moved, individually and collectively, by the Stoneman Douglas students caught up in the shooting who spent their last moments or what they feared might be their last moments texting and Instagramming their parents and siblings with messages of love. Social media is how this generation connects, and the faculty has developed a new appreciation of that reality.

Curriculum changes were also made. Principles of psychological first aid (PFA) and responding to natural disasters and other traumas have become a standard part of our curriculum. One of the PFA trainings was videotaped and is publicly available to view on our program website (www.cahss.nova.edu). We made significant changes to our International Perspectives in Counseling and Therapy course to address global mental health in humanitarian contexts, including trauma, ambiguous loss, and resilience. As a part of the requirements, students now complete the National Child Traumatic Stress Network (NCTSN) Psychological First Aid Online course. Adding this material to our family therapy curriculum both better prepares us for crisis, and connects us more intensively with those working in the field worldwide. Our students were surprised to learn how widespread the use of PFA is

globally (http://www.who.int/mental_health/publications/guide_field_workers/en/);
they responded positively to learning about the techniques and would like to see
them incorporated in more classes.

Our involvement in the community, already extensive, has deepened. A few
months after the school shootings, we were contacted by the Humane Society of
Broward County to provide PFA training to volunteer workers in the Animal
Assisted Therapy Program. Several animal assisted dog teams were on-site the day
after the shootings and they have continued to provide services to survivors for several months post-crisis. They reached out to us to get training in how to be better
prepared as first-responders in traumatic situations, and to receive support services
for themselves. We continue to provide equine family therapy at no charge for survivors and affected family members as well. We remain integrally involved with the
school district with the PROMISE program. The school district has recently hired
additional family counselors, and set up a permanent Resilience Center near the
Stoneman Douglas campus, staffed with these family counselors. The Resilience
Center offers family counseling, spiritual care from clergy, language translation as
needed, and referrals to community services (www.browardschools.com/crisissup-
port). Our graduates are among those employed by this center.

In addition to this type of community involvement, students have become accustomed to seeing faculty take an active part in the political issues of the day, as when
Beliard spoke on the record to People magazine about responses to school shootings
and Rambo attended town hall meetings in defense of PROMISE, covered by
national media. This has led to an increased awareness of the political aspects of
therapy, which shows up in classroom conversations and in clinical training.
Almonte describes seeing this as a logical outgrowth of the faculty's caring for and
commitment to students. Students have become more politically active as well,
marching in gun control demonstrations with the Stoneman Douglas survivors, participating in online debates, and attending town hall meetings including those seen
on CNN. Almonte, together with another student (Natacha Celsis), presented in a
public forum after the school shootings, and brought attention to the need to involve
voices from people of color.

Faculty continues to spend more time in classes on processing recent events, and
on the need for self-care. Some of the experience of hierarchy between faculty and
students seemed to lessen, as we definitely went through these storms together, and
we are now fighting on the same side in the resulting battles for needed services.
Our doctoral students have always seen themselves and been seen as colleagues of
the faculty, but in our much larger MS in MFT program, with beginning students,
there may have been more of a distinction in the past. Rambo can remember when
she would have hesitated to give out her personal cell phone number to incoming
MS in MFT students; now she finds it routine to get a midnight text from a master's
student, "just checking in".

Some students have reported symptoms of trauma, both direct and vicarious.
Almonte experienced symptoms soon after her internship site began accepting and
directly treating Stoneman Douglas survivors. She sought support from her clinical
supervisor and from other faculty. One faculty member (Douglas Flemons) with

training in hypnosis held a processing group specifically for those experiencing such vicarious trauma. There are also student counseling services available through the university. Our students have shown tremendous strength in coping with these consecutive traumatic events while reaching out to help others.

Changes to the Landscape

Both the hurricane and the school shooting have permanently altered our physical and social landscape. Some of these changes are obvious, some are subtle, but all are part of our "new normal" (Walsh, 2015, p. x).

Now, 8 months after the hurricane, the Florida landscape has altered and adjusted. Oak trees were uprooted and lost, but palm trees bend, and most survived. Beach erosion caused by Irma will leave us more vulnerable to the next hurricane yet has also created new dunes and interesting inlets (Hamilton, 2017). The number of Puerto Ricans who have moved to Florida is now over a million, and this has permanently altered the political and cultural landscape of the state (Alvarez, 2017). Many parts of Puerto Rico are still without power (Alvarez, 2017).

Since the Stoneman Douglas shootings, an estimated 185,000 US high school students, in all 50 states, have participated in walkouts to demand gun control (Grinberg & Yan, 2018). It will be interesting to see how this generation now coming of age will alter the political landscape, with their early exposure to activism. The building in which the shootings occurred will be torn down, so no one has to reenter it; but the larger school campus remains and near it the new resilience center for family counseling.

For us, here on campus, much looks the same. Our campus once again sparkles in the sunshine, and palm trees abound. Our master's students walk to and from classes busy with everyday activities like checking their phones and deciding where to have lunch. But for us also, nothing will ever be exactly the same. Even after the "MSD Strong" T-shirts, sold to raise money for the Stoneman Douglas survivors, are not as commonly seen as they are now, faculty and students will remember the experiences we shared. Our master's in family therapy mission statement is the same, shaped in large part by administrative and accreditation concerns (www. cahss.nova.edu). But our actual sense of mission now comes much closer to Desmond Tutu's description of community: "My humanity is bound up in yours, because we can only be human together" (www.tutufoundation.org).

References

Alvarez, L. (2017, November 17). A great migration from Puerto Rico is set to transform Orlando. *New York Times*. Retrieved April 29, 2018 from www.nyt.com

Beliard, C., Cunningham, P., Fontus, F., & Moye, D. (2018). Therapists of color: Surviving long enough to keep fighting. *Journal of Systemic Therapies, 37*(1), 18–26.

Dixon, D. (2018, January 2). Florida has handled nearly 300,000 Puerto Rican refugees since Hurricane Maria; Gov. Scott says state will welcome more. *The St. Augustine Record*. Retrieved April 29, 2018 from www.staugustine.com

French, D. (2018, March 2). Did lax Obama era school discipline policies enable the Parkland shooter? *The National Review*. Retrieved April 29, 2018 from www.nationalreview.com

Grinberg, E., & Yan, H. (2018, April 16). A generation raised on gun violence sends a loud message to adults: Enough. *CNN*. Retrieved April 29, 2018 from www.cnn.com

Hamilton, H. (2017, October 6). Before and after: Coastal changes caused by Hurricane Irma. *United States Geological Survey*. Retrieved April 29, 2018 from www.usgs.gov

Hobfoll, S. E., Watson, P., Bell, C. C., Bryant, R. A., Brymer, M. J., Friedman, M. J., … Ursano, R. J. (2007). Five essential elements of immediate and mid-term mass trauma intervention: Empirical evidence. *Psychiatry, 70*(4), 283–315.

Kelly, S. (2016). *Diversity in couple and family therapy: Ethnicities, sexualities, and socioeconomics*. Toronto, ON: Praeger/Kelly.

Keneally, M. (2017, September 11). Breaking down Hurricane Irma's damage. *ABC News*. Retrieved April 29, 2018 from www.abcnews.com

Kolayjian, A., & Paloutzian, R. (2009). *Forgiveness and reconciliation: Pathways to conflict transformation and peace building*. New York, NY: Springer.

McDowell, T., Knudson-Martin, C., & Bermudez, M. (2017). *Socioculturally attuned family therapy: Guidelines for equitable theory and practice*. New York, NY: Routledge.

McGoldrick, M., Giordano, J., & Garcia-Preto, N. (2005, 3rd edition). Ethnicity and Family Therapy. New York: Guildford Press.

Mendel, D. (2018). *An evaluation of the efficacy of the PROMISE program in Broward County* (Unpublished dissertation). Nova Southeastern University.

Montgomery, B. (2017, April 5). Why cops shoot. *Tampa Bay Times*. Retrieved April 29, 2018 from www.tampabay.com

National Child Traumatic Stress Network, National Center for PTSD. (2006). *Psychological first aid field operations guide* (2nd ed.). Retrieved from https://www.nctsn.org/sites/default/files/resources//pfa_field_operations_guide.pdf

Rambo, A. (2018). "Through the Storm: How one MFT program survived a hurricane". Family Therapy Magazine January/February 2018, pp. 36–41.

Substance Abuse and Mental Health Services Administration. (2005). *Psychological first aid for first responders: Tips for emergency and disaster response workers [Fact sheet]*. Retrieved from https://store.samhsa.gov/product/Psychological-First-Aid-for-First-Responders/NMH05-0210

Travis, S. (2018, February 2). Nikolas Cruz refused mental health services once he turned 19, Runcie says. *Sun Sentinel*. Retrieved April 29, 2018 from www.sunsentinel.com

Walsh, F. (Ed.). (2015). *Normal family processes: Growing diversity and complexity* (3rd ed.). New York, NY: Guilford Press.

Chapter 3
Disasters Are Never Natural: Emerging Media to Map Lives and Territories at Risk

Gonzalo Bacigalupe

Situating the Author

My grandparents' house always had letters with stamps that told us about our relatives. As the grandchild of the Spanish diaspora in Latin America, I collected stamps and little did I know that I was collecting the memories of those exchanges across the hemispheres. That was the technology that connected us across geographical distance. Telephones were scarce, telegrams were expensive, and travel was slow and inaccessible for those in the working class. What would have been the life of my grandparents if they had access to cheap and effective communications technology like Skype or WhatsApp? Emerging technologies enable immigrants across the globe and those separated by long commute distances in large urban enclaves to communicate effortlessly only very recently. Would this media have prevented my grandmother from losing contact—letters decreased through the years—with her relatives and addressing the longing for the family connection as she was becoming blind? Family history does inform my interest on the way technology may enable, maintain, intensify, and shape relationships in families as well as clinical work (Bacigalupe & Askari, 2013; Bacigalupe & Cámara, 2012; Bacigalupe & Lambe, 2011). A focus that continued to expand as I began fieldwork research in Chile to study how communities utilize emerging media to confront crisis elicited by extreme natural events—earthquakes, tsunamis, fires, landslides, floods, droughts, etc.

G. Bacigalupe (✉)
Department of Counseling and School Psychology, College of Education,
University of Massachusetts Boston, Boston, MA, USA

National Research Center for Integrated Natural Disaster Management (CIGIDEN),
CONICYT/FONDAP/15110017, Santiago, Chile

© Springer Nature Switzerland AG 2019
L. L. Charlés, G. Samarasinghe (eds.), *Family Systems and Global Humanitarian Mental Health*, https://doi.org/10.1007/978-3-030-03216-6_3

After the 2010 earthquakes in Chile and Haiti, I began exploring the power of social networks for helping individuals and communities to deal with the emergency and the initial recovery phases immediately after even if geographical distance is present (Bacigalupe & Velasco-Martin, 2018). Through the use of social networks and crowdsourcing of data, volunteers were able to locate relatives and friends, learn about needs, find ways of volunteering more effectively on the ground, and prevent as much as possible the negative impact humanitarian deployment in the site of the catastrophes that were unfolding in both countries. Studying the power of volunteers that use social media to inform, calm, and direct resources, and overall foster resilience in times of crisis, was instructive in expanding the notion of a strength-focused approach that informs my clinical work (Bacigalupe, 1996; Lawless, Gale, & Bacigalupe, 2001). This clinical approach is coherent with framing the work with others as a conversation, as a retelling of stories, and as a discursive exercise where what we talk constitutes reality and not just represents it in the search for the "truth" (Bacigalupe, 1998a, 1998b). Therapeutic conversations that question expert knowledge are consistent with participatory forms of engaging in the world (Bacigalupe, 2009). Technology can extend and intensify those conversations across distance and in difficult circumstances. The ability to archive and participate asynchronously also adds new forms of participation that bring forth all sort of new capabilities to families and communities. Communication information technologies were not necessarily designed for these purposes but fill the need for connecting as well as to overcome social norms that regulate face-to-face relationships that may inhibit experts meeting non-experts, the older sharing with the younger in nonhierarchical ways, as well as enabling the breakdown of other rigid cultural and social boundaries. The affordances of technology (Bucher & Helmond, 2017) can also amplify and intensify the deleterious impact of inequality when communities do not appropriate them. Moreover, emerging media—as the more traditional media—exists within a neoliberal logic in which surveillance of individuals to expand and test its capabilities is a central feature. Paradoxically, the behavior of those at the margin may not be of such interest to business although could be the focus of government control agencies. Our communications could be encrypted, but communities utilizing them to organize and find ways of gaining agency could also become the target of surveillance. In my work, however, emerging media affordances inspire and intensify forms of community participation that were before reserved to the most privileged. In the same way that immigrants have become de facto transnational as they maintain continuous communication with their families and communities abroad (Bacigalupe & Cámara, 2012), the ability of local communities to adopt emerging media to learn, advocate, and gain agency could be transforming of the ways experts define marginality particularly in the context of disasters and climate change adaptation. The local adoption of emerging media and the introduction of sophisticated technologies that emphasize participation from those at the bottom remind us that "small changes from below" (de Mel, 2017) can spread and extend through communities in shared and distant territories.

Lives at Unequal Risk

Vulnerable individuals, families, and communities often live in territories already characterized by the lack of security, marginality, and lack access to basic goods for survival. Extreme natural events put them at extreme risk. Disasters, therefore, are never natural (Gaillard & Mercer, 2013; Ismail-Zadeh, Cutter, Takeuchi, & Paton, 2017; Wisner, Gaillard, & Kelman, 2012). Disasters deepen and sustain social inequality (Gould, Garcia, & Remes, 2016). It is in these communities in which a disaster risk reduction strategy cannot alone or at the center be about intervening after a disaster occurs. Education, preparedness, and mitigation become central in preventing the occurrence of a disaster or catastrophe that threatens the lives of those populating these territories. Even dialogical and collaborative post-disaster humanitarian interventions may maintain the unequal conditions that make a natural event to become a destructive crisis. For clinicians, educators, building professionals, and all other experts, in supporting the recovery or addressing the immediate emergency, it is pivotal to educate in the messy and complex process of supporting a resilient approach founded on social justice and not just repair and rebuild approach. We need to prepare for creating just environments rather than attempt repairing the people and their habitat delinked from what eliminates social vulnerability and the overall identity of lives at risk.

Despite the unequal impact of disasters, dominant approaches are informed by a militaristic and bureaucratic approach to intervene (Coyne, 2013). The restoration of order seems to prevail after extreme natural event strikes. A hierarchical approach to the emergency after the impact of an event, palliative interventions with individuals, and the development of highly technological- and expert-driven solutions drive post-disaster action. The interventions by experts, professionals, and public and private institutions—government and nongovernmental—are often focused on the emergency or the palliation of the crisis rather than in strengthening the ability of people to develop a disaster risk strategy based on their needs, in sustaining resilience (Atallah, Contreras Painemal, Albornoz, Salgado, & Pilquil Lizama, 2018). Similarly, the exchange between experts and these communities is often fraught with a lack of understanding of how risk is construed in these territories. Emerging media—social networks, co-design thinking, aerial robotics, and digital cameras—offer innovative ways of engaging in the assessment of risk and points of resilience.

Conversations about risk and resilience are not common among communities living at risk. Emerging media offers ways of engaging anew with their territory. To create these conversations and interventions, it is crucial to develop a transdisciplinary approach that includes architects, sociologists, psychologists, social workers, etc. This approach intends to focus on the problem as lived and its potential solutions without centering it on a disciplinary question. It intends to address systemically the question of resilience in the context of disaster in a dialogue with individuals and families living as a norm in territories at risk (Atallah, Bacigalupe, & Repetto, in press). Transdisciplinary work requires thinking about how the distinctions each of us makes can become the source of a problem and/or a solution. This is similar to the way discursive and narrative therapies have insisted on the role that our professional roles have on defining and redefining reality as we make distinctions of what matters and what doesn't (Combs & Freedman, 2012; Tomm, George, Wulff, & Strong, 2014) and thus on making clear how our interventions are never free from validating or challenging inequity. Mapping risk and resilience interrogates not only what needs to change in these territories and communities but also how we, professionals, need to rethink our subject of intervention.

Emerging Media: Engaging in Conversations

Emerging media is per se attractive; children, adolescents, and adults are drawn to objects that call for a different representation of their relationships and the place they live in. Emerging media may also represent and construct information in ways that may have not been accessible before; in the hands of communities, these technologies can suggest new ways of engaging with knowledge and power. A strong temptation is to put the technology at the center rather than the possibilities that may evoke for a truly dialogical, inspirational, and participatory engagement. Engaging with emerging media can have the capacity to question and deconstruct the often naturalized ways of defining problems and creating solutions. It is not the technology per se, but the proposed interventions are also not devoid of the power of emerging technologies having to offer either. Technological interventions can be top-down and cutting edge, but they can also sustain bottom-up action. We can utilize technology to inspire action, to seduce into participation, to advocate for change, to empower communities to engage with those having the power to reassign resources, and to rethink how we engage with others.

Media can determine how communities construct their territory. The utilization of novel media cannot only offer a new perspective but also bring new voices into the conversation, thus reconstructing the territory anew. A map generated with the information that a drone collects can inspire a different cartography of the territory that people inhabit (Bacigalupe & Ojeda, 2018). This experience is not only a perceptual cognitive experiment but also a collective and dialogical one, which can undermine the hierarchical and often paternalistic approach of experts engaging with the most vulnerable. The ability to modify the way we perceive a territory, the place we live in and/or work, can be substantive in shaping our actions on the same place. When a family or a community mobilizes their scarce resources to build a house in what becomes an informal settlement, they are making implicit and explicit assessments of risk (Ojeda, Bacigalupe, & Pino, 2018). Evaluating risk for these families may not have the characteristics of a professional or expert assessment but can be accurate and informative. This is in part because these families live in conditions of risk that are intrinsically linked to their transgenerational identity; their memories and lived experiences are intimately connected to the place they live in. Informal settlements do not only emerge as part of social movements or organizations but also as intergenerational and extended family strategies to obtaining a house to live. Living at risk is the normal. Indeed, informal settlements (tomas), in countries like Chile, often referred as poblaciones (shanty towns), can last for generations. Informal settlements may never be integrated fully into the formal functioning of a city. They may not have access to water or electricity, or the roads may never be paved or have access to public services like schools or health clinics. When an extreme natural event occurs, that informality becomes visible to everyone. If the house burns, how does the family demonstrate that this is their place or how do they support their claims for assistance if they don't have any legal document that testify to the characteristics of the house? Assisting families and communities, in that context, does often lead to the deepening of these families' vulnerability since the fire does not only destroy their house and their belongings but also the claim to a piece of land. It is as if they are to start again with the search of another place.

Disasters are not natural; they occur as communities occupy spaces that are predictably dangerous and exposed to natural and anthropogenic hazards. Societies can invest resources to mitigate and prepare for these extreme events and organize their territories and where people live in ways that place those with the least resources at the most risk. Safe infrastructures, fast response during an emergency, resources for reconstruction, and the ability to create safe spaces are unequally distributed within cities, regions, countries, and the world. Some of the most vulnerable communities live in places that face multiple hazards with few resources to challenge rare but devastating events like fires, landslides, and earthquakes. It is in these territories where collaborative systemic interventions that integrate as many voices as possible are necessary. It is in these places where mental health interventions cannot be isolated from urban planning or the strengthening of community resilience.

Mapping Risk and Points of Resilience with Communities

Territories are the subjects of interpretation—a notion not foreign to practitioners, ethnographers, and other researchers who embrace a constructionist stance. The map is not the territory (Bateson, 1972, 1979) highlighting the role that context has in determining meaning, all essential assumptions informing postmodern systemic therapies (Freedman & Combs, 1996; McNamee & Gergen, 1992). These ideas, however, may encompass not only conceptually but literally a renewed meaning in the work with people at risk of suffering as a result of a disaster or a catastrophe. Radical geography does suggest that the map we construe of our territory is the result of contentious sociopolitical and cultural struggles. The map reflects society although its creation is today left to some expert technicians or scientists who often deliver on the views that represent the most privileged. The map is a discursive product in which those living at peril have little input as is the norm for the most vulnerable leaving in territories at risk; there, people are "uncounted, unrecognized, unseen" (Tironi & Rodríguez-Giralt, 2017, p. 90). Engaging everyone in a critical assessment of the map may be empowering and helpful in engaging with those in the expert role. Participatory mapping has been, indeed, a critical research tool for communities to understand and construct their territories in ways that capture their aspirations, frustrations, and needs.

Maps today are available in multiple forms. Satellite images are accessible via digital maps—i.e., Google Earth. Growing is the availability of images produced locally with drones. Participatory mapping—also called community-based mapping—is a general term used to define a set of approaches and techniques that combine the tools of modern cartography with participatory methods to represent the spatial knowledge of local communities (Cochrane, Corbett, & Keller, 2014; Warner, 2015). The basic premise is that local inhabitants possess expert knowledge of their local territories (Wall, 2018), which can be expressed in a geographical model, easily understandable and universally recognized. Participatory maps often represent a socially or culturally distinct understanding of the landscape and include information that is excluded from mainstream or official maps. Maps created by local communities represent the place in which they live, showing those elements that communities themselves perceive as important such as customary land boundaries, traditional natural resource management practices, sacred areas, and so on.[1] Creating maps with the community is interactive and has been developed in order to integrate the traditional knowledge and ideas of the people living within a community into the planning and development of a project. Community mapping enables a local community to analyze risky areas through multiple forms of representation that facilitate the understanding of the socio-environmental conditions of the community. Participants are invited to draw a physical map of their community and encouraged to share their observations and rationale with the members of the research team. Maps can be simple or very sophisticated. They can be basic drawings or sophisticated constructions created with geographical information software. Researchers working with a community encourage heterogeneity in the maps that emerge from interviews, conversations, and ethnographic notes while walking in the neighborhood, etc. To engage with public officials, these maps are to be transformed into the usual cartographic conventions that may help the community to communicate. The maps, although a representation, also constitute an experience that creates identity. The experience may, therefore, redefine the identity of a community. Moreover, in informal settlements, often the ones at the most risk for extreme natural events and high levels of social vulnerability, the territory is changing as people settle and create spaces for constructing their houses as well as common spaces, roads, etc.

Conversations in the Territory

With an interdisciplinary team and researchers at universities associated with the Research Center for Integrated Disaster Risk Management in Chile (CIGIDEN), we have engaged with communities in territories at multiple risks. The community

[1] https://www.mappingforrights.org/participatory_mapping

DroneLab, as we have identified the team, initiates conversations with the leaders of these communities to offer a series of citizen science-based activities (Ceccaroni & Piera, 2017; Jollymore, Haines, Satterfield, & Johnson, 2017; Marchezini et al., 2017; Paul et al., 2018) always carefully assessing with the leaders how our intervention will enhance, deepen, and/or expand the community organization work. Thus, the interventions are tailored to community needs rather than centering on the specific research interests that our team members or the institutions we belong may have. Our ways of engagement is negotiated and the researchers are there not just to observe, although we do take notes, and prepare ethnographic notes, survey, etc. However, neighbors may have very different ideas about what they see as a preferred outcome. Some communities may need a community place to meet or install a library for the children. Others may desire to have the tools to advocate for trash removal or better water distribution on the part of the municipality. The mapping, therefore, can take on different meanings for the people in the territory, while also the researchers are creating research questions that could mobilize a different assessment of disaster risk on the part of the same community.

We have offered to run workshops for youngsters to learn how to fly a drone and activities to which people of all ages and families join. More sophisticated offerings have included the building of a 3D model of a neighborhood with discussions informed by videos produced with drones in situ. As some of these citizen-based actions have gained some popularity, other communities have found out about us and requested us to create community events in which learning about their community was the centerpiece. We have joined organized communities, supported by an NGO or a group of organized volunteers who were building a pedestrian paved road or plan for rebuilding new housing to replace those that were destroyed by a fire.

We offer the possibility of expanding their efforts at knowing the characteristics of their community through aerial mapping in which the technical expertise joins the local knowledge in an assessment of risks and resilience. Researchers and leaders of the community generate information that it is made available to the community through aerial photographs, videos, and 3D models that can be used for a more systemic understanding of disaster risk. The gathering of the data through actual drone flights and then the sharing of the data encourage discussions that assess their knowledge of risk in what has been named as countermapping (Dalton & Stallmann, 2018; Wall, 2018). This critical mapping results in analog 3D models to enable NGOs, public agencies, and those living in that territory to have a comprehensive knowledge of disaster risk.

A drone and a satellite, the detailed tridimensional map that can create, cannot capture the stories of a community. Collecting those stories, however, demands a particular kind of engagement that a drone flight may support. Experiencing the drone flying over their community can foster conversations adding to a map that becomes attached to stories and a shared history of the territory. We have found, for instance, that conversations around a map of the place lead to a qualitatively different assessment of points of resilience and risk. Agreeing, disagreeing, and building up a story that it is consensual while also recognizing that the stories can be contested is an exercise that highlights how a territory cannot simply be represented in map; the territory is a complex story under continuous construction.

Our team has developed a flexible protocol to engage with communities. We ask many questions; we are inquisitive about the potential outcomes of learning about their territory from above. It is an opportunity to assess carefully who may be missing and who may need to be a participant. Having this preliminary knowledge highlights the importance of creating knowledge that does not alienate parts of the community or that it does not include crucial voices. After we have reached support for a wide group, we plan on having an activity that consists of first getting them to know whom we are and becoming familiarized with the technology. We set up a tent and invite children, adolescents, and whole families to play with toy drones. This is, at the core and for the most part, a ludic activity to encourage informal conversations and trust. We also have a semiprofessional and a professional drone available for participants to experience the flights using a virtual reality lens. A professional drone pilot flies the drone, while community members put the virtual reality lenses and experience "flying over" their community. In parallel, data is collected. The "flying over" alone elicits rich conversations about risk, vulnerability, and points of resilience. At one of these community experiences, one of the neighborhood leaders who have lived for 20 years in the upper section of a hill was surprised of the existence of a forest at the bottom of a creek—a hazard that otherwise would be forgotten in a territory where fires are common. In the community where that neighborhood leader lives, the presence of eucalyptus is of significant risk since the non-native trees are particularly dangerous during a fire. This new awareness brings to the conversation a new way of thinking about risks and vulnerability and of how the natural of a disaster is not its connection with how nature behaves but of how these terms become naturalized despite being contested and socially constructed.

Once data is collected, it is possible to create detailed maps and models. With the help of architects and urban specialists, we have created models and detailed maps that represent an area. The model and maps are then utilized as the springboard for discussions about the situation in the present and the past. The map is intervened with additions by inhabitants who add demographic data, stories, important milestones, etc. The conversations do also address the question of what will happen if government offices and business decisions lead to the destruction of the community—the building of a large road that could destroy the sense of community that a largely pedestrian but dirty road now fosters. It also therefore leads to brainstorming about desired futures responding to the question of what will make this community much more resilient and prepared to withstand the impact of a natural or anthropocentric hazard.

Territories, like Minds, Are Relational

Communities, like families, have complex and rich stories to tell (Breckenridge & James, 2012; Imber-Black, Roberts, & Whiting, 2003). The less privileged these communities and families are, the larger the chance of lives being overly determined by the action of the state and the forces that sustain inequality and for disasters to intensify these trends (Gunewardena & Schuller, 2008; Loewenstein, 2015). The tools employed to naturalize this reality are often the ones that professional and experts construe as the objective and the evidence-based or the ones carrying a cost-benefit analysis that legitimizes an understanding of disasters are natural or as unpredictable (Knowles, 2011; Marsh, 2018; Steinberg, 2006; K. Tierney, 2018; Tironi Rodó, Rodriguez-Giralt, & Guggenheim, 2014). I propose in this brief writing that some technological tools can draw the attention of these communities and enhance their agency to engage in more effective ways with those that have the power to shape their territory as well as help the same communities to create a discourse about risk and resilience that is in tune with their needs and desires for a better and just life.

When our team of researchers leaves the territory where the meetings with the community occur, we are always intrigued by how conversations evolve in the privacy of their networks and the families we engage with. We have been surprised by how organized communities integrate the models and maps we create into the fabric of their organizations. A model may be intervened to have additional information on it as added by community members, or a WhatsApp closed network conversation about the work we did is the source of conversations about what to do next. The community DroneLab activities have generative outcomes that are often invisible to experts.

My stamp collection had a thick set of pages with the stamps that my grandmother gave me and still constitutes a rich set of memories about my own identity. The stamps told the story, in not so subtle terms, of the hopeful and tragic diaspora that marks my family. The stamps, in addition to posed black and white photos, create a story that captures pieces of the family history, not the history but a snapshot that will continue to be modified. The technology of the time, with its power and constraints, enabled not only a representation of the time but a particular way of bringing the world to us. Technology is not neutral, nor on its own determines a specific path or way of understanding. The maps and models we create with the communities and the conversations that ensure may have a similar quality—a rich set of stories about resilience, risk, territories, and the interventions by the communities that inhabit them.

References

Atallah, D., Bacigalupe, G., & Repetto, P. (in press). Centering at the margins: Critical community resilience praxis for global mental health equity research. *Journal of Humanistic Psychology.*

Atallah, D. G., Contreras Painemal, C., Albornoz, L., Salgado, F., & Pilquil Lizama, E. (2018). Engaging critical community resilience praxis: A qualitative study with Mapuche communities in Chile facing structural racism and disasters. *Journal of Community Psychology, 46*(5), 575–597.

Bacigalupe, G. (1996). Writing in therapy: A participatory approach. *Journal of Family Therapy, 18*(4), 361–375.

Bacigalupe, G. (1998a). Cross-cultural systemic therapy training and consultation: A postcolonial view. *Journal of Systemic Therapies, 17*(1), 31–44.

Bacigalupe, G. (Ed.). (1998b). *Consulting and training in the land of others: Special issue, Journal of Systemic Therapies* (Vol. 17). New York, NY: Guilford Press.

Bacigalupe, G. (2009). Mapping transparent consultations with health and protective services teams. *Journal of Systemic Therapies, 28*(3), 77–88.

Bacigalupe, G., & Askari, S. (2013). E-health innovations, collaboration, and healthcare disparities: Developing criteria for culturally competent evaluation. *Family, Systems, & Health, 31*(3), 248–263. https://doi.org/10.1037/a0033386

Bacigalupe, G., & Cámara, M. (2012). Transnational families and social technologies: Reassessing immigration psychology. *Journal of Ethnic and Migration Studies, 38*(9), 1425–1438.

Bacigalupe, G., & Lambe, S. (2011). Virtualizing intimacy: Information communication technologies and transnational families in therapy. *Family Process, 50*(1), 12–26. https://doi.org/10.1111/j.1545-5300.2010.01343.x

Bacigalupe, G., & Ojeda, L. (2018, May–June). Tecnologías emergentes para la participación comunitaria en la reducción del riesgo de desastres: El DronLab, Una iniciativa de CIGIDEN-CINVIT-ADRA. [Emerging technologies for community participation in disaster risk reduction] COTA: Ciudad, Observación, Territorio, Arte.

Bacigalupe, G., & Velasco-Martin, J. (2018). *Are crisis platforms supporting citizen participation?* Paper presented at the International Workshop on Complex Networks.

Bateson, G. (1972). *Steps to an ecology of mind.* Northvale, NJ: Jason Aronson Inc.

Bateson, G. (1979). *Mind and nature. A necessary unity.* London: Wildwood House Ltd..

Breckenridge, J., & James, K. (2012). Therapeutic responses to communities affected by disasters: The contribution of family therapy. *Australian and New Zealand Journal of Family Therapy, 33*(03), 242–256. https://doi.org/10.1017/aft.2012.29

Bucher, T., & Helmond, A. (2017). The affordances of social media platforms. In J. Burgess, A. Marwick, & T. Poell (Eds.), *The SAGE handbook of social media* (pp. 223–253). London/Thousand Oaks, CA: SAGE Publications.

Ceccaroni, L., & Piera, J. (2017). *Analyzing the role of citizen science in modern research.* Hershey, PA: Information Science Reference.

Cochrane, L., Corbett, J., & Keller, P. (2014). *Impact of community-based and participatory mapping.* Institute for Studies and Innovation in Community-University Engagement. University of Victoria.

Combs, G., & Freedman, J. (2012). Narrative, poststructuralism, and social justice: Current practices in narrative therapy. *The Counseling Psychologist, 40*(7), 1033–1060.

Coyne, C. J. (2013). *Doing bad by doing good: Why humanitarian action fails.* Stanford, CA: Stanford University Press.

Dalton, C. M., & Stallmann, T. (2018). Counter-mapping data science. *The Canadian Geographer/Le Géographe canadien, 62*(1), 93–101.

de Mel, N. (2017). A grammar of emergence: Culture and the state in the post-tsunami resettlement of Burgher women of Batticaloa, Sri Lanka. *Critical Asian Studies, 49*(1), 73–91.

Freedman, J., & Combs, G. (1996). *Narrative therapy: The social construction of preferred realities.* New York, NY: W. W. Norton.

Gaillard, J.-C., & Mercer, J. (2013). From knowledge to action: Bridging gaps in disaster risk reduction. *Progress in Human Geography, 37*(1), 93–114.

Gould, K. A., Garcia, M. M., & Remes, J. A. (2016). Beyond "natural-disasters-are-not-natural": The work of state and nature after the 2010 earthquake in Chile. *Journal of Political Ecology, 23*(1), 93–114.

Gunewardena, N., & Schuller, M. (2008). *Capitalizing on catastrophe: Neoliberal strategies in disaster reconstruction.* Lanham, MD: AltaMira Press.

Imber-Black, E., Roberts, J., & Whiting, R. A. (Eds.). (2003). *Rituals in families and family therapy.* New York: WW Norton & Company.

Ismail-Zadeh, A. T., Cutter, S. L., Takeuchi, K., & Paton, D. (2017). Forging a paradigm shift in disaster science. *Natural Hazards, 86*(2), 969–988.

Jollymore, A., Haines, M. J., Satterfield, T., & Johnson, M. S. (2017). Citizen science for water quality monitoring: Data implications of citizen perspectives. *Journal of Environmental Management, 200*, 456–467.

Knowles, S. G. (2011). *The disaster experts: Mastering risk in modern America* (1st ed.). Philadelphia, PA: University of Pennsylvania Press.

Lawless, J. J., Gale, J., & Bacigalupe, G. (2001). The discourse of culture and race in family therapy supervision: A conversational analysis. *Contemporary Family Therapy, 23*(2), 181–197.

Loewenstein, A. (2015). *Disaster capitalism: Making a killing out of catastrophe*. London/New York: Verso Books.

Marchezini, V., Trajber, R., Olivato, D., Munoz, V. A., de Oliveira Pereira, F., & Luz, A. E. O. (2017). Participatory early warning systems: Youth, citizen science, and intergenerational dialogues on disaster risk reduction in Brazil. *International Journal of Disaster Risk Science, 8*(4), 390–401.

Marsh, G. (2018). *Community engagement in post-disaster recovery*. London/New York, NY: Routledge, Taylor & Francis Group.

McNamee, S., & Gergen, K. J. (Eds.). (1992). *Therapy as social construction*. Newbury Park, CA: Sage Publications.

Ojeda, L., Bacigalupe, G., & Pino, A. (2018). Coproduction after a disaster: The reconstruction of an informal settlement in Chile. *Environment and Urbanization, 30*(2), 1–20. https://doi.org/10.1177/0956247818790731

Paul, J. D., Buytaert, W., Allen, S., Ballesteros-Cánovas, J. A., Bhusal, J., Cieslik, K., … Stoffel, M. (2018). Citizen science for hydrological risk reduction and resilience building. *Wiley Interdisciplinary Reviews: Water, 5*(1), e1262.

Steinberg, T. (2006). *Acts of god: The unnatural history of natural disaster in America*. New York, NY: Oxford University Press.

Tierney, K. (2018). Disaster as social problem and social construct. In J. Trevino (Ed.), *The Cambridge handbook of social problems* (Vol. 2, pp. 79–94). Cambridge: Cambridge University Press.

Tironi, M., & Rodríguez-Giralt, I. (2017). Healing, knowing, enduring: Care and politics in damaged worlds. *The Sociological Review, 65*(2_suppl), 89–109.

Tironi Rodó, M., Rodriguez-Giralt, I., & Guggenheim, M. (2014). *Disasters and politics: Materials, experiments, preparedness*. Malden, MA: Wiley-Blackwell.

Tomm, K., George, S. S., Wulff, D., & Strong, T. (2014). *Patterns in interpersonal interactions: Inviting relational understandings for therapeutic change*. New York, NY: Routledge.

Wall, K. (2018). *Who needs experts? Counter-mapping cultural heritage*. London/New York, NY: Taylor & Francis.

Warner, C. (2015). *Participatory mapping: A literature review of community-based research and participatory planning* (pp. 1–20). Cambridge, MA: Massachusetts Institute of Technology, Social Hub for Community and Housing, Faculty of Architecture and Town Planning.

Wisner, B., Gaillard, J. C., & Kelman, I. (2012). Framing disaster: Theories and stories seeking to understand hazards, vulnerability and risk. In *Handbook of hazards and disaster risk reduction* (pp. 47–62). London: Routledge.

Chapter 4
Paved with Good Intentions? The Road of the Humanitarian Project of DNA Identification of the Missing in Post-Conflict Cyprus

Anna M. Agathangelou and Kyle D. Killian

Introduction

In Cyprus, violence comes in various forms, some emerging out of development and governance projects, however well intended. Here we examine the humanitarian project of DNA identification of the missing in Cyprus and its effects on the professionals and families involved. Interviews with anthropologists, psychologists, and surviving family members shed light on the social and political complexities inherent in the identification and symbolic "return" of lost family members. This chapter draws on interviews with human rights activists, forensic scientists, and the relatives of those missing and disappeared in nationalist violence to trace how evidence and claims making are pivotal in both state making and healing. It shows how state officials, relatives, and forensic scientists, are guided by different epistemologies, and desires and find themselves constantly negotiating healing and justice claims.

Humanitarian Projects, DNA Forensics, and Identification of the Missing

Cyprus gained independence from the British Empire in 1959 and was juridically divided along ethnic and racial lines: Greek and Turkish Cypriots as the two major political groups embodying the postcolonial state, with Britain, Greece, and

A. M. Agathangelou
York University, Toronto, ON, Canada

K. D. Killian (✉)
Capella University, Minneapolis, MN, USA
e-mail: kyle.killian@capella.edu

© Springer Nature Switzerland AG 2019
L. L. Charlés, G. Samarasinghe (eds.), *Family Systems and Global Humanitarian Mental Health*, https://doi.org/10.1007/978-3-030-03216-6_4

Turkey as guarantor powers. Starting in the 1950s and 1960s, the attempts of different actors to co-constitute the sovereign led to a series of conflicts, culminating in a war between the Republic of Cyprus (led by Greek Cypriots) and Turkey. Turkey colonized the island, dividing it physically into North and South. About 200,000 Greek Cypriots were displaced, and the majority of the Turkish Cypriot community was relocated to the North. About 2000 Greek and Turkish Cypriots were designated "missing" during the series of conflicts pre- and post-independence.

The search for the missing was triggered by humanitarian concerns (CMP, 2018). While the search, exhumation, and identification began much earlier, the newly emerging technology of forensics (Agathangelou, Forthcoming; Agathangelou, 2017a, 2017b) has intensified the humanitarian move. In fact, forensic science has been brought together with humanitarianism in practices worldwide (Moon, 2016: 50). When capital is added to the mix, it creates what Agathangelou calls a humanitarian forensic empire (Forthcoming). These three co-produce each other and the global political order.

Humanitarianism as a process and ordering mechanism dates to the eighteenth century when a diplomatic delegation led by Sir Henry Bartle Frere arrived on Zanzibar to discover that 20,000 Africans were deported each year to the Arab World. Appalled, Frere reported to London, characterizing the Zanzibar slave market as inhumane, with Africans treated like animals instead of "beings with human dignity" (cited in Klose & Thulin, 2016: 10). The Royal British Navy intervened, and the Sultan was forced to end the slave trade in June 1873. The British built an Anglican Church on the site, triumphantly showing the transformation of a place "of inhumanity into one of European humanity" (Klose & Thulin, 2016). This European intervention to suppress slavery, though lauded, is itself based on racialized positionings, however. More recently, humanitarian and "humane" projects in the name of (European) humanity range from interventions to stop wars to assistance with ecological catastrophes, including the use of forensic technologies and juridical mechanisms to protect the rights of people in situations where the state does not fulfill its sovereign rights. This humanitarian orientation to rights is now embedded in international humanitarian law (IHL). The "forensic turn," as "an emergent sensibility attuned to material investigation," has allowed states to co-produce a certain rational order and eradicate "the very irrationality, sometimes madness" of the violent elements among us (Weizman, 2013: 10).

Since the 2000s, DNA technology (i.e., forensic science) has reshaped scientific and legal questions around the "missing" (Agathangelou, 2017a, 2017b; Smith, 2013; Loucaides, 2011; Rosenblatt, 2010), but much of the literature on Cyprus (Fics, 2016; Kovras, 2013) misses that the introduction of DNA evidence, together with law enforcement and legal practices, materializes and (de)materializes the question of the sovereign and the missing and the "transition" of the state and its sovereign powers within the global order of capital. At the same time, it establishes a connection between a particular body and a particular crime. Thus, forensic evidence is a material technology, a metaphysical device, a set of discourses, an institution, and a technology of governance (Jasanoff, 2006: 283–284).

As this chapter shows, forensic technologies and the missing and disappeared are continually de/materialized through humanitarian bio-industries and their scientific practices and co-materialized differently as subject positions around the question of tending to traumas and healing in global spaces.

Bioconstitutionalism: The Un/Making of the Postcolonial State Through the Missing and the Disappeared

From 1974–1977, several formal meetings on the missing were held, with no significant decisions on how to address this question. Between 1977 and 1981, negotiations in Nicosia, Geneva, and New York led to the establishment of a Committee on Missing Persons (CMP) in April 1981, with an agreement between Greek and Turkish Cypriots under the auspices of the UN. For 20 years, Greek and Turkish Cypriots conducted investigations to establish the fate of the missing and disappeared to negotiate a common official list. DNA samples were collected from relatives to aid identifications. In 1997, the two leaders agreed to provide each other with all information already at their disposal on the location of graves. CMP turned to the Cyprus Institute of Neurology and Genetics (CING), a bicommunal, non-profit, academic, biotechnology center with a focus on DNA training. CING's Laboratory of Forensic Genetics (LabFoG) uses state-of-the-art DNA-based typing methodologies to study evidence from civil, criminal, and missing person investigations. Simultaneously, the Argentine Forensic Anthropology Team (EAAF) was recommended by the International Committee of the Red Cross (ICRC) and mandated by CMP to design, set up, and initially coordinate this Global South humanitarian project (Smith, 2013) to search for, exhume, and identify the missing. From the start of the project in August 2006 until the end of 2007, international forensic experts from EAAF coordinated and trained a bicommunal forensic team of over 60 Cypriot archaeologists and anthropologists under the auspices of CMP. Scientific labs in Cyprus, Bosnia (International Committee of Missing Persons), and the USA became involved and have access to about 4000 DNA Cypriot samples. These labs have a DNA bank and a computer database of relatives (Agathangelou, 2017a, 2017b; Fics, 2016; Kovras, 2013; de Cassia, 2006; Peterson, 1999).

The search for the missing and disappeared is both scientific and legal, what Jasanoff calls *bioconstitutionalism* or "the power of human subjects to articulate new claims vis-à-vis governing institutions, thereby demonstrating the productivity of constitutional ideas as resources for bottom-up self-fashioning" (2011: 290). She orients us to how different populations work through forensic investigations and simultaneously challenge the biopolitical ordering and the demands by capital and the state through institutions of science and their contingent technologies (i.e., DNA) and the law (i.e., amnesty law). In Cyprus, a series of contestations at different scales speaks to multiple attempts to practice and express bioconstitutionalism. Racialized Cypriots challenge the "given" biopolitical ordering of individuals, including who deserves to be searched for, identified, and integrated into practices of commemoration and whose life is to be obliterated. While the state pushes for certain "transitions" and certain forms of citizenship, the relatives and human rights activists, including lawyers, contest such attempts. As such, bioconstitutionalism is "a dispersed and active process of reordering – indeed reconstituting – knowledge and society" (Jasanoff, 2011: 290) and does not belong to only certain actors (i.e., just the state). By focusing on the political practices of multiple actors in Cyprus, we can trace the narrowness of the notion of who deserves attention, push for a broader notion of the subject and its health, and point to gaps and breaches in the structure, including healing.

The introduction of DNA technology in Cyprus was met with considerable excitement. It could allow the seemingly impossible: attaching a name to anonymous bodies. For the first time, people could identify their missing with "absolute" certainty (Interlocutor 10, 2015). But it has also shifted the deliberation of what a human is and what is possible in redressing human trauma and achieving justice. It opens up the possibility of identifying the missing in a racialized conflict while generating opportunities to make connections between a certain human and a particular conflictual event. As Jasanoff reminds us, DNA evidence is multifaceted (2006: 284). The missing and disappeared can be understood as continuously reterritorialized through material techno-scientific practices and through subject positions and social (global) spaces. Public-private relations (i.e., industry and academic sites) are pivotal, but this relationship is being reconfigured in humanitarianism, embodied in the relations among international organizations, the state, forensic labs, and, of course, relatives, friends, and communities.

Much of the forensic work is informed and shaped by affective economies, especially around notions of the "dead" and their "bodies." On the one hand, for the forensic humanitarian professionals, the human remains embody a certain subject, a life cut short by conflict. On the other, as scientists, they detach from this life. Leighton says, "Some [archaeologists] stated that they felt they ought to see them [human remains] as people, but in the course of study they inevitably were treated as objects" (2010: 86). In the process of collating bones into a skeleton, the forensic workers detach/attach affectively in various ways. Some see themselves as redressing the larger Cyprus problem:

> The work I do here is redressing a major problem that has been amidst us for a long time. When…the DNA, for example, says those body parts… belong together…but I see with my eye that is not true, something is happening…something is…wrong, and I feel concerned and scared at moments. Why is that happening? Why can't we figure this out? How do we solve this problem? (Interlocutor 3, 2015)

To "solve this problem," in fact, CMP workers follow "carefully coded and circumscribed" standard operating procedures (SOPs), with "best practices guiding each step of the analysis" (Smith, 2013: 3). A forensic anthropologist turned from her table full of bones to show me the SOP guidebook. I (first author) was not allowed to take a photo of it, though I went through its pages. I asked how much information in this guidebook came from other labs and how much from Cyprus. She said:

> We want scientific rigor in the work we do. We want objectivity. We want as much guidance and direction as we can to avoid subjectivism and interpretations which ought to be mitigated.

> A humanitarian SOP guidebook collated elsewhere is helpful to us. In the process though we are adding to it based on our learning here in this lab. We are innovators here as much as followers of certain known procedures. The best practices though till today have come to us from the Argentine Anthropology Team and we are thankful for that insight and empirical knowledge. Both the work we do here and the work of the DNA lab documents facts on the table. It is only then, when we have the facts, that we can deal rationally with the issue at hand, rather than with unverifiable emotional speculations. Our job is to establish "facts" by following standard operating procedures and guidelines. This is the only way we also develop ourselves as the experts of this global emerging phenomenon. (Interlocutor 5, 2013)

The type of scientific rigor she is discussing has been systematically generated through a "decade of humanitarian forensics" (Ktori & Baranhan, 2018: 4), including objectification (i.e., science as objective and neutral politically). The scientific objectification of the remains also allows them to be viewed as "questions" or "puzzles" which require solving (Williams, 2004: 265). Other forensic workers show much attachment to what they do and how they carry out this scientific rigor, with some wanting to participate in "healing." Whether they know it or not, these humanitarian "healers" are also participating in the emergence of new global publics:

> [The] respatialization of our sense of the public brings the opportunity of a more complete repoliticization of the public than would otherwise be available. Investigating the means of making and remaking public space provides a unique window on the politics of the public sphere, suggesting an even more powerful imperative to the focus on public space. (Low & Smith, 2006: 7)

The conversations of the forensic anthropologists are professional and focus on the samples in front of them. Yet many feel they must be very careful how they deal with the "loss" and the pain of the families. Some even feel this "loss." An anthropologist in the CMP forensic lab explains the difficulty involved in speaking to families about remains:

> The difficult part is to make them trust you...You need to trust yourself that you're sure about what you're saying. You need to find a way to present yourself. So the family, from one point of view, can see you as a scientist so they can trust you. But from the other point of view, they can see this person who understands and shares their feelings. The whole situation is complicated....With little other information, sometimes seeing the mark of a gunshot, perhaps an indicator of a quick death, can be a comfort for family members. (Eleftheriou cited in Gannon, 2018)

This moving back and forth between the need for empathy versus science as an "objective fact" that can be trusted by the families reveals much about the desire to legitimate the humanitarian project as a transitional one redressing conflict and allowing closure. One of the anthropologists at the forensic lab showed me (first author) a skeleton, and said she was affected by the "loss":

> In the process of assembling the bones toward identification I always think. Who is this person? How did s/he die? What if s/he was alive? What kind of a life would s/he be leading? What kind of work would s/he be doing? During this time, I am not really emotional about the whole thing. It is just a job like any other. Other times, when we have finally identified the person and have to return the bones to the families that moment is really emotionally complicated for me. It is as if, I am now for the first time connecting the bones with the living person. (Forensic Anthropologist 1, 2013)

The distinction between a detached form of labor (just another job) and attachment labor is interesting. This anthropologist links production and reproduction through the artifact of the human remains, understood "as having social agency through their continuing relationships with the ...bodies of the living" (Williams, 2004: 267). In the field and labs, anthropologists mentioned other work issues that go to the heart of value and valuation:

> Those countries that invest in this kind of work (I'm not talking here about Cyprus only) are concerned with us gaining this insight and then disappearing. And that may happen sooner or later as the new generation is not concerned with suffering and solutions to any kind of crisis but rather with turning themselves into skillful entrepreneurs. (Interview, June 2013)

Birch says, "Any analysis of value in the bio-economy has to analyze a range of valuation practices, especially those valuing knowledge" (2017). While Birch is talking about corporations and how they embody practices beyond biology, a similar logic appears in humanitarian innovation valuation. These sites of search and identification bolster state conditions and open up the space for corporations to enter countries post-conflict. Humanitarianism does not just indirectly serve bourgeois interests in a way that is impossible to prove; it is explicitly involved in opening up new markets for companies with an interest in testing their products at the "bottom of the pyramid" (Smith, 2016). The search for the missing in Cyprus is a project of humanitarian innovation. The burial sites are landscapes where the calculations of humanitarian work and value can clearly be observed.

The labor that goes into exhumations is an embodied phase of "experimentation" (Snow cited in Rosenblatt, 2015: 53) common to conflict sites of forensic investigations. Rosenblatt says it was only after the "experimental" phase in the former Yugoslavia that the needs of families reemerged, demanding humanitarians be attentive to their empowerment. Sharma argues that such kind of work requires the constitution of a biopolitical, self-disciplined subject:

> Empowerment, it is argued, acts as a biopolitical technology, which constructs self-interested and self-governing disciplined individuals – *homines oeconomici* – needed for the smooth functioning of a market economy out of the culturally differentiated great mass of humanity. It has become a preferred tool with which to produce self-governing and self-caring social actors, orient them towards the free-market, direct their behaviors towards entrepreneurial ends, and attach them to the project of rule. (Sharma, 2006: 16)

In Cyprus, we see a mixture of this, especially among international workers.

In interviews, scientists at the Neurology Center in Cyprus argued against the sale of DNA databases to corporations but told us DNA identification was outsourced to a US corporation (Prainsack & Aronson, 2015). Problematically, the assembled "regimes of value in space and time" (Appadurai, 1986: 4) in the form of emerging socio-technical configurations open the door for states and humanitarian organizations to "sell their knowledge assets – capitalized and converted into financial assets (e.g., biotech firms)" (Birch, 2015: 25). While the original purpose of the use of the DNA was to be used to redress the violence and trauma of wars of the families, in the process much has changed about its uses. When human life is regarded in terms of market value, families of the missing become a form of currency used by humanitarian innovations to generate possibilities for scientific work relegating to the side some of their own concerns and struggles around trauma and terror.

The lab also collates other forms of data, such as "antemortem data," further objectifying the process, following ICRC principles, whereby "all the data and the specific characteristics of a missing or deceased person are catalogued" because "previous research has demonstrated the value and importance of artifacts and how they are handled by the CMP scientists, especially at this early stage of the identification process" (Ktori & Baranhan, 2018: 8–9). Some scientists speak of affective attachment to collation, thus suggesting the agency of the dead: "This skull has a gunshot here in the occipital bones. I wonder what happened. How did this man feel? Did he die immediately? I try to put all my feelings aside but it is very difficult. What was the fear on his face when he saw the gun approaching him?" (Interlocutor 6, 2015). Others note the pain of collation, especially when they find materials that point to the life of the person:

> You saw in the grave the keys that this one dead had in his pocket. You saw the watch that has stopped at a certain time. Seeing the pieces of their pants, the keys in the pockets and the money. They remind me that this person had a life that was cut short and they would never look at their watch, never use their keys to open their door, and never buy anything for their kids. (Interlocutor 9, 2015)

These material items have acquired a certain evocation power that unmakes the familiar and the political. They turn forensic experts into sites of meaning making about suffering and the possibility of healing. The experts speculate and affectively invest themselves in reciting certain stories that are both interesting and problematic. These affective investments, in turn, may require further action, even therapeutic support, if they are to maintain their "professionalism" and their physical health. An anthropologist shared his struggles with me:

> I have been struggling with my health for a long time.... I think the stress is a lot. You may have dug and dug, searching for the missing, knowing all the while that their relatives are waiting. Time is running out. And I go down the lane thinking that these efforts may be in vain. And that intensifies my pain....The more I work on the search, exhumations and identification of the missing and disappeared, the more I realize how I have been part of this dialogue even before I was born. Yet, we ought to be professional and detached. We ought to work only with hard facts. In the process I also realize my own precariousness as a Cypriot of the working class. Many of these were kids when they went to the war. Even younger than me today. Most of them were asked to be in the front. My own perspective about what I am doing has changed. I hope to remain a part of it in a way that makes possible a livable transformation. (Interlocutor 3, 2011)

This anthropologist orients us to the complex relations in the making of scientific evidence which itself mediates and co-produces the expert and the missing. The political dialogue is not just about the hard facts. It positions subjects, dead and alive, even when the bones do not speak for themselves but are made to speak through the application of scientific methods such as analysis, interpretation of scientific expertise, and the translation and interpretation of scientific knowledge into something commensurable and easily understood by different institutions and audiences (Keenan & Weizman, 2011). For bones to speak, "A person or a technology must *mediate* between the object and the forum, to present it and tell its story" (ibid italics ours).

This interlocutor highlights two significant questions in the co-production of the expert and humanitarianism: What are the stakes about this work and whose life and death is being made possible, acknowledged, analyzed, and commemorated in humanitarianism? This unevenness is what humanitarian projects cannot register or grapple with explicitly, especially if the goal is to create the conditions for a certain bicommunality toward peace and, through that, to create a professional who can excavate the public secrets of the un/making of the state and the political subject. Da Silva refers to the methods used in post-Enlightenment strategies of socio-scientific power as the "analytics of raciality." These analytics "presupposed that scientific reason accounts for the various existing modes of being human" and produced "race difference as a category connecting place (continent) of 'origin,' bodies, and forms of consciousness" (Da Silva, 2007: 422). The term "raciality" evokes an "onto-epistemological toolbox that has transmutated the spatial "others of Europe into historical 'others of whiteness'" (2007: 367). Though this interlocutor does not explicitly speak of the Enlightenment, he speaks of the unevenness of life and, by extension, the value accorded to those subjects, dead and alive, within the humanitarian projects that can easily integrate into them and the zero value and death of other subjects within the sovereign. Though the humanitarian project to identify the missing has opened many spaces to redress the terror and violence of sovereign-making projects, it has relegated the relatives and friends to the margins unevenly. And this unevenness appears in the "healing" work with which psychologists and other healing professionals are grappling.

Regimes of Translation and Its Stutterings: Workers as Mediators?

When we consider the problem of the missing in conflict zones, we tend to consider this as a national problem. The state apparatus and its reproduction depend on the drawing of boundaries for stable – territorialized – identification. Humanitarian projects are translating sites and the un/makers of boundaries. In *Mourning Processes and Commemoration*, ICRC notes:

> The humanitarian workers to whom it falls to transmit information to the families of missing persons are faced with a number of problems and difficulties. They bring the news of death, with or without a body.... Humanitarian workers are faced with people suddenly deprived of all hope of ever seeing a loved one again. (ICRC, 2002: 6)

For stable, territorialized identification processes to occur, experts in addition to the forensic anthropologists are needed. "Transmitting" is expressed through psychologists in Cyprus as well. The CMP has psychologists who speak to the relatives and families. Two we interviewed (first author) spoke extensively of their work and the struggles around healing. One said:

> These relatives have been living with unconfirmed loss for a long time. Many of them are experiencing traumatic grief, as well as severe depression. Part of my work is just to listen. I do listen and I sense the grief following the loss of a parent, the father, the son, the child

forty or more years ago. This loss is characterized by intense longing and yearning for the lost relative. Sometimes, the relatives of the missing express feelings of hopelessness and emptiness. (2011)

This psychologist acknowledges that waiting generates feelings of depression, anxiety, and ongoing grief. Part of her job, as she claims, is "just to listen." So she does. And she attempts to figure out how to best counsel those in this predicament. She knows that some have been living with "false hope." Others' hopes have changed over time. In the laboratory/mortuary, in addition to the anthropologists and geneticists, the psychologist is present as family members hear the details about the deaths of relatives. They are also confronted for the first time with the bones/remains:

Feelings of anger, guilt, or hopelessness may overcome the survivors. Some of them cry uncontrollably, others just stand there, others need a shoulder to cry, and others may attempt to harm themselves. I am there to help them manage these kinds of reactions. Though not easy to respond to the relatives, friends and family members, effectively, I try to be there to support them through this devastation. At times, it is very distressing and difficult but my job is to support them to see through what many of them experience: an incessant dwelling on the missing and disappeared relative. (2011)

The psychologists play a significant role in the alleviation of suffering, at least, for a short time. Part of their job is to "manage" the chronic insecurity infusing the lives of the "survivors." In this capacity, they become translators and transition workers in the humanitarian project. Another psychologist who has seen the relatives as clients explains:

Those who lost family members experience anxiety and severe depression, including suicidal thoughts. Those who lost a family member to the war experience a prolonged grief, which ultimately interferes with their daily life and even has led for some to collapse in the long run. Some family members have not worked for years. Some have been drinking themselves to death. What could one or two psychological conversations do? For some, this grief has been going on for 40 to 50 years. Who has come to support these families beyond feeling a sense of empathy or even a sense of pity for them? (2011)

This psychologist highlights that the grief of almost five decades cannot be eradicated in a few sessions. Although psychologists in humanitarian work are expected to remove the suffering which acts as a "block" to transitioning to a bicommunal peace, this kind of work is difficult, even overwhelming. In effect, it represents an ordering mechanism of the survivors, the collating of grief into units of time and space, to be made commensurable on a world scale and thereby function as one unitary, seized, and harnessed state body. In *mourning process and commemoration*, the ICRC notes how humanitarian workers may struggle to respond to family members' grief, pointing exactly to this work of "transmission" and "transition":

The relationship with other human beings and their suffering is often a major source of psychological stress for humanitarian workers: how are they to strike the balance between empathy for the victims – which means to some degree identifying with them – and maintaining the detachment required to cope with the atrocities of war while fulfilling the objectives of their humanitarian mission? (2002: 6)

As noted above, a "detached" approach is crucial in allowing humanitarian workers, including anthropologists, forensic scientists, police officers, and psychologists, to uphold their professional identity. Sovereign law concerns itself with the management of personhood through the management of the dead, the management of the physical-moral aspects of the material existence of the body through the search for and the exhumation and identification of the dead. However, the question of the missing and the disappeared exposes the limitations of sovereign law and detachment. A certain mode of social practice displaces the conditions generating terror and violence in the name of the im/possibility of a bicommunal peace. Can peace be made without such a derangement? If so, what would this entail?

For the relatives and two movements in Cyprus, humanitarianism is a view from above, a view that seizes and harnesses the "organized social forces" (Marx, 1986: 190), but this is not enough. Instead of simply transitioning by realigning the process of violence, the humanitarianism detachment consists of "moving away, away from the remains, away from what made them possible…in order to save – to kill and thereby save" (Interlocutor 10, 2013). The stutterings in the work of professionals as well as more centrally the work of relatives and these movements orient us to a decisive point: community as a creation, as the possibility of a different way to order our lives, has more to do with the logic of humanitarian projects or with the fantasy of rational mastery or detachment from life and death. For them, this sociality cannot be made possible in the nation or the state in its current form. As Fanon reminds us in his work, community is an invention in which all life matters, blacks, persons of color, whites. Community cannot go back, and as Marriott comments, the struggle for a decolonial form of world and its healing is neither a revindication nor a "politics of ascent" (2016: 63).

Creation and Invention: Stutters, Ruptures, and Healing

Ironically, in the search for, identification, and return of remains to the families as a form of transitioning, the formation process of the subject-identifying mechanism called "nation" evades the process by which these families remained "silent" in their pain and suffering unless it was to be used to localize global power (i.e., and its capital relations) in a certain "gradient and use… its enclosure of that gradient to legitimate its own existence" (Walker, 2012: 71). In other words, we miss how the operation of this "national" element is continually re/made in tandem with the remaking of capital on a global scale, including the ways the state mobilizes those absent to do the workings of capital. A relative says bitterly:

> They spoke of our pain and loss when it would benefit them. Publically acknowledging our suffering and loss, so crucial to healing our dignity, was never allowed to us who lost our friends, relatives, parents. They spoke of us when it was expedient politics. They turned us into sites of impunity. If we wanted to speak against those responsible for this terror and war, to speak of our missing, was to rattle the gates of the highest echelons of power. And that's a no no. Speaking about punishing those who brought this unspeakable terror to us and punishing their crimes is not possible. I am a Christian but I *curse curse curse* those who brought this terror to us every day. (Interlocutor, 2015)

Christian or not, this woman occupies a radical position. True healing, she said, was not going to happen by focusing on the transgressions of abstractions and figure-heads: the state security apparatus and religious leaders. She said the amnesty law did not bring closure on multiple scales, or what Alexander calls the "palimpsest": "Time is scrambled and palimpsestic, in all the Worlds….The central idea is that of the palimpsest—a parchment that has been inscribed two or three times, the previous text having been imperfectly erased and remaining and therefore still partially visible" (2005: 190–191). Alexander's point mirrors the interlocutor's. The state's refusal to provide evidence to the relatives and families about their missing has prevented any kind of healing or closure. But this interlocutor also points to the palimpsestic character of time that the ideology of distance (i.e., an event that happened long ago) creates, and she challenges all strictly legal notions of closure.

The state does not create subjects; that is the job of capital. Rather, the state concerns itself with the management of personhood and the physical-moral aspects of the material existence of the body to maintain the "rational individual" to furnish labor for capital and its contingent projects. Postcolonial states are inflected with coloniality, manifested in the theft of territory through war, a capital economy, and an apparatus which separates subjects to be obliterated from those to be "exploited" and those to be saved. This apparatus generates the postcolonial sovereign anew. The missing orients us to the limits of such a sovereign structure and its reading. They allow us to read for the uneven terror underlying its making. The interlocutor's vision exceeds the limits of time and reason of the postcolonial sovereign: "I have seen God and defied death; when my children and I were captured by the Turks in that August 17, 1974,….they told us: 'we are keeping you here because your people [Greek Cypriots] have captured a woman with her four kids and are not letting her go…We will let you go when they let them free." She knows now the truth of the world:

> Of course my comrade is not dead. He could never be dead until I stop thinking and feeling about him. His face, look at his face [pointing to a photo], speaks to us of love and light, of healing of gentleness, of peace. Here is peace. Theirs, whatever that is, is war is terror. Wherever he is, I call him every day to come and see so much life, his grandchildren and his great grandchildren. (2013)

In the language of the helping professionals, this interlocutor may be exhibiting complicated grief. She understands that existence exceeds the short time between birth and death, that feeling and thinking are just as real as seeing and knowing. Her comrade's soul still wanders free, and the whole world and everything in it are at her fingertips, forever. Yet she still curses "those who brought all these things upon us."

Fanon argues we ought to confront such a situation, forcing it to "admit its own void, those elements whose exclusion or absence structures the interior of the situation, but which do not exist within it as such" (Walker, 2012: 215). We might even argue that the wars of the state are a form of enslavement and colonization. Such processes of terror and force are involved in the un/making and enclosure of territoriality and the zoning of those subjects who can be healed though with drugs and those who are healed to forge the nation-state to ensure a violent "concatenation of elements into a putative national unity" (Walker, 2012: 74). In Cyprus,

Turkey specifically spoke of this territorialization (i.e., colonization) as a "resolution" to the postcolonial state's emerged particularity within three years of the independence. The state's double sidedness, "two kinds of produced, aspirational spaces" (Walker 2016 citing Lefebvre 2000[1974]), if you will, led to the two components' emergence as enclosed territoriality signalizing what was to come later through the colonization of the island by Turkey. This racialized aspirational state experimented with a kind of a new double-state as part and parcel of the reproduction of the hierarchy of the world order around the West and the Rest. The state, thus, is bound up with the enslavement and colonial index of modernity. Enslavement and colonization are sedimented and irredeemable elements of the nation-state itself. And this becomes apparent in the way the USA (the first to demand the use of DNA technologies for a US citizen of Greek Cypriot descent killed in the 1974), the Republic of Cyprus, Greece, and Turkey contest the missing.

We cannot think of any contemporary 1987 war and its multiple deaths without engaging with the interrelated forces at work in the historico-epistemological "production" of "species/bones" and "subjects" and those at work in the historico-epistemological "production" of "backwardness" and "national particularity" (racialized) regionally. A CMP psychologist said the following about the search for and identification of the missing:

> What is at stake in the "missing-disappeared-question" is nothing less than the ontology of social being. The postcolonial-humanitarian state manages and regulates the relationships of persons with time, the relationships with themselves, their work, their bodies, their desires, their fears, their households, the market and of course, their dead. When our ministers insist on reformation of the state, they are also insisting to retroject the missing and the disappeared in that restructuring. And they do. However, as psychologists we are accountable to the families, to the people, to the next generation. (Interlocutor 4, June 2015)

The responses to the missing and disappeared point to how the co-production of some subjects as "homo nationalis from cradle to grave" (Balibar, 1991: 93) and others as exterior flesh (Spillers, 2003 [1996]) and the state as "transitional sites" echo the original appropriation and division of the savage/homo and the world. Cyprus as a site is a reminder of conflict and war as a technology central to that division and hierarchization. Cyprus as a "postcolonial" site is still contested. The contestation is over its land and its peoples – alive or dead. The Republic of Cyprus and the three major "guarantors," Greece, Turkey, and Great Britain, are vying for the lands and for the dead. But this structure depends on mechanisms whose traversal might expose capital's limitations:

> The missing…this absence haunts all presence in our society, in our world. The missing force the contemporary situation to confront this absence, which cannot find a place to be buried or body inside or outside this system. This absence demonstrates the system's finitude. What do our missing tell us? Simply that their concrete absence gestures exactly to the ways the system agglomerates the living dead, a wraith that concatenates into one ghostly absence/presence the totality of life. (Interlocutor 4, June 2013)

For some relatives and families, the collection of DNA and the identification of the missing in the anthropological lab are simply placeholders, moments spent waiting for something else to happen. Families are waiting for their daily conversations with their lost ones, their displaced neighbors, and friends. These moments where emptiness resides – often in place of other meanings – constrain the families' attempts to challenge those governance (death) projects. Some challenge humanitarian innovations (i.e., "taking DNA") as impoverishing their attempts to live a meaningful life with their loss. One man, a Greek Cypriot whose brother has been missing since 1974, said: "Not only have they made possible the loss of my brother now they want me to give my DNA. For what purpose? For what benefit? I also heard that they are now going to be using the data from DNA for other purposes even when they did not ask us to sign such a form" (June 2011). To this man, giving his DNA represented another form of enslavement (i.e., the obliteration and stolen life), with no benefit to him or his family with no return of those networks and kinships, that his missing brother that the war ruptured and disappeared.

Of course, finding and identifying the missing is important to the families; they can assuage their suffering by burying a loved one, and they can take the state to court. When I asked a lawyer to explain his involvement, he explained that if he wins, he becomes a major transnational player, able to defend other families against a state that claims to be protective of all its citizens but did not do so in the case of the missing persons. The relatives question some of the premises of the humanitarian project. Showing us bones in a small coffin, a woman said:

> Remains they call my brother. Remains in a small coffin box they call our sons. All these people in the lab standing apart from us [the family members], the brown envelopes tucked under their arms while they present to us like business people the extermination of my brother. I could not really breathe or remember much detail. A hand was the only thing moving in the room, pointing to a bunch of diagrams. A murmur from another Mister. I think we move to another room. A set of bones on a table. My mother backs away. She screams. *These bones are not my son.* But the DNA bears the name heard soaring over rooftops on that July summer night in the village.

Her comments suggest paralysis, cognitive dissonance, and perhaps avoidance; the humanitarian forensic project has certainly not "spoken" to some of the relatives of the missing and disappeared as elsewhere. As such, this DNA of embodiment – the traumatic ongoing effects of war and conflict and the political commitment archived in this woman's body and the rest of the family and the absent body of her brother – comes alive as disruptive and dissonant of a liberal imperialist epistemology and ontology that uses genetic testing to resolve terror that uses this technology for a possible deranged integration into these transmuted structures. This interlocutor mobilizes breathing in such somatic relationalities as a ceremony to deal with conditions of attrition. This question of breathing and memory implies a radical breathing (Agathangelou, 2011) that encounters the state and the violence making it repeatedly possible, in an asphyxiating world; the radical breath is both literal, a breath necessary for survival, and figurative, a breath with political vitality in spite of the foreclosure of postcolonial presents and futures.

Burials of Greek and Turkish Cypriots (in many cases, for a second, third, or fourth time, as remains were often moved) are often accompanied by religious and political practices. In effect, the individual body is integrated into the national body by means of a commemorative ceremony and physical interment. The politics at work in official burial ceremonies contains a logic wherein the one who was missing and disappeared is returned to the community, given both a physical and a symbolic presence.

In July 2017, I (first author) attended the burial of a Greek Cypriot. The body was brought to the church to be reburied with political national presence (i.e., soldiers with military ware who were to carry the "body" to the cemetery) in a Greek Cypriot ceremony, but the speeches before and during it gestured to cracks in the state. For example, his brother said:

> We have been notified by the CMP that remains of my brother Antonis have been identified. He has been missing since 14th August 1974, last seen on Mount Koutsoventis exactly where his remains have been found. Next Friday we will be visiting the Anthropological Laboratory to meet with what remains of our brother. We will bury him in Dhali on Saturday the 29th July 2017 at 10:00am. We are planning a *simple family* and friends funeral, in recognition of the tragic events of 1974 and the conflict that led to these, in a manner that we are sure Antonis would have liked. (Eftymiou 11 July 2017)

The brother's comments indicate this "funeral" is going to be "simple," not framed as the loss of a comrade at the hands of the enemy, as the nation-state wants to do. This speech orients us toward a Cypriot community, a possibility underscored by a comment made by one of the nieces at this funeral: "A few hours of this ceremony at the village's graveyard is a kind of a healing that extends out into concentric circles of the lifeblood of a Cypriot comradeship, solidarity and community." Healing is a process of synthesizing multiple senses; it acknowledges the whole self, all its capacity and all its ways of connection. By the same token, decolonization requires a healing process open to multiple events. It must include imagining the destruction of the nation-state as we know it.

On August 15, 2016, when 33 Turkish Cypriots were to be buried, Turkish soldiers carried the coffins, thus symbolically inscribing the power of the state to integrate this event into its governance process (Associated Press, 2016). In stark contrast to the move by the state, the villagers and family members said it was important to have found the bodies as they could now "rest in peace and … hear their families' prayers nearby instead of the heavy trucks driving over their earlier mass grave" (Associated Press, 2016). Put otherwise, the process and dominance of the sovereign at the moment of burial were at odds with the needs and imaginaries of the families. The co-production of the state depends on securing the missing within its territorial and governing processes; in this case, the state attempted to code and integrate the event as part of its own political sovereign-making project.

Even graves have political statements, some revealing a major issue with which CMP is grappling: the "race against time" (UNDP Cyprus, 2017). One widow's gravestone simply says: "If you find my husband, please bury him next to me" (UNDP Eurasia, 2017). Similarly, UNDP Cyprus, the organization "responsible for the day-to-day administrative, financial, and procurement implementation of the project," articulates this feeling about the race against time: "The identity and dignity of so many Cypriots—so cruelly snatched from them some 40 or 50 years ago—must be restored before it is lost forever" (UNDP Eurasia, 2017).

Turkish Cypriot graveyards simply have the name of the person along the dates that he/she went missing and others the date of the burial or sayings from the Qur'an. One may attempt to accept Turkey's colonization of the island to resolve once and for all in support of the Turks the sovereign question which the British empire along with Greece and Turkey constitutionally "resolved" unevenly through the establishment of the Republic of Cyprus premised on a minority and majority racialized populations: "And do not say about those who are killed in the way of Allah, 'They are dead[!]" (Interlocutor, 2016). Some of the poetics speak not only to Islamic and Christian understandings of life (i.e., sacrifice, heroism), and life after death, but also to the importance of making present the terror and violence by questioning whether this kind of obliteration is not itself hinging on the idea of global raciality and its notion of gender and class. Greek Cypriot graveyards are decorated with the names of the persons or with a series of different sayings expressing either the sacrifice and/or heroic nature of the person who was killed in the name of the state. Next to the graves of several missing is the following: "See…you are not lost. You are here never dead." Closure is sometimes impossible (Killian, 2016). For example, some remains cannot be buried in cemeteries. For some Muslims there is a prohibition against burying a body until all bones have been collected.

Though the violence is ongoing and the "biotechnological response" to the missing and disappeared does not easily address these complex social, economic, religious, symbolic, ethical, and healing questions (2010: 8), what goes on gravestones and how it is integrated into certain nationalist projects are contested processes. In a commemoration of my uncle (first author), among others, government officials, priests, and members of the nationalist-popular party showed up. With their presence, the painful memory of the terror my uncle experienced during the Turkish colonial war was exacerbated by our knowledge of the state's inattention to his burial post-Turkish colonization, even when it clearly had information, including the material collected from his military post. The whole family grapples in

Photo: Anna M. Agathangelou (July 2017)

different ways to challenge and rupture the dominant attempts to integrate his death into a certain memory project. At the event, one of the women from the village started a lamentation:

They did this to us. They brought this hell upon us.
Their desires ate our children.
Our sons were obliterated.
But our sons are here (υπαρχουν).
Look at their children.
I see our sons' faces. The terror still marks them and all of us.
Now, they raise their fists high up to the heavens.
The princes of war have been amassing at our borders.

Her lamentation speaks to how desires for expansion and colonization are destroyers of life, and it ruptures logics of national sacrifice. This lamentation animates and poetically buries the dead. It is also a lamentation and ruptures the sociality that comes with the state and with that the notion that integration of the missing and disappeared into the nation is going to entail healing.

If the question of the disappeared is dis/placed or dislocated as a question of conflict and war, which it is, without attending to what kind of healing humanitarian projects imagine and engage in, the social, political, economic, and symbolic relations, then much is being missed/disappeared in the conversation. One interlocutor challenged the retrospective stabilization of the national healthy subject through the missing and disappeared:

The courage does not come in the words of any humanitarian organization or a state and its attempts to attend to trauma. The courage comes in our poetries. Leave behind the mythologies of our origin, the promises to come. We know that this land was one of the first plantations, our ancestors were enslaved. Let's break with these dominant origin myths. Let's invent poetry that orients us to revolution that revolutionizes by dispersing itself. No one has the right to use those whose lives were obliterated in the name of a nation-state or any humanitarian project. (Interlocutor 15, 2015)

Let us engage in the creation of new grounds: the continual act of invention of anti-memories that do not depend on the transmutation of the lives of our dead. Let us find new ways of relating which do not depend on enslavement, but are created and inscribed without slaves of any kind. Let us find new ways of healing that does not depend on the unfreedoms and death of others.

References

Agathangelou, A. (Forthcoming). Regrets and remains: The "missing" and (in)securities in Cyprus. *Theory and Event.*
Agathangelou, A. (2017a). Living archives and imperial wars. *Critical Military Studies, 3,* 206–211.
Agathangelou, A. (2017b). Humanitarian innovations and material returns: Valuation, bio-financialization, and radical politics. Special issue on global techno-assemblages: Entanglements of inventions, markets, and labor. *Science, Technology and Society, 22,* 78–101.

Agathangelou, A. M. (2011). Bodies to the slaughter: Slavery, reconstruction, Fanon's combat breath, and wrestling for life *Somatechnics Journal, 1.* (1), 209–248.

Alexander, J. M. (2005). *Pedagogies of crossing: Meditations on feminism, sexual politics, memory, and the sacred.* Durham, NC: Duke University Press.

Associated Press (2016). 33 missing Turkish Cypriots laid to rest after 42 years. http://www.dailymail.co.uk/wires/ap/article-3741368/33-missing-Turkish-Cypriots-laid-rest-42-years.html

Balibar, E. (1991). *Race, nation, class: Ambiguous identities.* New York: Verso Press.

Birch, K. (2015). *We have never been neoliberal.* Winchester, UK: Zero Books.

———. (2017). Rethinking value in the bio-economy: Finance, assetization, and the management of value. *Science, Technology & Human Values. 42*(3), 460–490.

Bartlett, B. (2017). Time-soaked: How trauma submerges in and out of time. *Psychoanalytic Dialogues: The International Journal of Relational Perspectives, 27*(3), 241–254.

Cassia, P. S. (2006). Guarding each other's dead, mourning own's own: The problem of missing persons and missing pasts in Cyprus. *South European Society and Politics, 11.*(1), 111–128.

Committee on the Missing Persons in Cyprus (2017). *The origins.* http://www.cmp-cyprus.org/content/origins

Cox, M., et al. (2008). *The scientific investigation of mass graves: Towards protocols and standard operating procedures.* New York: Cambridge University Press.

Da Silva, D. F. (2007). *Toward a global idea of race.* Minneapolis, MN: University of Minnesota Press.

Espiritu, Y. L. (2006). Toward a critical refugee study: The Vietnamese refugee subject in US scholarship. *Journal of Vietnamese Studies, 1*(1–2), 410–433.

Espiritu, Y. L. (2005). Thirty years after war: The endings that are not over. *Amerasia Journal, 31*(2), xiii–xxvi.

Fics, K. (2016). *Healing through the bones.* Lanham, MD: Hamilton Books.

Interlocutor. (2016). *Interview and transcript.* Kyrenia, Cyprus.

International Committee of the Red Cross. (2002). *The missing: The mourning process and commemoration.*https://www.icrc.org/en/doc/resources/documents/misc/5eyd9z.html

Jasanoff, S. (2006). Biotechnology and empire: The global power of seeds and science. *OSIRIS, 21*(1), 273–292.

———. (2011). *Reframing rights: Bioconstitutionalism in the genetic age..* Cambridge, MA: MIT Press.

Keenan, T. & Weizman, E. (2011). *Mengele's skull: The advent of a forensic aesthetics.* Berlin/Frankfurt: Sternberg Press.

Killian, K. D. (2016). Time, trauma and ambiguous loss: Working with families with missing members in post-conflict Cyprus. In L. Charles & G. Samarasinghe (Eds.), *Family therapy in global humanitarian contexts: Voices and issues from the field* (pp. 77–89). New York: Springer.

Klose, F. & Thulin, M. (ed.) (2016). *Humanity: A history of European concepts in practice from the sixteenth century to the present.* Göttingen, Germany: Vandenhoeck & Ruprecht Gmbh & Company.

Kovras, I. (2013). Explaining prolonged silences in transitional justice: The disappeared in Cyprus and Spain. *Comparative Political Studies, 46*, 730–756.

Ktori, M. & Gülseren, B. (2018). Development and future perspectives of a humanitarian forensic programme: The committee on missing persons in Cyprus example. *Egyptian Journal of Forensic Sciences, 8*, 25–36.

Lefebvre, H. (2000[1974]). *La production de l'espace.* Paris: Anthropos.

Leighton, M. (2010). Personifying objects/objectifying people: Handling questions of mortality and materiality through the archaeological body. *Ethnos, 75*(1), 78–101.

Loucaides, L. (2011). Is the European Court of Human Rights still a principled court of human rights after the Dermopoulos case? *Leiden Journal of International Law, 24*(2): 435–465.

Low, S. & Smith, N. (ed.) (2006). *The politics of public space.* New York: Routledge.

Marriott, D. (2016). Corpsing, or, the matter of black life. *Cultural Critique, 94*, 32–64.

Marx, K. (1986). *"Instructions for the delegates of the provisional general council" in MECW* (Vol. 20). Moscow: Progress Publishers.

Moon, C. (2016). Human rights, human remains: forensic humanitarianism and the human rights of the dead. *International Social Science Journal, 65*, 49–63.

Peterson, S. (1999). DNA detectives on divided Cyprus. *The Christian Science Monitor.* http://www.csmonitor.com/1999/0528/p6s2.html

Prainsack, B., & Aronson, J.D. (2015). Forensic DNA databases: Ethical issues. *International Encyclopedia of the Social and Behavioral Sciences, 9*, 339–345.

Rosenblatt, A. (2010). International forensic investigations and the human rights of the dead. *Human Rights Quarterly, 32*(4), 921–950.

Schmitt, C. (2003). *The nomos of the Earth in the international law of the Jus Publicum Europaeum.*, trans. G.L. Ulmen. New York: Telos Press.

Schweitzer, R., Melville, F., Steel, Z., et al. (2006). Trauma, post-migration living difficulties, and social support as predictors of psychological adjustment in resettled Sudanese refugees. *Australia New Zealand Journal Psychiatry, 40*, 179–188.

Smith, L. (2013). "Genetics is a study in faith": Forensic DNA, kinship analysis, and the ethics of care in post-conflict Latin America. *S&F Online, 11* (3), Summer. http://sfonline.barnard.edu/life-un-ltd-feminism-bioscience-race/genetics-is-a-study-in-faith-forensic-dna-kinship-analysis-and-the-ethics-of-care-in-post-conflict-latin-america/

Smith, L. (2016). Identifying democracy citizenship, DNA, and identity in postdictatorship Argentina. *Science, Technology and Human Values, 41.* (6), 1037–1062.

Spillers, H. (2003[1996]). "All the things you could be by now, if Sigmund Freud's wife was your mother": Psychoanalysis and race. *In Black, white, and in color: Essays on American literature and culture.* Chicago, IL: University of Chicago Press.

UNDP Cyprus (2017). A new generation of Cypriots uncovers the missing: Healing the wounds of a divided island. Retrieved July 1, 2018 at https://medium.com/@UNDPEurasia/a-new-generation-of-cypriots-uncovers-the-missing-57389ae396c3

UNDP Eurasia (2017). *A new generation of Cypriots uncovers the missing: Healing the wounds of a divided island.* https://medium.com/@UNDPEurasia/a-new-generation-of-cypriots-uncovers-the-missing-57389ae396c3

Wagner, S. (2010). Tabulating loss, entombing memory: The Srebrenica-Potočari memorial center. In E. Anderson et al. (Eds.), *Memory, mourning, landscape.* Amsterdam: Rodopi.

Walker, G. (2012). *The sublime perversion of capital: Marxism and the national question in modern Japanese thought.* Dissertation, Cornell University.

Walker, J. (2016). Enclaves and states in (post)colonial Congo: Spatial logics and epidemiological metaphors. *Somatosphere: Science, Medicine and Anthropology.* http://somatosphere.net/forumpost/enclaves-and-states-in-postcolonial-congo-spatial-logics-and-epidemiological-metaphors

Weizman, E. (2013). Introduction: Forensis. MIT Architecture. Retrieved June 21 2018 from https://architecture.mit.edu/sites/architecture.mit.edu/files/attachments/lecture/Weizman_Introduction-Forensis-libre.pdf

Williams H. (2004). Death warmed up: The agency of bodies and bones in early Anglo-Saxon cremation rites. *Journal of Material Culture, 9*(3), 263–291.

Chapter 5
Undocumented and Unafraid: Resilience Under Forced Separation and Threat of Deportation

Catalina Perdomo and Tiffany Adeigbe

Introduction

The Community Counseling Service (CCS) is a mental health clinic that serves as the clinical training center for Our Lady of the Lake University's master's and doctoral level students. The CCS is located in the West Side of San Antonio, Texas, where the population is predominantly low-income families of Mexican origin. The CCS uses a co-therapy approach to deliver therapeutic services to the neighboring underserved and marginalized communities of low-income families at a sliding scale fee. The student clinicians at the CCS offer individual, couple, marital, and family counseling as well as psychological testing in both English and Spanish. When scheduled appointments are unavailable, families are invited to walk-in at their discretion during set hours of the work week. At the CCS we receive and provide live supervision from a brief therapy perspective, therefore clients decide if they need more than one session, not the clinician. Due to the geographic location of San Antonio, and the nearby border of Mexico, there is a large population of Latin American immigrants, both documented and undocumented. Working at a clinic that predominantly serves historically marginalized and underserved populations provides us with a unique opportunity to engage in therapeutic conversations that explore various aspects of diversity within and between Latin communities. The majority of our clinical work revolves around addressing experiences of crisis. In this chapter we include examples of our clinical work within the context of undocumented immigration and deportation.[1]

Now that we have introduced the training clinic where we work, we would like to introduce ourselves. We met one another during our studies at Our Lady of the

---

[1] Identifying information changed throughout the chapter.

C. Perdomo · T. Adeigbe (✉)
Our Lady of the Lake University, San Antonio, TX, USA
e-mail: cperdomo@ollusa.edu

© Springer Nature Switzerland AG 2019
L. L. Charlés, G. Samarasinghe (eds.), *Family Systems and Global Humanitarian Mental Health*, https://doi.org/10.1007/978-3-030-03216-6_5

Lake University. We both completed a master's degree in Marriage and Family Therapy where our time overlapped briefly. A few years later, we reunited as health psychology doctoral students, once again at Our Lady of the Lake University in San Antonio, Texas. As we progress in our program together, we have found similarities that continue to shape our professional and personal lives.

One important connection is our shared family history of immigration. Both of our fathers immigrated to the United States as international students; Tiffany's father from Nigeria and Catalina's from Colombia. We both have Latin American roots, Tiffany through her mother's Mexican heritage and Catalina through Colombia, which led to Spanish-English bilingual upbringings. We also share a mutual interest in serving undocumented families. This led to similar practicum experiences and the shared authorship of this chapter. We were both mentored and trained in biopsychosocial evaluations for immigration purposes by our clinic director Dr. Bernadette Solórzano, who we discuss in further detail at the end of our chapter. These evaluations become part of families' immigration applications to prove extreme hardship to the government. If approved, individuals can stay with loved ones and prevent deportation. Additionally, our combined clinical experiences include providing individual and group therapy to survivors of torture, asylum and refugee seekers, unaccompanied minors in a shelter, and services for families recently released from immigration detention centers. Throughout this chapter, we will present our stories individually and collectively through case examples and reflections.

Theoretical Framework

There are key theoretical underpinnings that guide our therapy work with clients. Our master's and doctoral training stems from a postmodern strengths-based approach to psychotherapy. Postmodernists believe that one's language, culture, and perceptions construct their reality. So what we believe to be true, or real, is created by our own lived experiences. The meaning we assign through language to those experiences becomes our reality (Goolishian & Anderson, 1987). Within this view, language is the origin and functional basis for the construction of reality (Gemignani & Pena, 2007). For example, the word *love* at face value is simply four letters put together in a sequence. Alone, it has absolutely no real meaning. However, through our own individual experiences and perceptions, we have each assigned different meanings to the word *love*. In our immigration work, *trauma* is a unique experience. Families that have similar lived experiences might not share the same meaning of *trauma*. This includes mental health workers. Our understanding of *trauma* may not necessarily fit how clients understand it.

At our training clinic, we learn to conduct therapy from a single-session mindset or the perspective that clients can receive benefits and results from even just a single therapy session. Immigration applications are time intensive and expensive. Coupled with the low-income status of most undocumented individuals, clients generally cannot afford the time away from work to engage in long-term therapy, even if our sessions are free. As a result, the single-session mindset works well at our training clinic. By working with clients in an efficient manner, our role is to guide the work toward their goals, not necessarily to meet goals fully in session. We work collaboratively with families to initiate positive, realistic, and achievable changes in their lives (De Shazer, Dolan, Korman, McCollum, Trepper & Berg, 2007). This means that we believe in the co-responsibility of therapy progress. The assumption of co-responsibility is that clients are also responsible for their outcomes and what they accomplish in a single session. Working from this perspective has been successful with undocumented families. This mindset is also effective with different models of therapy and is further explored in Slive and Bobele's *When One Hour is All You Have* (2011). Additionally, we borrow from our Latin American roots by adopting the literary style of magical realism to engage in meaning-making conversations that align culturally with clients, many of which are from Latin America (Polanco, 2010). In the second case presentation, I (Catalina) show the incorporation of magical realism in a co-constructed letter.

In conjunction with magical realism, we also share the theoretical perspective of narrative therapy as explained by Michael White and David Epston (1990; White, 1988/1989). We see clients as the experts of their lives and reinforce the familiar phrase that the person is not the problem, the problem is the problem. In our case presentations, the collaborative process takes its form as the co-creation of a list and a letter. In both of our clinical practices, we use externalizing language and work with clients to enrich the alternative story or preferred identity. We work from the perspective that people can evaluate their lived experiences in the context of their culture through conversations and stories. This means that our culture, beliefs, and values influence how we understand our own lived experiences. For example, if a male client reported feelings of failure or worthlessness after losing his job because he can no longer provide for his family, we would inquire how his culture and personal beliefs have lead him to that conclusion. We might explore how his culture influenced his understanding of his roles as a man, father, husband, etc. In the following case presentation, Tiffany explores immigration work through the lens of our postmodern strengths-based framework. The case presentation focuses on long-term family therapy after the deportation of a family member. We will then delve into the historical and legal contexts of immigration work.

Case Presentation I: Strengths-Based Counseling

Tiffany Adeigbe

The family you are about to meet has profoundly impacted my work with undocumented families. For the past 2 years, I have worked with David and his children in therapy conducted in Spanish. David has been separated from his wife, Sara, for more than 8 years due to her undocumented status and subsequent deportation.

At the first appointment with David and his children, I learned they had been separated from Sara for approximately 6 years. Together, the couple has three children: Alexis who is 11, Mia who is 10, and Chris who is 9. When the family was separated, David and Sara decided it would be best to have the children remain in the United States. They were worried for their children's well-being and safety living in Mexico. The city where Sara lives is incredibly dangerous. Gang- and cartel-related violence are prominent, and women and children are often targeted. David knew he would be unable to protect their children from these dangers if they lived in Mexico. Since their separation, David tries to travel every weekend with their three children to visit Sara. Their children have now lived most of their young lives without their mother.

I first met with David to conduct a biopsychosocial evaluation to prove he was suffering extreme psychological hardship stemming from Sara's deportation. Since Sara had been deported, they were trying to obtain a visa and needed to apply for an immigration waiver or pardon. Essentially, asking the government for forgiveness for Sara living in the United States illegally. After conducting David's biopsychosocial evaluation and clinical interviews, David and his three children began therapy.

Our therapy work initially focused on their emotional and psychological distress. David wanted a space for his children to talk openly about their pain, fears, and worries. At that time, he was also struggling to cope with the overwhelming pressure of caring and providing for his family without his partner by his side. David also shared that his wife Sara was beginning to lose hope that they would ever be reunited. This led David to feel further pressure and distress. In our initial meetings, he appeared desperate to find a solution to the family's collective distress. Without the ability to obtain Sara's documentation, he was searching for some alleviation to his family's suffering. David shared that he did not know how to help his family. An excerpt from a session transcription is included below[2]:

David: I don't know. It's too much now. I just don't want to worry about this anymore. Sometimes I just want to stop trying. It's just too much. Sara isn't sleeping, and she calls me crying all the time. Sometimes I call her in the middle of the night to make sure she is okay.

Alexis: Hearing her voice makes me happy but sometimes when I hang up I will go to the bathroom, so I can cry and let my feelings out. But no one knows that I cry. I don't let them see.

Mia: My favorite day is Friday and Saturday because we go to see my mom. I don't like any of the other days. I don't like them because my mom isn't with me on those days.

---

[2] All transcriptions translated to English.

When David and his children were sharing their distress, I worked from a strengths-based position to carefully listen for exceptions, or times when the problem was not occurring. I searched for examples of when the emotional distress was not present in their lives. As a strengths-based practitioner, I have learned that asking clients what is going well in their lives and highlighting their strengths helps initiate positive change. At times clients change the meaning of previously problematic words in the course of therapy. I recall working with a woman who was seeking political asylum after being physically and sexually assaulted by her partner and several gang members. As the session progressed, she shared feeling worthless, ashamed, and tired of fighting to feel normal. I held on to her use of the word *fighting*. *Fighting* meant something unique to her and I was curious. I began asking what she was fighting for and how it had helped her in the past. As we explored, I learned that despite being tired, her life was worth the fight. She shared that *fighting* previously helped her survive. Through conversation, *fighting* no longer seemed exhausting, instead becoming a strengths-based alternative and a symbol of freedom. In my strengths-based work with families like David's, I focus on these alternative understandings.

As our therapy progressed, I learned that David and his children had not seen Sara in 3 weeks. The children were crying and David held his head down. It was clear to me that the only thing that would make them happy was to be physically reunited with Sara in the United States. Since, like David, I could not bring Sara to them, I was unsure how to be helpful. As my mind raced I learned that it was important to provide a space for David and his family to express their distress. I acknowledged the frustration and sadness they were feeling. The therapy room became a place to share their pain. They missed Sara desperately and wished for her return. After some time, I asked how they were managing the pain of not seeing Sara. David's children, Chris and Alexis, immediately shared their tactics while their father listened, surprised at their resiliency.

> Chris: I cooked with my dad. He doesn't cook very well though. I'm going to be a chef when I grow up. A chef with a big mustache and I am going to cook my mom's favorite foods.
> Alexis: I'm going to be an immigration lawyer, so I can help my mom and she can be with us again (...) and then I can help other people too.

David was visibly emotional as he wiped tears from his eyes. He explained how proud he was of his children and how much he loved them. He felt relieved to know that despite missing Sara, his children were doing well in other areas. I reflected to the family how incredible it was that they were able to find ways to include their mother in their day-to-day lives. I shared that I saw Sara in Chris' cooking, since he often attempted to make his mother's favorite dishes. David and Alexis knew their mother valued education, so they worked hard to excel academically. Alexis' separation from her mother led to a vocational calling in immigration law.

In our last meeting, we co-created new ways to honor Sara as a family. We specifically focused on the periods of time between their visits, since they shared these gaps to be particularly difficult. Their ideas stemmed from their stories of resiliency. The co-constructed list included (1) going to their favorite *fruteria*[3] for ice cream, (2) cooking Sara's favorite meal together, and (3) using a calendar to count down the days until their next visit. During a follow-up call, David stated they were doing fine and would call if needed.

There are times when I think about this family and their experience of deportation. I sometimes wonder if Sara is still in Mexico, if the children continue to do well in school, and if David still engages in the co-created list. Although these questions remain, my belief in the co-responsibility of therapy leads me to trust that David and his family will continue to show resiliency in the face of uncertainty. Through this case presentation, a small glimpse of the human experience of immigration was brought forward. Often, immigration policy and reform are discussed with such legal and political jargon, that it is easy to forget how policies directly affect not just those deported but the families that remain. The historical and legal context of immigration is often complex and frustrating for families and clinicians. In sharing our understandings of this complexity, we hope it might inform your work and possibly somewhat diminish your own feelings of frustration.

Historical and Legal Context

Just like a genogram can help us learn the historical relationships of clients, we believe it is important to highlight the historical relations of the United States with the home countries of undocumented Latin immigrants. The relationship between the United States and Latin America could be described as contentious and unstable. The United States has participated in the shaping of politics through political coups, paramilitary training, and CIA-funded insurgencies (Worthington, 2015; SOA Watch, 2017; *U.S Code: Title 10, Section 4415;* Main & Johnston, 2009). The results of these actions often left countries politically unstable. It's possible that the US involvement in Latin American political and economic endeavors contributed in part to the influx of immigrants that continues today. When you add factors like civil war, natural disasters, gang activity, corruption, poverty, oppression, and persecution, the influx of immigrants begins to make sense (American Psychological Association, Presidential Task Force on Immigration, 2013). These factors are not unique to the Americas; countries across the globe face these issues on a continuum. With such dire conditions, immigration becomes a global occurrence. This was evident in the 2015 flow of unaccompanied minors from Central and South America to the United States, which mirrored the waves of migrants seen in Europe (Rietig, 2015). The political crisis that followed these waves in Europe paralleled the US political divisions.

---

[3] Type of fruit store that serves Mexican desserts, beverages, and popular snack foods.

Immigration was identified as a central issue in the 2016 U.S. Presidential Election by 79% of registered voters (Pew Research Center, 2016a). With over 1.7 million unauthorized migrants arriving from Central America alone, the United States needed to find ways to control immigration (Pew Research Center, 2016b). The U.S. Department of Immigration and Customs Enforcement, in combination with the presidential office, has passed and enforced divisive laws that vilify sanctuary cities in an effort to control immigration at a national level (*Exec. Order No. 13768, 3 C.F.R. 8799–8803. 2017*; Yee, 2017). Another way the government has attempted to control immigration is through the development of explicit avenues and procedures for documentation. The federal and state governments establish and enforce certain procedures to obtain permits and documentation.

The families we encounter in our work apply through a variety of avenues including, U-Visa, T-Visa, VAWA, Asylum/Refugee Status, and Extreme Hardship (USCIS, 2017). Although multiple paths exist, there is a set country quota per visa, and the numbers of applications can make the process take years. In 2016 alone, there were over 261,000 petitions received through relatives with 1,062,620 still pending processing (USCIS, 2017). In our work as psychologists in training, we have collaborated with families from across the world pursuing any of the aforementioned paths. There are times when we have utilized the services of interpreters and family members to gather the necessary information to write the biopsychosocial evaluation which becomes a part of their immigration application. This evaluation requires a detailed account of the client's life focusing on the suffering they would experience if they, or a loved one, are deported. In essence, although not directly associated with immigration law or the federal government, mental health workers become part of the immigration process.

Mental Health Workers

One crucial element of our work in immigration is our role as an evaluator of suffering. Our work must align with the government's immigration system in language and medical lens. We have found that our systemic training helps us balance a strengths-based perspective of resiliency with the diagnostic lens of the medical model. Our immigration work with families is translated on paper, not just into English, but also into the diagnostic jargon for immigration officials. The clients and their lawyers hope that the biopsychosocial evaluation will show an immigration judge that the individual is suffering extreme psychological hardship, derived from the government term of extreme hardship that has no set definition (USCIS, 2017).

We not only balance perspectives but also our privileged position as US citizens. In order to work with undocumented families, we learned that it is important to recognize the benefits we have accrued as a result of the US role in Latin America and potential contribution to the influx of immigration seen today. Balancing perspectives and privilege has led us to not only focus on the hardship families experience but also the resiliency despite the uncertainty of their futures. Although we recognize that immigration work occurs in different countries and languages, for the purposes of this chapter, we have chosen to focus on our work in Spanish since we have direct access to this language. Now that we have briefly explored the historical and legal contexts, the experiences of families must be further explored.

Nos Estamos Apagando[4]

The constant fear experienced by individuals and families facing deportation is profound. The ongoing emotional distress often stems from living in a state of sustained uncertainty, never really knowing whether they or their loved one will be deported or pardoned. According to Cohen (1993), when faced with an experience that cannot be changed or controlled, ideas of the past and near future become unattainable, leaving the individual stuck in a constant state of emotional distress. In addition to the ongoing emotional distress related to the immigration process itself, their experience is compounded by discrimination and exploitation. They face racism, insults, and threats of deportation and are often exploited at their jobs due to their lack of civil protections (American Psychological Association, Presidential Task Force on Immigration, 2012). I (Catalina) remember a therapy session with a young man who worked in construction. He was hired to lay a concrete driveway. When the job was finished, the contractor refused to pay him and threatened to call immigration. I recall feeling disgusted that someone could be so malicious. Even worse, the young man I was working with went through this experience without a legal avenue for justice. It is in those moments that we as clinicians become witnesses to testimonies of injustice. I knew during that session that it was crucial to believe my client, to acknowledge the injustice, and to listen fully to the recount of his pain.

Families with a member under threat of deportation worry that their loved one will be detained at a routine traffic stop. They fear passing immigration checkpoints and therefore avoid travel. I (Tiffany) worked with a client who, having just finished eating dinner at a restaurant with his family, was pulled over on his drive home by local police officers. He was told that he fit the description of an individual they were looking for. The officers asked for his driver's license, and since he was unable to produce one, they decided to call immigration and customs enforcement. He was then handcuffed in front of his family and placed in the vehicle. He professed that he would never forget what it felt like to know his children saw him handcuffed. During his 2-month detention, their cries replayed in his mind every single day. He was finally released when his family raised enough money.

Not only do families fear every day commutes, but we often hear stories of guilt for missing the funerals of loved ones in their country of origin due to their immigration status. In our experiences working with clients seeking asylum and trafficking visas (T-VISA), their fear of returning is palpable, and their views of deportation

---

[4] A quote from an undocumented client: "We are shutting down."

as a death sentence are clear. As we continue to bear witness to these experiences of fear and suffering, we knew it was important to write this chapter. We believe it is relevant to the current immigration discourse and important for those interested in working within the context of immigration. Driven by these shared experiences, we are constantly motivated to find better ways to serve the needs of undocumented individuals and their families. In the following case presentation, Catalina shares an example of adapting therapy to meet the immediate needs of a client who is seeking a trafficking visa.

Case Presentation II: Single-Session Letter[5]

Catalina Perdomo

Maria was born in Mexico in a family that raised her to believe women were "born incomplete so men could finish forming them." She was taught that physical violence is a normal part of relationships. When she met her first husband, Jesus, she saw an escape from her home life. Instead she was forced into marriage and repeatedly physically and sexually abused. After the birth of her son, Jesus sold Maria to corrupt police officers. The officers sexually trafficked Maria and forced her into drug use. Eventually Maria succeeded in escaping, noting her son as the motivation for her freedom. When she attempted to press charges, the judge told her to accept that she was a prostitute, recant her claims, and flee the country within 72 hours. Jesus forced Maria to let him travel with her, by kidnapping their son and threatening harm. After the birth of her second child in the United States, Maria was able to leave Jesus with both children. She became an informant for the FBI after experiencing immigration fraud and eventually remarried a generous and respectful man.

As part of her immigration application for a trafficking visa (T-VISA), Maria was required to retell her past experiences of trauma. Undocumented applicants write a victim declaration, share their past with their lawyers, undergo evaluation, and retell their story in court under interrogation. The multiple experiences of retelling her story for her application were re-traumatizing. Maria began to experience dissociative amnesia related to her posttraumatic stress disorder. When she called to make the therapy appointment, she wanted help to move forward and away from her past. Applying for the trafficking visa was a long and intensive process. Maria was tired of repeated appointments which were constant reminders of her past. She shared not wanting long-term therapy, so, instead, we worked together in a single session.

In our single therapy session, Maria and I co-created a strengths-based narrative informed letter that mirrored her trauma-focused biopsychosocial evaluation. The co-created letter employed magical realism to focus on Maria's hopes, values,

---

[5] Case presentation further explored in *Undocumented and Deportable: Re-Authoring Trauma within the Context of Immigration in a Narrative Informed Single Session* (Perdomo, 2018).

preferences, and dreams while destabilizing the biopsychosocial evaluation. Essentially, by using the same format as her immigration evaluation, the narrative informed letter became an alternative to the accepted reality of posttraumatic stress disorder (Polanco, 2010). Her richly detailed memories of motherhood exist in the same world as the narrative of posttraumatic stress disorder. Aligned with the magical realist paradox, Maria simultaneously balances the biopsychosocial narrative of her immigration experience with the strengths-based narrative informed letter (Faris, 2004; Polanco, 2010).

English Excerpt of Maria's Alternative Narrative of Motherhood
On October 1, 1989, Maria gave birth to Peter. She felt an immediate peace knowing that he was hers. She had feelings of tenderness toward her son, and when she held him to her breast, she pictured his future. She dreamed that he would study and have a great career and a family one day.

On April 22, 1994, Maria welcomed Amanda into the world. Even though Amanda had to spend some time in the NICU, Maria still remembers what it felt like to be with her daughter. At first, she joked, "Are you sure she's mine? She's so big!" She felt so much love for her daughter. Maria remembers when Peter met his sister for the first time in the hospital. He came with a big pink balloon that read "Congratulations! It's A Girl!" and a doll. When Maria asked Peter if he wanted to meet his sister he replied, "No! I only brought her this doll. The balloon is mine!" Maria tried to teach Peter that he must share with his sister, but he was a little jealous. The nurses gifted Amanda lots of pink gifts and clothes. Peter found the only little gift with a blue string on it, it was a baby cap and he placed it on his head proclaiming that it was his. Maria still laughs when she remembers this moment; she stated that "he looked like a little Jewish boy because the cap was so small!"

Not only did Maria share her joys of motherhood, but through collaboration, we developed new psychological diagnoses that would fit the alternative narrative. These new diagnoses, described in Maria's words, subvert the Western empirically based *Diagnostic and Statistical Manual of Mental Disorders* (Faris, 2004). One of her diagnoses is tied to the alternative storyline of motherhood. Given Maria's past experiences of trauma, and abuse from her own mother, some might see Maria's mothering ability as extraordinary. In the alternative letter, Maria's rich description of her extraordinary mother abilities is rooted in everyday activities and made mundane. From the magical realist perspective, this allows the miraculous to be seen in the everyday (Geetha, 2010).

New Psychological Diagnoses
Maria is proud of her children. She loves them unconditionally and is willing to sacrifice her happiness for their own. Maria enjoys watching her daughter develop into a young woman and hopes for the best in her son's future. She has instilled in her children nobleness and strength. Throughout their lives she has made sure they are safe and protected, even at the cost of her own safety. She puts their lives above her own. These symptoms more than meet the criteria for *Amazing Mother Syndrome*. Amazing Mother Syndrome may develop in only certain individuals who can establish a secure, structured, hopeful environment for their children.

As I reflect on my time with Maria, I have come to conceptualize our work as embodying key elements of posttraumatic growth. The premise of this concept is that after a person experiences a traumatic event or negative life circumstance, growth can be achieved if the person begins creating a new meaningful life goal (Diener, 2009; Davis & Nolen-Hoeksema, 2009). The period between the conception and implementation of the new goal(s) is the crucial period of growth. In my opinion, Maria contacted me in the midst of this period. Although her goal of documentation was out of our control, the reconnection to her ideas of motherhood became instrumental to her identity. Maria's experiences of trauma, connection to motherhood, and reasons for emigrating are not unique to Mexico and the United States; in fact they occur on a global scale.

Practical Implications

A Global Experience Deportation and detention are not region specific but a global occurrence. People across the world have voluntarily and involuntarily emigrated for centuries. Reasons might include religious persecution, natural disasters, employment, education, finding family members, and at times seeking refuge in foreign countries for their own survival (American Psychological Association, Presidential Task Force on Immigration, 2013). Many arrive with hopes of living a safer and more peaceful life. Leaders of countries across the globe are facing the same challenges as the United States regarding unauthorized immigration. These challenges often take place in a back and forth between human rights and political issues. The work that we shared in this chapter took place in San Antonio, Texas, but it is not in isolation. The ideas have practical applicability across the globe where themes of suffering and resiliency are present on a daily basis.

Tearing Down Walls Immigration clients seeking mental health services face seemingly insurmountable barriers. At times they risk deportation just driving to their therapy appointments. Most immigration clients are uninsured, may work irregular hours, and balance family life with legal appointments (American Psychological Association, Presidential Task Force on Immigration, 2013). At our training clinic, services are offered at a sliding scale fee, and times are available for clients to walk-in when convenient. Additionally, intake forms were adapted for clients to preserve the privacy of their immigration status. These structural changes can make a huge difference.

Services that are culturally and linguistically congruent can also remove barriers. At times when we do not have access to a client's native language, like *Tigrinya* from Eritrea, we collaborate with interpreters. In therapy we refer to experiences of distress in the client's language, intentionally circumventing the Eurocentric bias of the *Diagnostic and Statistical Manual of Mental Disorders*. When exploring goals, we inquire what values clients bring instead of imposing western beliefs, like the need to participate in therapy or the value of independence (American Psychological Association, Presidential Task Force on Immigration, 2013). We cannot stress enough the importance of collaborating with culturally congruent community resources to understand and meet the needs of immigrant clients. We have partnered with refugee and resettlement programs, schools, immigration lawyers, religious leaders, curanderos, elders, as well as family members. Through those relationships, we have tailored services to better meet the needs of immigrant communities.

The Power of Hope Since we see our work as bi-directional, there are times when we too feel stuck in the uncertainty of our client's immigration status. We hear clients express how their problems would be resolved with the resolution of their immigration status. Yet, we feel helpless in providing that resolution since it falls outside the scope of our services. It has taken some time to learn that the uncertainty we feel about clients' futures is only helpful in that it gives us a small glimpse into their own uncertainty. Instead, we have found that it is more beneficial to focus on the things that are working in their lives, despite uncertainty. For us, we relate that not just to our theory of practice but a belief in the power of hope in uncertain times. Working from a strengths-based perspective helps us cultivate feelings of hope not just for clients but also for ourselves.

Strengths-Based Therapy Based on our own experiences, we would recommend aspects of strengths-based therapy when working with immigration clients. In our therapy sessions, we often reflect on families' strengths and resiliency despite separation or uncertain futures. As a reader we invite you to not only recognize and acknowledge the distress experienced by families but the resiliency that exists beneath the surface. Furthermore, we hope that the ideas of strengths-based therapy have become more tangible through our case presentations. We believe that regardless of clients' experiences of trauma or distress, highlighting strengths and moments of resiliency will open the door for conversations that are often overshadowed by the presenting problem. It has been our experience that incorporating tenets of narrative therapy, offering brief services, and considering posttraumatic growth fits seamlessly into immigration services. Not only has this incorporation received positive appraisal from clients, but from our own experiences, and that of our colleagues, it has countered clinical burnout.

Advocating for Change Another important lesson we have learned in our work is the reciprocal nature of therapy. When we are open to change, the alleviation of suffering becomes bi-directional. Our work with families sometimes includes highlighting posttraumatic growth. In turn, we have experienced growth as practitioners, advocates, women, Latin Americans, and human beings. This has led to our proposition that initiating changes on an individual level can in fact impact the social discourses of immigration. If you are engaging in this work, we ask you to consider your services as acts of *daily advocacy* for a community that faces opposition from people, countries, and institutions across the globe.

Mentorship

Our first introduction to biopsychosocial evaluations stemmed from our work as Spanish interpreters for our training clinic director, Dr. Bernadette Solórzano. Shortly after, seeing our eagerness to become involved, she mentored us in conducting our own biopsychosocial evaluations. Through her mentorship students have attended immigration court, accompanied her on evaluations at detention centers, and performed evaluations under supervision. Her open-door policy allows for constant consultation. Having a mentor that first listens to your concerns, then, shares what has worked for them, and, finally, still allows you to creatively construct your own interventions is how we have continued in this field. With this particular type of work, we believe it is beneficial to have conversations not just about personal well-being and therapeutic boundaries, but regarding feelings on public policy and the impact of immigration news on our motivation.

Having a mentor lead by example is also pivotal. Witnessing small things like waiving fees, seeing clients outside her regular schedule, working with interpreters, and constantly reiterating the importance of working with clients in their native language shaped how we work. Not only should mentors share their practical, literary, and legal knowledge, but the reasons they are working in their field. The *why* of work is important. In our self-exploration, we have found three main answers to the *why* question: (1) our own family's connection to immigration, (2) a sense of duty to our society and community, and (3) the importance of social justice advocacy. We invite you to engage in self-exploration to understand your *why* question. This process is as equally important as surrounding yourself with supportive mentorship.

Conclusion

Our work in biopsychosocial evaluations and therapy for immigration clients has led us to a lifelong commitment to advocacy for undocumented individuals. In this chapter we have highlighted the role of posttraumatic growth and resiliency when working with immigration clients. Through our case presentations, we have shown how strengths-based and single-session therapy can benefit your practice regardless of theory. We included the challenges immigrants face and the resiliency they exhibit when reconstructing new and positive realities. As we have mentioned, our local experiences and ideas are not unique to the Texas-Mexican border. The emotional distress, discrimination, uncertainty, and fear that undocumented families face in San Antonio, Texas, are shared across the country and the globe. It is our wish that the practical implications we included in this chapter serve you in your practice, mentorship, and most importantly, advocacy. Lastly, we offer our gratitude to the undocumented families that made this chapter possible by honoring us with the testimonies of their lived experiences.

References

American Psychological Association, Presidential Task Force on Immigration. (2012). *Crossroads: The psychology of immigration in the new century*. Retrieved from http://www.apa.org/topics/immigration/immigration-report.pdf

American Psychological Association, Presidential Task Force on Immigration. (2013). *Working with Immigrant-origin clients: An update for mental health professionals*. Retrieved from http://www.apa.org/topics/immigration/immigration-report-professionals.pdf

Cohen, M. H. (1993). The unknown and the unknowable: Managing sustained uncertainty. *Western Journal of Nursing Research, 15*(1), 77–96. https://doi.org/10.1177/019394599301500106

Davis, C. G., & Nolen-Hoeksema, S. (2009). Making sense of loss, perceiving benefits, and posttraumatic growth. In S. J. Lopez & C. R. Snyder (Eds.), *The oxford handbook of positive psychology* (2nd ed., pp. 641–649). Oxford, UK/New York, NY: Oxford University Press, Inc.

De Shazer, S., Dolan, Y., Korman, H., McCollum, E., Trepper, T., & Berg, I. K. (2007). *Haworth brief therapy series: More than miracles: The state of the art of solution-focused brief therapy*. New York, NY: Haworth Press.

Diener, E. (2009). Positive psychology: Past, present, and future. In S.J. Lopez & C.R. Snyder, (2), The oxford handbook of positive psychology (pp. 7–11). Oxford, UK/New York, NY: Oxford University Press, Inc.

Faris, W. B. (2004). *Ordinary enchantments: Magical realism and the remystification of narrative*. Nashville, TN: Vanderbilt University Press.

Geetha, B. J. (2010). Magic realism in Gabriel Garcia Marquez' one hundred years of solitude. *Rupkatha Journal on Interdisciplinary Studies in Humanities, 2*(3), 345–349.

Gemignani, M., & Pena, E. (2007). Postmodern conceptualizations of culture in social constructionism and cultural studies. *Journal of Theoretical and Philosophical Psychology, 27-28*(2–1), 276–300. https://doi.org/10.1037/h0091297

Goolishian, H. A., & Anderson, H. (1987). Language systems and therapy: An evolving idea. *Psychotherapy: Theory, Research, Practice, Training, 24*(3), 529–538. https://doi.org/10.1037/h0085750

Main, A. & Johnston, J. (2009). *The millennium challenge corporation and economic sanctions: A comparison of Honduras with other countries*. Center for Economic and Policy Research CEPR. Retrieved from https://www.files.ethz.ch/isn/105218/mcc-sanctions-2009-08.pdf

Perdomo, C. (2018). Undocumented and deportable: Re-authoring trauma within the context of immigration in a narrative informed single session. *Journal of Systemic Therapies, 36*(4), 3–15.

Pew Research Center. (2016a, July). *2016 campaign: Strong interest, widespread dissatisfaction.* Retrieved from http://assets.pewresearch.org/wp-content/uploads/sites/5/2016/07/07-07-16-Voter-attitudes-release.pdf

Pew Research Center. (2016b, November). *Unauthorized immigrant population trends for states, birth countries and regions*. Retrieved from http://www.pewhispanic.org/interactives/unauthorized-trends/

Polanco, M. (2010). Rethinking narrative therapy: An examination of bilingualism and magical realism. *Journal of Systemic Therapies, 29*, 1–14. https://doi.org/10.1521/jsyt.2010.29.2.1

Rietig, V. (2015). Top 10 of 2015-Issue #8: A shared challenge: Europe and the United States confront significant flows of unaccompanied child migrants. *Migration Policy Institute*. Retrieved from http://www.migrationpolicy.org/article/top-10-2015-%E2%80%93-issue-8-shared-challenge-europe-and-united-states-confront-significant-flows

Slive, A., & Bobele, M. (2011). *When one hour is all you have: Effective therapy for walk-in clients*. Phoenix, AZ: Zeig, Tucker & Theisen.

SOA Watch (2017, n.d.). *What is the SOA?* Retrieved from http://soaw.org/about-the-soawhinsec/what-is-the-soawhinsec

U.S. Citizenship and Immigration Services (USCIS), 2017. *Humanitarian*. Retrieved from https://www.uscis.gov/humanitarian

White, M. (1988/1989). The externalizing of the problem and the re-authoring of lives and relationships. In M. White (Ed.), *Selected papers* (pp. 5–28). Adelaide, Australia: Dulwich Centre Publications.

White, M., & Epston, D. (1990). *Narrative means to therapeutic ends*. Adelaide, South Australia: Dulwich Center.

Worthington, D. (2015, April). The USA and Latin America: A history of meddling? *New Historian*. Retrieved from http://www.newhistorian.com/the-usa-and-latin-america-a-history-of-meddling/3476/

Yee, V. (2017, February). Immigrants hide, fearing capture on 'any corner.' *The New York Times*. Retrieved from https://www.nytimes.com/2017/02/22/us/immigrants-deportation-fears.html

Chapter 6
"Do You Know the Tale of Cinderella?": Case Study of the Use of Metaphor and Proverbs with a Newlywed Syrian Couple in a Refugee Camp in Sidon, Lebanon

Rima Zeid Nehmé

"Metaphors represent the logic upon which the biological world was built. It is the main characteristic of the organization of mental processes."(Bateson, 1979)
   "In fact the symptom itself presented by the identified patient, often expresses metaphorically an individual and family difficulty, that can't be expressed in another way. And it is just in its metaphorical dimension that the symptom often proposes the double and paradoxical need 'to say' and, in the same time, 'not to say,' 'to change' and, in the same time, 'not to change.'"(Bateson, 1979)

Introduction

I have been working with Syrian refugees as a psychotherapist in Ein El Hilweh Camp, in the south of Lebanon, in the city of Sidon, since 2013. This camp had originally hosted Palestinian refugees since 1948 and is now also hosting, since 2011, Syrian refugees. During my work experience as a psychotherapist, I have observed that the use of multiple functions of metaphors and popular proverbs has had a positive application in the therapeutic process. It builds a link or a bridge between the fact and the solution, in a nonthreatening way to the clients, and improves the collaboration between the psychotherapist and the client. In this case, the resolution of the main problematic issues raised during the therapy process and the application of the metaphors and proverbs assisted the client to adopt more adequate normative standards for family life. It also encouraged the family to develop a vision of the future and offers support as to determine the skills, resources, and abilities needed to achieve that vision successfully.

R. Z. Nehmé (✉)
Clinical Psychologist, Beirut, Lebanon

© Springer Nature Switzerland AG 2019   69
L. L. Charlés, G. Samarasinghe (eds.), *Family Systems and Global Humanitarian Mental Health*, https://doi.org/10.1007/978-3-030-03216-6_6

Focus of the Case Study

A short description of the geohistorical situation in the near countries of Lebanon will be significant to perceive my work environment:

> The 1948 Palestine war, known in Hebrew as the War of Independence or the War of Liberation and in Arabic as The Nakba or Catastrophe refers to the war that occurred in the former Mandatory Palestine during the period between the United Nations vote on the partition plan on November 30, 1947, and the official end of the first Arab–Israeli war on July 20, 1949. The demographic consequences were that Palestinians were expelled to various near countries, Egypt, Jordan and Lebanon. They were placed in refugee camps were they mostly remain. (Esber, 2009, p. 28)

Moreover, the ongoing multisided Syrian civil war started in March 2011 between the Syrian Arab regime and various forces opposing both the government and each other in varying combinations. The result was that Lebanon received and kept until now the highest number of refugees, living in several camps.

At the time of this case, I was working as a psychotherapist in the "Ein El Hilweh" Palestine refugee camp (EHC), located in the south of Lebanon. As noted earlier, the camp first settled in 1948 by refugees from northern Palestine. According to a recent report published by the UNOCHA (2017) on ReliefWeb[1]:

> EHC is the country's largest camp in terms of both area and population; an estimated 80,000 people reside in and around the camp, in an area of 1.5 square kilometers. An estimated 6,000 Palestine refugees from Syria (PRS) have settled in the camp since the beginning of the conflict, joining Palestine refugees in Lebanon (PRL) who already face high levels of multigenerational poverty and vulnerability. Camp residents – both PRS and PRL – suffer from high rates of poverty and unemployment and remain heavily dependent on The United Nations Relief and Works Agency for Palestine Refugees (UNRWA) and other NGOs services for housing, health care, and education. (UNOCHA, 2017, p. 1)

The lack of security is a major concern in EHC. The camp is a microcosm of the Palestinian political universe. This situation has produced a tense and confrontational environment characterized by lawlessness and frequent breakdowns into brief episodes of armed violence (UNOCHA, 2017).

Working in the Community of the Camp

I am a fully trained psychotherapist in Lebanon with a Master's Degree and have been working in the field over 10 years. I am Lebanese, living in Beirut. My first language is Arabic; I grew up and was educated in Lebanon. I also speak French, which I learned at school, and have learned English as an adult. My psychotherapy studies were at the Faculty of Letters and Human Sciences, Lebanese University; I've also had postmaster's training and earned a diploma from the Tabyeen Center, which was done in collaboration with the Institute of the Family and Human

---

[1] https://reliefweb.int/report/lebanon/south-lebanon-ein-el-hilweh-camp-profile-2017

Systems Studies in Belgium and under the supervision of Mony Elkaim and Abbas Maky. Further, I have completed further postmasters' training and certifications in drama therapy, cognitive and behavioral therapy, and mindfulness-based cognitive therapy.

As much as I've learned, I found that working with the community in the camp was really challenging. As psychotherapist who studied both analytic and systemic approaches, as well as drama therapy, it was critical to integrate several types of therapy to best suit the issues people bring unto the therapy room. This is especially true when working with couples or families experiencing times of strain and difficulty, who need space to understand and seek to resolve underlying issues and overcome their challenges of developing, repairing, or ending their struggles.

I wasn't really certain that I could use family or couple therapy inside the camp. We were practicing CBT (cognitive behavioral therapy); the sessions were for individual therapy only. Coming to the clinic was felt by the refugee as being stigmatized; many of them were coming to therapy in secret without telling anyone they were seeing a therapist. I was not sure they would collaborate and come as a couple or as a family for therapy to the very small clinic room (1.5×2.5 m) that limited the possibility of using many techniques or to receive all members of large families.

I learned more about Palestinians' and Syrians' habits, beliefs, religion, and culture through the use of family therapy techniques. They provided me with tools to understand and deal better with their conflicts, difficulties, and interpersonal problems. Working with them, I found that clarifying the solution or the problem was easier by using popular proverbs or metaphors. These techniques assisted me in making the therapeutic approach more adequate to the culture. After many years of experience in NGOs, I have learned that Syrians who were living in remote areas encouraged early marriages; the girls between 14 and 16 years old were obliged to marry and to live with husbands in their family house, where all brothers with their wives shared the parents' house.

In this chapter, I will share with you my first experience of family therapy with refugees, through which I learned the importance of psychosocial support for families who have suffered from all aspects of life, how their circumstances have turned them into enemies in this confined space, and how they have been unable to find a solution.

A Room Divided by Sheets

In 2016 one of those families I worked with, upon moving to Lebanon, consisted of four adult sons who shared one room, divided by sheets. The sheets were there to give a type of private place for the four couples; two of those couples had children. Further, one of those couples was newly married. The newlywed wife, whom I will call Nada,[2] had been previously married; she had been a widow at the age of

---

[2] Nada and all other people mentioned in the case are pseudonyms as agreed by the family.

22 years. Nada had come from Syria to marry her cousin, who was 21 years old. That was the family decision.

The day she arrived, in Sidon-Lebanon refugee camp, the marriage ceremony was done. Nada was to spend the night with her husband in a room where he lives with family inside a small house. She had not been made aware about their living arrangements.

Once Nada came into the room and saw the sheets, her husband Feysal explained to her that he was sharing this room with three of his brothers with their children and that they left this entire room for them for their honeymoon week. The three brothers, and their families, went to stay with their relatives. Feysal's mother and two of his sisters with their children occupied the other room.

Nada felt disappointed at the living arrangements and scared about the future. She stated that her night was horrible. Day after day she became sad and anxious. She was spending all her days cleaning and cooking with her mother-in-law, or teaching the children, who filled the house. She didn't have any second of privacy in the room or outside in the hall.

After 5 months of her marriage, Nada was referred to me by the social worker who does home visits to the refugees. The mother-in-law talked to her about her worries regarding Nada due to changes she showed recently: crying, spending most of the time sleeping, and less interested in her obligations regarding the home or toward her relationship with her husband.

Nada came accompanied by her mother-in-law, Om Omar, who explained the problems Nada and her son were facing and her worries about their marriage. I thanked Om Omar and then asked her to let me meet with Nada alone.

With her tearful eyes, Nada hesitated in the beginning to talk. She told me that for her nothing is going to change and all she knows is that she is not herself any more, she is unhappy, and she feels sleepy and tired most of the time and restless.

Nada told me she was the eldest girl in her family, has two other sisters aged 20 and 19 years old, married with children. They still live in Syria. Her mother had remarried 4 years after her husband died of cancer.

Nada was married in Syria, to their neighbor Ahmad, 3 years older than her. He was a foreman, handsome, hard worker, and a good husband. Nada, at 16, had her own apartment, located above her in-laws. She reported that she loved Ahmad who was supportive and accepted that she continued going to school and had her high school degree. They didn't have children; however, the doctors assured them that they didn't have any fertility problem.

In 2015 Ahmad died in an explosion after 4 years of their marriage; Nada went back to her mother's house, but there was no place for her beside her five brothers and sisters. After 1 year, her family agreed that it is better for her to marry her cousin.

Feysal, 21 years old, came illegally with his family to Lebanon in 2012 and stayed in Ein El Hilweh camp; he worked occasionally with his uncle. Feysal had left primary school early, before grade 6. He spent most of his time with his friends playing games. His mother thought that by getting married he will become more responsible.

Nada could no longer withstand sex with her husband; she spent the days cleaning, cooking, and looking after all the family. She didn't have any physical problem. Everyone had been accusing her to be faking an illness; however, she simply did not feel at all good nor happy.

Nada had a regular sexual relationship with her husband in the first week, when they were alone in the room. But later, as Nada and her husband were sharing the bedroom with other couples, their intimacy became an issue of disagreement. This was due to the fact that at night Nada could hear the whispers, sounds, and breathings of the other couples in the room. In the morning, she felt scrutinized by the family when she or her husband went to shower (it is a habit that after intercourse, they have to take a bath before praying).

The house chores never ended for Nada. After 3 months spent with her mother-in-law, she was not going out. She accompanied her to the vegetables market, but she never went out for a visit or a journey. Feysal never asked her if she liked to have anything or to go anywhere. Feysal was asking money from his mother who was deciding on every single thing at home, what to eat, what to wear, and when and how to clean. Feysal was giving his salary to his mother who was managing the home expenses and controlling every daily detail such as food, cleaning, and clothing.

Nada tried several times to talk to Feysal about her emotions and to explain the reasons why she was tired at home. She felt he never seemed to understand her thoughts and needs.

Nada then tried to go to learn sewing or makeup or enroll in an association nearby or to try to find a job to have her own income, but her mother-in-law refused and discouraged her doing so, telling her that she has to think about having a baby to fill up her days.

Day after day, Nada became more introverted and stayed in her part of the rooms; she was losing weight and energy. When the session ended that day, I asked Nada to bring her husband and her mother-in-law for the following session.

I insisted that the social worker see them all together. I couldn't get her to bring all the family members, but at least I could involve the husband and the mother-in-law in the sessions, especially since Nada asked our help.

Family Session

A week later, the three of them came. The mother-in-law came in first and followed by her Feysal; Nada was behind him. I welcomed them and asked them to sit where they wanted, where the six seats were placed in a circular way.

Nada and Feysal sat next to each other, the mother-in-law Om Omar was facing them, and I took my place next to her and beside Nada, in between a bit. I presented myself and asked them to introduce themselves. The mother-in-law took the lead. She explained that she is a mother of nine children, six of them live with her in Lebanon, three others still are in Syria, now she has a new daughter Nada, and she worries about her, because she became different recently: "She is not as she was when she first arrived."

Feysal did not say a lot, just his age and that he is the youngest in the family and that he works sometimes and has lots of friends. I asked him if he agreed that Nada is different, how had she changed since her arrival? He agreed by saying she is sleeping most of the time and not assisting anymore with the household chores.

Nada mentioned that she did all the heavy household chores, but she couldn't do it anymore as she felt she was obliged to do so. She found herself indirectly forced by her mother-in-law who continuously stated that all other women at home are busy with their children. She also reported that her mother-in-law kept on repeating that being with her in the kitchen is a privilege to Nada, as cooking is an exclusive job of the mother-in-law, flattering her good food. Instead, Nada had to wash the dishes, assist the children with their homework, and engage in other chores.

Nada claimed that this situation became extremely tiring for her. While expressing herself, Nada was crying and stated that "I couldn't find time for myself ...I felt I am Cinderella." Feysal reacted strongly and blamed her, saying "Every woman has to work," and "You are helping my mom, and this is why you are hiding in the room!!!????" The mother-in-law told Nada, "You are the youngest and you don't have children; therefore, I was depending on you. I didn't mean to hurt you."

Nada, in expressing her feeling as Cinderella, had found in that tale a good comparison to express her inability to defend herself or to find some space for her in this family. This then gave me an idea and inspiration for my intervention; I have to "spread the magic" in the session, I thought. I asked Om Omar: "Do you know the tale of Cinderella?" She did not. I tell her briefly about the Cinderella tale and how the fairy godmother helped her. I tell the mom you are the godmother of this couple, by your magic they are going to overcome their problem.

> "You see Om Omar, the Godmother helped Cinderella when she was suffering from unfairness, what will you do to help Nada?? I have a question for you: When your daughters were young did they work at home?"

> Om Omar answered: "Yes, I put a plan and each one had a turn. And there where things they did together." I then asked her: "If your daughters were in their houses did they have to do the house obligation even if they have children?" She answered Yes."Do you think if Nada had her own house she can handle her duties?"
> She answered yes.
> "As a fairy Godmother mother, do you think that Nada was tired from doing all the jobs alone? What would you do for her? Is it time to share these duties between all the daughters?"
> Om Omar didn't answer but shook her head....

Nada was looking, wondering at me. I asked her: "Did you tell her how you are feeling about your home duties?" She answered "No, I didn't want to upset my mother in law." So, I explained the importance of talking and communicating with each other.

Then I stopped talking for few minutes and I asked Nada: "Did you know what I thought or felt during those minutes?" She said No. "You see Nada, when you have something you have to talk about, to let the other hear you, they cannot know about your suffering if you don't tell about it." Nada replied: "I did and I told Feysal but he wasn't listening to me. Nobody cared." Feysal anxiously replied: "You didn't listen to me, you are in your cocoon, as you are single and you don't have husband to take care about."

I asked Feysal about a husband's duties toward his wife and vice versa. It made him thoughtful, and then I told him that he and Nada will be doing a homework for the next session; I said: "You will have to prepare a list of positives and negatives-features found in your partner."

At the end of the session, I said to Om Omar a popular proverb, very common, "You know the proverb Om Omar, God bless the house from which a house comes out and each house has his sanctity. As a fairy Godmother, help this couple to find their sanctity."

Discussion and Follow-Up

I saw the family for four sessions, where I implemented in later sessions psychoeducation to teach them about marriage duties, communication, and conflict resolution. In particular, I explained privacy, especially in the relationship and why Nada should not have sex with Feysal while the family was in the room, as that is inappropriate not only for Nada but for all the other couples (each house must have his sanctity) and will affect the children in this room too. For me, I had to define the official program (explicit) and world map (implicit) of the couple and build the link to modify the family dynamics where each one finds his/her place and defines his/her role. Metaphors, stories, and that final proverb all facilitated my work and made a sense to link new acts and new thoughts for everyone in the family.

Further, I explained that Nada's symptoms were real and not false pretense; actually, her body was talking on her behalf, when she couldn't talk about her emotions or need. I involved the social worker in my action plan. She assisted Nada to participate in many workshops and integrated Feysal in a group of men to reeducate the youth and young men about the role of women alongside the man in society. One month later, Feysal and Nada started working, and the social worker helped them get a room sponsored by an NGO. At the end, the family therapy method of intervention opened a new perception for this couple.

Conclusion

Providing family therapy for vulnerable families can help the family members improve communication, resolve conflicts, and help them to listen and support each other. Through different techniques such as playing roles; creating, drawing, and sculpting their thoughts and ideas; and using metaphor, behaviors, problems, and emotions can be represented with a metaphorical image, allowing for symbolic understanding. The use of imagination helps people disclose private parts of themselves that they would not confront directly (Jennings, 1990). Also, common proverbs explain and reflect some of life advice and experience, and every culture has them. They are very useful in therapy. The story of this family and my work with them shows how we use all the methods we can, even in the small and unusual space of the camp.

Family therapy is often considered a brief, short-term therapy. It may include all family members or just those able or willing to participate. Together family members can feel and understand different perceptions and be in the shoe of the other. Family therapy also improves troubled relationships with partners, children, or other family members. The therapist teaches the participant skills to deepen family connections and get through stressful times, leading them to a better understanding about themselves and how to support each other. In my case study, the use of metaphors and proverbs and the story of Cinderella facilitated the communication and the understanding of the core problem in the family and couple dynamics. It helped me, the psychotherapist, to guide and facilitate the comprehension of the message by talking broadly yet in a directly related way, to the main issue arising.

References

Bateson, G. (1979). *Mind and nature: A necessary Unity*. New York: E.P. Dutton.
Esber, R. (2009). *Under the cover of war*. Alexandria, VA: Arabicus Books & Media.
Jennings, S. (1990). *Dramatherapy with families, groups and individuals*. London: Jessica Kingsley.
UNOCHA (2017). *Ein El Hilweh profile*. Geneva, Switzerland: Author. Accessed September 6th, 2018 at: https://data2.unhcr.org/en/documents/details/61175

Chapter 7
Between Family and Foreign Policy: A Gendered Approach to Understanding the Impact of Foreign Policy Failure on Human Security in the SIDS of the Caribbean

Simone Young

Introduction

The world of diplomacy and international affairs is, at first glance, far removed from that of mental health and support for families in crisis situations. Yet there is growing evidence that these ostensibly disparate worlds are not only inextricably linked but that success in one may often predict and support success in the other.

In 2001, the World Health Organization (WHO) identified mental health and neurological disorders as the leading cause of disability and ill health globally (WHO, 2001b). Back then, the paradox was that addressing the issue seemed to rank as a clear non-priority for the international development community and indeed for governments. This, even as the consequences and costs of foreign policy failure in the aftermath of the end of the Cold War, on the integrity of states, on the stability of the Westphalia nation state system – that was ushered in with the Peace of Westphalia that ended the Thirty Years' War in 1648 and is regarded as the catalyst for the creation of the modern day nation state system (Farr, 2005) – and on the overall well-being of the communities comprising these states, Rwanda and the former Yugoslavia come to mind, became writ large and was seen particularly in the impact on human security.

More recently, this appears to have changed with a growing awareness of the impact of mental health on overall well-being. Moreover, as the repercussions of inadequate healthcare, conflict, famine, periods of instability and high levels of crime on the overall development trajectory of countries became clearer, the idea that mental health, general well-being and "whole" countries are built from "whole" communities has taken root, and the international development community is paying attention, even as the Sustainable Development Goals (SDGs) have come to

S. Young (✉)
Trinidad and Tobago Fulbright Humphrey Fellow 2016, Washington, D.C., USA

© Springer Nature Switzerland AG 2019   77
L. L. Charlés, G. Samarasinghe (eds.), *Family Systems and Global Humanitarian Mental Health*, https://doi.org/10.1007/978-3-030-03216-6_7

reflect this understanding (UN, 2015), one that the professionals who care for such communities need to be cognisant of.

> Why? Because while diplomats may negotiate and sign peace agreements, it is the communities that provide the fertile foundation upon which peace is sustained, nourished and thrives. It is only in peace we can speak of truly achieving human security.

Thus, the Millennium Development Goals associated with health such as those related to HIV and malaria, child mortality and maternal health (WHO, 2015) morphed into Sustainable Development Goal 3 (SDG 3) that went beyond health and addresses well-being for all at all ages.

A recent example of a commitment to a more holistic approach to health and development goals can be found in Trinidad and Tobago's achievement of no maternal deaths over a 6-month period (PAHO, 2018). This goal was achieved due to the direct involvement of the Government of Trinidad and Tobago in committing to the provision of support for initiatives and programmes that improved the health of women attending prenatal clinics (PAHO, 2018).

Moreover, in accessing support and technical assistance from the Pan American Health Organization (PAHO), the World Health Organization (WHO) agency responsible for health in the Americas region, the government was able to synchronise health policies with a demonstrated commitment to achieving SDG 3 on health and well-being for all. Critical to accomplishing this also was understanding the specific needs of women and in particular, the peculiar needs of pregnant women as a demographic and as an interest group that had been facing challenges reflected in the country's maternal morbidity and mortality rates (PAHO, 2018).

Thus, in seeking a greater understanding of human security, the key may be understanding the all-encompassing impact of gender-based inequities on the achievement of the same for as a parameter, gender remains the biggest single determinant in how a person is treated as an individual and as part of a group.

A key example is the differential in wages paid to women as compared to those paid to men. The International Labour Organization (ILO) – the United Nations specialised agency that addresses labour and employment and pays special attention to social justice in this context – estimates that reducing the employment gaps between men and women could generate approximately $1.7 trillion in output globally; for Latin America and the Caribbean, if the gender gap drops from 26% to 17.2% between 2012 and 2017, there would be $223 billion in additional GDP (ILO, 2012).

Building on the acknowledgement of gender as the most influential determinant of how a person is treated Hudson, Caprioli, Ballif-Spanvill, McDermott, & Emmett (Hudson et al., 2008) explain that societal-based differences in gender-status beliefs as reflected in beliefs, practices, customs and treatment under the law in turn have consequences for politics and the way a state organises and interprets its security. These findings can have important implications for the way countries view domestic and international security – the assumptions they employ in adopting foreign policy positions and domestic policy positions in economics, employment, health, social services, education and law and justice.

Consequently – and as has been seen through many examples – policy failure in these areas, which can occur for a number of reasons, can have a dire and lasting impact on human security. The recent past is replete with examples of the impacts of policy failure where gender-related issues were not adequately incorporated in key areas that sustain human security such as migration and employment.

Current migration issues in the Caribbean bear testimony to the nexus between (forced) migration, gender-based violence and economic, personal and psychosocial insecurity. An influx of migrants in search of better opportunities for employment and education can sometimes underscore the special issues that affect girls and women (Franklin, 2018).

The specific case of Venezuelan women and girls forced to migrate to Trinidad and Tobago due to social and economic upheaval in their native country is well-documented with countless accounts of girls and women enduring human trafficking and forced prostitution (Kong Soo, 2018).

In the case of employment, the consequences of policy failure are broad as they are deep, for employment is not only central to self-actualisation but expanding the menu of life options a person has available to them and is particularly central to access to education and healthcare. As Verveer noted, gender equity is integral to economic prosperity (Verveer, 2012) with a 2015 McKinsey Global Institute report bearing this out, estimating that in a scenario where women participated in the labour market as fully as men do, $28 trillion could be added to the global annual GDP by 2025 (Woetzel et al., 2015). Cuberes and Teignier noted that if the gender labour gap was completely closed, per capita GDP would be 15% higher among OECD countries; for Latin America, the per capita gain from closing the gap would be 17% (Cuberes & Teignier, 2016).

Why Human Security Matters

Human security recognises the widespread and cross-cutting issues that threaten the viability of not only states but the people and communities that comprise them. Its point of departure is grounded in the fact the traditional concept of security goes beyond that of threats to people, communities and states posed by crime, war or terrorism.

As an approach, human security reflects the fact that while one of the main goals of every state's foreign and domestic policy is to achieve or to enhance its security, the insecurity that citizens can experience from, inter alia, persistent poverty, famine, disease, gender, race and other forms of inequity can feed directly into perpetuating and creating a less secure state – economically, socially, culturally and defensively.

As Gomez and Gasper elaborate (Gomez & Gasper, 2013), the human security approach was introduced in 1994 via the global Human Development Report (HDR) where the focus was on the two (2) main components of human security: "freedom from fear" and "freedom from want". These were inspired by the Universal

Declaration of Human Rights and are central to the four human freedoms Roosevelt referred to in a famous speech in 1941 (Gomez & Gasper, 2013). In the 1990s, the freedom "to live in dignity" was also added with the increasing focus on not just identifying threats but analysing the root causes underpinning these threats.

Thus, in the context of the SIDS of the English-speaking Caribbean, a common and consistent threat is vulnerability to external economic events. However, a human security would advocate for undertaking the relevant analyses to determine what the causal factors are that sustain this vulnerability and seek to identify the main groups affected with a view towards having them and also to develop and implement possible solutions.

Essentially then the concept sought to expand the parameters of security analysis and policy from one mainly focused on the security of states and its attendant issues to one where there was an equally significant focus on the quality of people's lives. In sum, human security, as an approach, sought to better understand what generally made one less "secure"; made one less able to access education; less able to be physically secure; less subjected to crime, victimisation and aggression; less vulnerable to all forms of discrimination; less able to be denied medical care; and so forth. Consequently, as noted by Gomez and Gasper (Gomez & Gasper, 2013), the seven (7) fundamental elements of human security were initially identified as:

- Economic
- Food
- Health
- Environmental
- Personal
- Community
- Political

The approach has been historically associated with HDRs where it has been employed in the crafting of national and regional development reports seeking to identify, analyse and treat with a variety of threats as described in the preceding paragraph (Gomez & Gasper, 2013). Consequently, as a tool, the human security framework has been described as a flexible approach as it can be customised to a wide range of contexts and topics (Gomez & Gasper, 2013).

This signals one of the most important elements of the concept: that of national ownership. As enunciated in the UNGA Resolution A/Res/66/290, the criteria for human security varies from place to place, from situation to situation and from person to person. Specifically, the resolution reminded that "….since the political, economic, social and cultural conditions for human security vary significantly across and within countries, and at different points in time, human security strengthens national solutions which are compatible with local realities." (p.2) Notwithstanding, the resolution underscores that there are essential freedoms and dignities that each person should inhere in keeping with their fundamental human rights.

As Gomez and Gasper have noted (Gomez & Gasper, 2013), one of human security's guiding principles is that it requires understanding the particular threats experienced by particular groups of people, as well as the participation of those people in the process of analysing these threats. The work of advocacy groups such as People Living With HIV and AIDS (PLWHA) and the Caribbean Vulnerable Communities (Caribbean Vulnerable Communities, 2016) that are staffed and administered by persons living with HIV and AIDS is a prime example in the Caribbean subregion, of client-driven advocacy geared towards improving elements of a particular group's human security.

In the case of those living with HIV and AIDS, it has come to mean security from eviction from homes, firing from jobs and discrimination and security in terms of ensuring access to healthcare (Caribbean Vulnerable Communities, 2016). Central to the approach then is that people have a say in determining what affects them and that this is inextricably linked to what then UN Secretary General Ban Ki-Moon reminded was the right to enjoy "freedom from fear, freedom from want and freedom to live in dignity" (UN, 2010).

Critical to tracing the evolution of human security as an operationalised concept is the parallel pillar of human development. As the UNDP reminds, human development and human security are interlinked but are by no means identical as the former is a broad concept, aiming at enlarging people's choices and freedoms, while the latter is focused on assuring priority freedoms so that "people can exercise choices safely and freely" (United Nations Development Programme, Human Development Report, 1994, p.23) and can be confident that the opportunities they have are protected.

Gomez and Gasper recall further that some elements of the UNGA Resolution A/RES/66/290 (UNGA, 2012) illustrate the links between human security and human development where it emphasises that "Human security calls for people-centred, comprehensive, context-specific and prevention-oriented responses..." (Gomez & Gasper, 2013).

As a framework within which mental health and healthcare practitioners can seek a greater understanding of the nature of threat, insecurity and their provenance, human security is particularly compelling with its focus on analysing threats with a view towards nullifying the same. However, it goes beyond identifying and seeking to eliminate and seeks, as its broadest aspirational intent, to eliminate the conditions that gave rise to the threat in the first place per UNGA Resolution 66/290 that explicitly stated that "Human security recognises the interlinkages between peace, development and human rights, and equally considers civil, political, economic, social and cultural rights" (UNGA, 2012).

A key example may be found in the employment standards for domestic workers. Historically an occupation dominated by women globally, domestic workers lacked a convention - a legal instrument that could provide universally accepted standards, benchmarks and guidelines for the employment of domestic workers that would reduce instances of job insecurity; child labour; inconsistent, stagnated or no wages; unsafe work conditions; physical abuse; and sexual exploitation, among others. As the ILO noted, these conditions of work have serious repercussions for domestic workers – more often than not, women and young girls – and their families (ILO, 2016).

Due in part to the sustained advocacy of domestic workers' unions globally and the advocacy of the ILO, the *Domestic Workers Convention, 2011* (No. 189) was passed in 2011, the first international standard that established minimum labour protections for domestic workers. The possible impact on the lives of hundreds of millions of women, young girls, their families and communities cannot be overemphasised with countries beginning the process of bringing their domestic laws in line with the convention (ILO, 2016).

In the process, such actions taken by governments have established a benchmark for the provision of protections that improve human security for these workers in critical aspects of their lives such as giving them the same rights as other workers (Brazil); providing minimum wages, social security and health insurance coverage (The Philippines); and creating a wage commission to set minimum wages for domestic workers (Namibia) (ILO, 2016).

In galvanising the support of its member states for this convention, the ILO took a critical step in fulfilling some of its key mandates: establishing and upholding labour standards, advancing human rights protections in the world of work and promoting "decent work" – a pillar of the organisation's remit that refers to fairly paid productive work carried out in conditions of freedom, equity, security and human dignity, all common elements of what constitutes human security. Trinidad and Tobago's bargaining body for domestic workers – the National Union of Domestic Employees (NUDE) – was very active in garnering local stakeholder support for the *Domestic Workers Convention, 2011* and was present in Geneva in that year, for its historic passage.

The Role of Gender: Perspectives on Human Security and Foreign Policy

Gender Inequity – How Insecurity Contributes to Conflict

As can be seen from the aforementioned example of the Domestic Workers Convention, 2011, one of the most critical determinants affecting human security is gender. In examining the nature of insecurity in international contexts, the role gender inequity plays is significant and one that merits the attention of the mental health practitioner, particularly those that provide vital services in conflict situations.

The work of Hudson et al. (2008) is relevant here and, as referred to in the introduction, compellingly sets out the case linking the chronic insecurity women experience to the insecurity of the state, where they posited that societal-based differences in gender-status beliefs as reflected in beliefs, practices, customs and treatment under the law, in turn, have consequences for politics and the way a state organises and interprets its security (Hudson et al., 2008, p.12).

Their use of evolutionary theory to further explore the physical security of women and the behaviour of nation states is insightful and is centred on the fact that the security of women can impact on the security of states, as does the security of children and young people. In so doing, the authors provided a thought-provoking rationale for the hypothesis that the treatment of females constitutes another key reason for conflict and insecurity between and among states. The example provided by Hudson et al. (2008) of the millions of women's and girls' lives lost due to societal devaluation of female life (Hudson et al., 2008, p. 9) signals the need for an immediate, critical and fundamental rethink of what constitutes true security and the role of the state in either sanctioning or not protecting women and girls from violence.

For the family therapists and professionals who work with communities recovering from conflict and other various types of trauma, this linkage underscores how critical it is for professionals who focus on family health, women's well-being and community sustainability to seek and develop a comprehensive understanding of the context within which foreign and domestic policy failure occurs but also, the consequences of inadequate or non-existent policy, both of which can be equally damaging. The example of the passage of child marriage legislation in Trinidad and Tobago in 2017 is relevant here and explored in section "The Case for People-Centred Foreign Policy: Child Marriage in Trinidad and Tobago" of the chapter.

In exploring Hudson and her colleagues' work in greater detail, what becomes evident is that they provided a plausible basis from which to understand how and why human beings organise themselves socially and politically by outlining the origins of patriarchy as rooted in the development of male dominance hierarchies (Hudson et al., 2008, p.14). Patriarchy as they quoted Wrangham and Peterson "has its ultimate origins in male violence" (Wrangham & Peterson, 1996 in Hudson et al., 2008, p.14).

As they observed, this violence is firstly directed against women who accede to it to prevent its recurrence to them and their children (Hudson et al., 2008, p.14). Hudson and her collaborators' work reads as a logical, coherent and persuasive argument drawing on anthropology, evolutionary biology, history and sociology to draw the line connecting male dominance hierarchies as the provenance of patriarchy to the fact that "human gender hierarchies is the most pervasive, persistent and pernicious of all types of inequality in the world" (Miller, 1993).

The application of this to analysing the origins of bellicose foreign policies and why they are preferred has important implications for the way we perceive ourselves, the foreign policy goals espoused and defended, the basic foundations of how and why we organise societies and policies the way we do and critically and the way we define and prioritise development goals, including health, well-being and human security that have traditionally been seen as "soft" issues.

Of critical importance is the argument the authors themselves offer by way of past not being prologue: that patriarchy and its associated violence need not be and are not inevitable. The reasons proffered in terms of female-bonding, cultural selection modifying women's behaviour and acceptance of violence and the impact of this on their female offspring are significant and point the way forward in terms of addressing the impact of toxic masculinities and femininities.

The example of democracy's diffusion being a consequence of greater equality for women and the lessening of violent patriarchy is significant in terms of how democratisation and nation-building is conceptualised and implemented. The authors' tracing of the arc of development of democracy and the possible link between that, the treatment of women, and the breaking of male dominant hierarchies remains important. This also applies to the norms of gender-based violence and its impact on domestic and international behaviour. The use of Galtung's work on violence is central to this as acceptance of violence as a mechanism to mediate conflict and exercise control in families speaks to the cultural mores, norms and values a society or a collective subscribe to and this can be transmitted to and influence the behaviour of political actors.

The idea that state violence can lead to higher levels of violence in the domestic sphere is also supported by numerous studies that show women who are in relationships with persons who are members of the military or the police often tend to suffer more varied forms of domestic violence (Ryan, 1994; Cheema, 2016), a pervasive and enduring source of familial and community trauma. While this may be attributable to the high-stress environment of these jobs, it has also been shown to be a direct result of the pervasive levels of violence these professions are often witness to (Friedersdorf, 2014).

As Hudson et al. (2008) reminded, "…gender roles lead to highly differential possibilities for personal security, development, and prosperity, even in today's world. An example of this kind of exploitation occurs when women 'naturally' receive less pay than men for equal work, or when domestic violence is considered 'normal'" (p. 20). While there has been remarkable progress in the decades since the women's liberation movement, as the authors note, structural violence may not need to be expressed overtly but is based on open or implicit violence in the private sphere of the home.

Thus, we continue to see that norms of cultural violence are widespread within religion, ideology, language and art, among other aspects of culture. As Galtung (1990) noted "..cultural violence makes direct and structural violence look, even feel, right—or at least not wrong.." (p. 291). The link between structural violence and cultural violence is central as it underscores how deeply entrenched attitudes are and how pervasive they can be in all elements of social, economic and political life. It further signals that this extends beyond a state's borders when the majority of states are headed by men and there are historic inequities globally.

Patriarchy, anchored in violence, still therefore serves as the fundamental underpinning for cultural violence in human political and social organisation – or as Hudson et al. (2008) term it, "human collectives" – the world over. To ignore this fact, given its persistent ubiquity and costs in blood and in treasure, would be to pay those costs forward and to ignore a useful path from which to redefine our approach to development goals as projected by a state's foreign policies.

In seeking to bridge the gaps between the world of diplomacy that safeguards the integrity of states and the world of the family practitioner that safeguards the integrity of the individual and his or her communities, both worlds may then find common ground with Hudson et al.'s (2008) conclusion that "to the extent that the security of women is a societal priority, the security and peacefulness of the state will be significantly enhanced. State security rests, in the first place, on the security of women" (p. 26).

Security of States, Security of Women and Intersectionality

In considering the need to locate the analysis of the security of states within the context of the security of women particularly in some of the SIDS of the English-speaking Caribbean, all of whom share a common colonial past characterised by *inter alia*, plantation slavery, indentured immigration, other types of migration and the plantation economy. Greater attention needs to be paid to the impact of race particularly in the evolution of the great European powers and the United States. Expanding this intersectionality beyond gender is of critical importance for four (4) key reasons.

Firstly, the double helix of slavery and colonialism was central to the rise of the great European colonial powers as well as that of the United States where these countries' economic and military ascendancy and continuing dominance are directly attributable to this twin legacy. Secondly, violence – particularly gendered violence – was a foundation of the colonial and slave state and it might be argued, found its expression in some of these countries' (foreign) policies.

Thirdly, these systems have created schisms that can make it difficult, but not impossible for women to form the sorts of the alliances that Hudson et al. (2008) suggest are central to creating systems that lessen and nullify male violence and dominance. The cleavages that exist among the various groups concerned with gender-based inequities and discrimination attest to this. To wit, the concerns of an urban-based women's business group may be far removed from that of rural jobless women from indigenous communities as also obtains in the provision of healthcare (Melamed, 2012), and clearly evidenced in the disparities in the availability of heath care for rich, urban women in India (UNIFEM, 2010).

Finally the transmission of these types of violence and dominance has bequeathed a legacy of inequity, inequality, violence and institutionalised oppression in slave-descended communities that persist to the present day and which continue to impact on state security and state behaviour. Johnson and Kochel (2012) examined this in the context of Trinidad and Tobago, exploring the influence of race and ethnicity on criminal offending, victimisation, fear of crime and interactions with the police. As Johnson and Kochel's (2012) findings indicated there were differences among the various ethnic groups in terms of their interactions with the police, with fear of crime and perceived safety, as well as access to justice but that this could be partly traced to the country's colonial past and legacy of historically disadvantaged groups, now concentrated in communities disproportionately affected by crime and criminal behaviour (p. 224). This reminds that one critical element of understanding what contributes to the security of a person is understanding the specific lenses and life experiences through which an individual inhabits the world.

In the case of gender, Tickner observed (1992) that women's lived experiences have not been reflected in international relations just as they themselves have not been portrayed as actors in international affairs and on the world stage. Like Hudson et al. (2008), Tickner's point of departure is that the pervasive existence of mail dominant hierarchies forms the basis for a gendered international relations perspective that affords primacy to men's knowledge. This is critical in seeking to understand the social, economic and political contexts within which an individual's security can be positively or negatively impacted.

Tickner is correct in asserting that the sphere of international relations is framed in its own set of binary distinctions – us versus them, men versus women and other versus default – and this extends naturally to the outside world where this becomes translated into stereotypical notions about those who inhabit "the outside". Like women, foreigners are frequently "otherised", where men are, by nature, the default.

In a manner reminiscent of Wallerstein and Gunder-Frank's world systems theory, Tickner reminded that feminist theories, which reflect the various experiences of women – who are usually on the margins of society and interstate politics – can offer us some new insights on the behaviour of states and the needs of individuals, particularly those on the peripheries of the international system (Tickner, 1992). Moreover, she highlighted that since women are frequently the first casualties in times of economic hardship, useful insights may be gained in understanding the link between military violence and economic hardships. For the mental health practitioner in conflict zones, these insights can provide an important window into the context in which conflicts occur and trauma is inflicted. The section "Recommendations for family and mental health practitioners: scaling up and expanding outward to deliver at the policy level" provides some practical and theoretical recommendations for health practitioners in this context.

How Sound Foreign Policy Matters to Human Security: Examples from the Field

Statelessness in the Caribbean – The Case of Haiti

One most recent example of foreign policy failure leading to one of the most underreported human security crises in the western hemisphere is the case of stateless persons in Haiti and the Constitutional Tribunal ruling of September 2013, where the need for an intersectional, human security approach could have arguably precipitated a more favourable outcome (Young, 2017a).

As one of the most troubling challenges of the modern era, for human security and for modern diplomacy, the question of stateless persons is one that has recently captured and continues to engage the attention of the international community. The UN High Commissioner for Refugees (UNHCR) recognises someone as stateless if he or she is not recognised as a citizen or national "under the operations of the laws of any country" (UNHCR, 2017).

The UN Human Rights Council, based in Geneva, has gone further by repeatedly emphasising the deleterious impact of statelessness on the enjoyment of human rights. The Council adopted a resolution in June 2016 on the arbitrary deprivation of nationality, focusing on the repercussions of arbitrarily depriving people of their nationality and the centrality of nationality as a fundamental freedom that impacts every element of a person's life, including his or her education, health, social inclusion, employment, housing and social security.

In the Caribbean, the repercussions of the deprivation of these rights were manifestly clear in the impact of the September 2013 ruling of the Constitutional Tribunal of the Dominican Republic (DR) that stripped citizenship from descendants of people who were deemed to have been in the DR illegally, retroactive to 1929. In effect, the ruling rendered more than an estimated 200,000 people stateless by removing their citizenship, refusing to issue them birth certificates and identity documents, thus denationalising them and creating what has been justifiably termed the "Western Hemisphere's worst refugee crisis" (Hindin & Ariza, 2016).

People of Haitian descent – including Dominicans – account for over 86% of the affected population. Thousands of Haitians arrived in the Dominican Republic in the 1890s and the first three decades of the twentieth century, under the aegis of the Dominican government to work on sugar cane plantations (Belton and Krzyzaniak, 2017). The newly arrived Haitians were given *fiches* or the equivalent of a work permit that permitted them to stay and work – and with which they registered their children, who became Dominicans through the principle of jus soli (Belton and Krzyzaniak, 2017). Although the Dominican government vehemently denied it, the crisis' antecedence in the historical *anti-Haitanismo* (Hindin & Ariza, 2016) that has formed part of Dominican culture towards Haitians and their descendants and that is also largely race-based is inescapable.

The Organization of American States (OAS), the Inter-American Commission on Human Rights (IACHR), Amnesty International, the Caribbean Community (CARICOM), the Office of the High Commissioner for Human Rights (OHCHR), the UNHCR and others all denounced the ruling. But it has not been repealed. In fact, the Dominican legislature followed the ruling with a Naturalisation Law in May 2014 (Wucker, 2015) that was touted for allegedly assisting disenfranchised Dominicans to reclaim their citizenship. However, it placed the burden of proof on the victims to provide records of their births and also their parents' births in the Dominican Republic and was plagued by implementation flaws (Human Rights Watch, 2015). Many of the births were either never registered – in many cases because Dominican government officials deliberately denied records to people of Haitian descent or because Dominican officials did not return original birth certificates to people who were deemed to "look" or "sound" Haitian when they presented their certificates for renewal (Belton and Krzyzaniak, 2017).

Records, while not completely reliable, show that up to 7000 persons were able to regularise their status before the expiration of a June 2015 moratorium. Those who were unable to regularise their status were required to register as foreigners in the country where they were born. Many of the affected had never seen Haiti, but between August 2015 and May 2016 – after the expiration of the June 2015 moratorium – it was estimated that over 40,000 persons were deported from the DR to Haiti (Amnesty International, 2016). A further 71,389 persons reported returned "spontaneously". Yet even during this "moratorium", there were documented reports of persons being summarily removed based, in some cases, only on their appearance.

With the fear of violence from Dominican authorities, misinformation, and deportation and removal driving the movement of people from the DR to Haiti, makeshift settlement camps housing tens of thousands of people sprung up in areas near to the Haitian-Dominican border. Human Rights Watch noted that the International Organization for Migration estimated that as of November 2016, an estimated 150,000 Haitian migrants and Dominicans of Haitian descent entered Haiti since the middle of 2015 (Human Rights Watch, 2016).

Statelessness for these persons means they are unable to access education, employment, public utilities, healthcare, housing and other basic necessities fundamental to daily, civilised life. Moreover, as has occurred in this instant case, statelessness also renders them vulnerable to arbitrary detention, arrest, expulsion and forcible separation from their families – and in many cases, from the only country they have ever known as home.

The silence of the international community as a whole – apart from concerned NGOs and some international organisations – since the start of the crisis has not been encouraging. The same goes for the tepid response of more influential actors who may have been better positioned to exert more pressure or use a more effective version of moral suasion on the Dominican government and to encourage the Haitian Government to respond in a more expeditious manner to the needs of returning nationals, notwithstanding the latter government's obvious capacity constraints.

There may not be easy answers in seeking to compel a government to honour the human rights of its citizens, yet perhaps it is precisely this simple: it *is* a question of the promotion and protection of human rights and constitutes a challenge to human security, to traditional security and to good governance in the region. This has been underscored not only by the violation of long-established norms and values on citizenship and the treatment of nationals by its government but also by the proliferation of serious health challenges such as malaria and the Zika virus in the makeshift camps on the Haitian-Dominican border as noted by Human Rights Watch (2016). It is a situation that, if left unchecked, could further erode gains made in the healthcare sector in Haiti and the region and exacerbate instability in Haiti.

The Case for People-Centred Foreign Policy: Child Marriage in Trinidad and Tobago

The recent amendment of child marriage laws in Trinidad and Tobago is a key example of the intersection between human security, gender-based inequities and the need for effective anchoring of more inclusive foreign policies within a human rights framework as Young (Young, 2017b) explored in 2017. A small island developing state, the twin island republic northeast of Venezuela, is the largest economy of the English-speaking Caribbean largely due to its petroleum and natural gas reserves. Apart from its energy reserves, Trinidad and Tobago is set apart from its Caribbean neighbours by its diversity.

As a direct consequence of the search by colonial plantation owners for cheap labour in the aftermath of the abolition of slavery, the result is a population of 1.3 million persons of African, Indian, Chinese, Syrian, Lebanese, Portuguese, French, Venezuelan, Spanish and Amerindian descent, inspiring Nobel laureate Desmond Tutu to christen the nation "a rainbow country" in 2004, as he did his native South Africa.

This multiculturalism also left a legacy of adherence to different faiths, with the Catholic and Anglican Churches and Hinduism having the largest number of members. Other religions represented are Islam, Presbyterianism, Baha'i, Pentecostal, Spiritual Baptists and Judaism. In the aftermath of independence from the United Kingdom in 1962, efforts were made to accommodate the multireligious nature of the country's nationals through the passage of marriage acts specific to each faith, not least because colonial authorities had also made it difficult and in some cases illegal for followers of varying faiths to be married in their religion. One lasting consequence was the regulation of marriage under four acts – the Marriage Act of 1923 governing Christian and civil marriages, which set the age of marriage at 18 for men and women, the Hindu Marriage Act of 1945 where the age was 14 for girls and 18 for men, the Muslim Marriage and Divorce Act of 1961 where the age was 16 for girls and 18 for men and the Orisa Marriage Act of 1999 where the ages were 16 for girls and 18 for men.

For decades since independence, Trinidad and Tobago has one of the highest GDP per capita incomes in the region, yet some of its statutes and the resulting inconsistencies still bear the remnants of a bygone era. This puts the country at odds with its development thrust and its human rights commitments as mandated by its signature and ratification of key human rights instruments such as the Convention on the Rights of the Child (CRC) and the Convention on the Elimination of all forms of Discrimination Against Women (CEDAW). In 2016, after several calls by civil society, the government announced its intention to amend the respective laws, triggering opposition from Hindu, Muslim and Spiritual Baptist leaders and an equally incensed response to this opposition, from those advocating for change. The UN office in Port of Spain also issued a statement recalling the country's obligations under the CRC and CEDAW and supporting efforts to end child marriage (UNIC, 2017). Although the law was eventually amended, the opposition party abstained (Sant, 2017) highlighting the divisive nature of the issue, the tension between realising a vision for human development and the politics of a multicultural society, as well as the desire by some for decision-making that takes cultural realities into account.

Critically, the episode also signalled the need to pay attention to a number of key issues. First, the absence of a clearly articulated vision for the promotion and protection of human rights has resulted in a failure to mainstream relevant issues into a whole-of-government approach. Second, the non-integration of gender as a pillar of foreign policy highlighted the gap between foreign policies that on paper professed a commitment to human rights and gender equity, but were not operationalised nor integrated in the implementation of domestic programming. This in turn facilitated the lack of structured analysis for issues such as child marriage, various forms of gender-based inequities, the state's obligations to protect its citizens within the overarching framework of upholding its human rights obligations and the consequent impact on the human and general security of girls and women and boys and men.

Third, while it may be said that the figures are relatively low for adolescents who marry – UNICEF estimated that 2% of girls were married by 15 and 8% by 18 (UNICEF, 2016) – the country's Attorney General noted that 3478 child marriages occurred between 1996 and 2016 (Ramdass, 2017). In a small country such as Trinidad and Tobago, this merits attention. Tellingly, of that figure, 3404 were girls, while 74 were boys under the age of 18, and further *analysis* on the age gaps between these child brides and their husbands showed that girls between the ages of 11 and 16 were married to men aged 36–52 years old (Ramdass, 2017). These figures point to the pervasive influence of long-standing beliefs about the role of girls and women.

The retention of such laws has thus indirectly contributed to the persistence of misogynistic attitudes and beliefs that are manifested in a variety of pervasive practices that negatively impact the security of women and girls. These find expression in a range of behaviours including the so-called "harmless" misogynistic speech often attributed to culture as embodied by the local phrase "after 12 is lunch", meaning that any girl over the age of 12 is deemed ready for adult relationships. The extreme has come to be epitomised in the country's alarmingly high cases of domestic violence, where it is estimated that 1 in 3 women are victims of domestic violence with approximately 10,000 applications for restraining orders annually (Hunte, 2016).

Additionally, these practices also manifest themselves in the way various types of families live on a day-to-day basis, how girls and boys are socialised, how families deal with varying types of trauma and how belief systems are incorporated and the educational goals and the overall menu of options available to individuals. In sum, this is the impact of gender as the single biggest determinant of how a person is treated, writ large.

Fourth, the non-integration of human rights and gender into foreign policy has contributed to a limited view of domestic and regional security that does not take into account some of the critical issues that create a climate of insecurity in specific subsets of a population. Simply put, a human security framework has not been adequately integrated for security cannot be limited to crime such as gun violence, armed robbery or gang activity. Moreover, a chronic lack of security can be the daily experience for a significant sector of the population due to gender-based violence.

The cumulative impact of this chronic – and in some cases *sanctioned* violence – creates economic, social, cultural and personal insecurity for some citizens that feeds directly into perpetuating an insecure and less resilient state as a culture of violence is perpetuated, economically active populations compromised, family units destroyed in some instances and the rights of women, boys and girls impacted. For the health practitioner, understanding these contexts and making these linkages are equally important. But what does the mental health practitioner need to keep in view?

Recommendations for Family and Mental Health Practitioners: Scaling up and Expanding Outward to Deliver at the Policy Level

Understand *the Context: Understand the Lay of the Land*

Of critical importance is understanding the context in which insecurity occurs and is sustained. This calls for a rudimentary understanding at least and a moderate appreciation at best, of the nature of the international system, its various actors, the nature of state behaviour, the impact of non-state actors and the factors that contribute to insecurity in its various forms. Central to this is also understanding that what may constitute a form of insecurity in one context may be viewed as "business as usual" in another.

Adopt *an Intersectional Approach*

Practitioners must also pay singular attention to the imperative of meeting every community on its own terms. This calls for a constant self-reflexivity and an understanding of the different cultural, social, psychosocial, economic and political contexts.

Identify *Crosscutting Issues*

In view of the complex nature of the issues that impact on health and overall well-being, and the consequent outsized impact health has on the socio-economic development of communities and countries, mental health practitioners should advocate for health and mental health to be treated as crosscutting issues. Relatedly, there is also a need to identify the crosscutting issues that impact on health and mental health.

Advocate *for the Inclusion of Health and Mental Health as Standing Agenda Items*

One option to consider is to ensure health and mental health programming are adopted as standing items on the agenda for certain UN agencies and bodies to ensure that the related programming is considered, allocated and budgeted for.

Use *a Gendered Lens*

A vivid example of how a more nuanced understanding of gender dynamics and its link to human security could have influenced international policies may be found in the "Washington Consensus" of the 1980s. The consensus's structural adjustment mechanisms had a disproportionate impact on female-headed households in some English-speaking Caribbean SIDS, underscoring that security transcends force, militarism, war and peace and encompasses public health, social security, the well-being of families and the resilience of communities.

Create *Partnerships in Security and Defence to Expand Definition of Security*

All elements of the security of English-speaking Caribbean SIDS face urgent, complex and interrelated challenges that traditional approaches to foreign policy and security are less capable of adequately addressing. Redefining the region's view of what security means will be key to engaging new and imaginative human rights-based approaches. The health sector overall has a unique role to play in this regard, given their points of entry into communities for whom security can assume varying forms. In this context, pursuing policies that safeguard the collective security of its nationals – including policies that address gender-based discrimination within the framework of the more robust promotion and protection of human rights – is central to ensuring all their citizens have the most basic capabilities for human development. This is a cornerstone of the human security approach which draws heavily on the work of Amartya Sen (Sen, 1999), who advanced the idea of "unfreedoms", of which one was gender inequity.

Ensure *Human Rights is at the Centre*

One key element to addressing the persistence of these "unfreedoms" is the acceptance of and adherence to the universality of human rights and their inalienable, indivisible and interdependent nature, for if there is no agreement that people derive certain entitlements as a result of their humanity and which safeguards their security, how does a society or a government ensure that they receive same? Moreover, as the WHO has noted (WHO, 2017a) the inability of communities and people to enjoy general well-being, avoid impairment and overall ill-health is steadfastly grounded in the lack of priority afforded to health as a human right and the consequent failure to promote and protect such rights.

Conclusions: Sound Policies, Sound Polities, Sound Families and Sound People

As noted above, the SIDS of the English-speaking Caribbean have unique vulnerabilities (UNDESA, 2002) associated with these countries' history, social development, geography and small economic size. Among these well-documented vulnerabilities are environmental issues such as small size, relative isolation, lack of resources, exposure to natural hazards and greater susceptibility to climate change. Economic concerns such as lack of competitive advantage, weak institutional structures, human resource constraints, high costs of basic infrastructure, energy insecurity and informal economies also confer a unique set of challenges (CEPAL, 2000).

It is precisely this scenario that constitutes day-to-day existence for Caribbean SIDS: what Otto terms in her 2011 article being "permanently suspended in states of crisis" (Otto, 2011). This is the reality for small countries, and it is one that she characterises as having rapidly reshaped what international peace and security means.

The impact of these issues is exponentially increased by social challenges that include, *inter alia*, the preponderance of female-headed households, the feminisation of poverty, the loss of human capital to metropoles – "brain drain" and health challenges such as HIV and AIDS and non-communicable diseases (NCDs), as well as drug addiction and the impact of narco and human trafficking with all the attendant impacts on human security.

Against this backdrop and the relentless march of globalisation with a concomitant multilateralisation of the international agenda, the idea has gained traction, as noted by Verveer (Verveer, 2012), that foreign policy cannot be effectively implemented and security not fully realised for any state, if the issues that affect half the world's population are not taken into account.

Slaughter's call (2012) for a "people-centred foreign policy" has therefore been instrumental in popularising the above idea that the field's focus should extend beyond the mainly traditional notions of security to encompass one where caregiving is valued differently. In Slaughter's formulation, the notion of security does not conceptualise women as passive agents of development and encompasses issues that the mental health practitioners are concerned with.

Among these are, *inter alia*, public health, well-being of families, social security and the integrity of healthcare systems. One needs to only examine the Ebola virus disease (EVD) crisis of 2013–2016 to grasp the unambiguously clear linkages between the severely compromised health systems of Ebola source countries and the resultant widespread impacts in terms of loss of life and those impacts as well as the socio-economic disruptions on a global scale, to understand that health and mental health are not "soft" issues. These "soft" issues are in fact the most urgent challenges, as Madeleine Albright reminded, ultimately jeopardising the sustainability of the "harder" version of security, often operationalised as efforts to maintain public order and safety (Albright, 2010).

As can be seen from the example of child marriage in Trinidad and Tobago, the value in achieving these objectives is not merely aspirational, but grounded in empirical findings (WHO, 2017a, 2017b): a *healthy* woman who lives a life without the possibility of child marriage, sex or gender-based violence (SGBV), limited educational opportunities, suboptimal participation in the labour force and restricted political participation is more optimally positioned to become and remain a productive member of her community and society and to lift her family out of poverty (Hakura, Mumtaz, Newiak, Thakoor, & Yang, 2016; WHO, 2017a, 2017b; Woetzel et al., 2015). One of the best ways to achieve this is to develop, maintain and expand the systems for the promotion and protection of the fundamental element of human security such that security will be less viewed through the traditional prism of crime, arms, drugs and nuclear proliferation.

Using a gendered lens – in the context of health and health-related issues – to examine issues related to foreign policy and human security highlights the importance of addressing issues related to power, inequality and access to and control of resources, as well as various other political dimensions (Tiessen, 2015) and the consequences for a person's security in every dimension.

It is critical then that practitioners and those in the field understand that that such a process goes beyond political rhetoric. This is of particular importance noting that international relations can be complicated and capricious. Foreign policymakers – and now the health and mental health communities and its practitioners – therefore have to be nuanced in their approaches secure in the irony and armed with the knowledge that international dynamics do not often allow for the luxury of nuance. Nevertheless, the bedrock human rights principles of empowerment, participation, accountability, transparency, non-discrimination and international cooperation within an intersectional framework are integral to creating societies and systems of governance that are resilient and enhance citizens' economic, social, personal and environmental security.

References

Albright, M. (2010). "On being a woman and a diplomat," *TedWomen 2010*, December 2010. http://www.ted.com/talks/madeleine_albright_on_being_a_woman_and_a_diplomat/transcript?language=en.

Amnesty International. (2016). Haiti/Dominican Republic: Reckless Deportations Leave Thousands in Limbo. Retrieved from https://www.amnesty.org/en/latest/news/2016/06/haiti-dominican-republic-reckless-deportations-leaving-thousands-in-limbo/.

Belton, K. & Krzyzaniak, J. (2017). *A Conversation on Statelessness*. Carnegie Council. Retrieved from https://www.ethicsandinternationalaffairs.org/2017/conversation-on-statelessness-with-kristy-belton/

Caribbean Vulnerable Communities. (2016, March 14). *Promoting Human Rights and Health for all*. Retrieved from http://www.cvccoalition.org/content/caribbean-vulnerable-communities-coalition-membership-brochure

Cheema, R. (2016). Black and blue bloods: Protecting police officer families from domestic violence. Retrieved from https://scholarlycommons.law.hofstra.edu/cgi/viewcontent.cgi?article=1009&context=hofstra_law_student_works.

Cuberes, D., & Teignier, M. (2016). Aggregate effects of gender gaps in the labor market: A quantitative estimate. *Journal of Human Capital, 10*(1), 1–32.

Economic Commission for Latin America and the Caribbean (CEPAL). (2000). The vulnerability of the Small Island Developing States of the Caribbean, March 13, 2000, Retrieved from http://www.cepal.org/publicaciones/xml/8/8118/G0588.html.

Farr, J. (2005). Point: The Westphalia legacy and the modern nation-state. *International Social Science Review, 80*, 156–159. Retrieved from http://www.jstor.org/stable/41887235.

Franklin, J. (2018). Venezuelan pirates rule the most lawless market on earth. *Bloomberg Businessweek*. Retrieved from https://www.bloomberg.com/news/features/2018-01-30/venezuelan-pirates-rule-the-most-lawless-market-on-earth.

Friedersdorf, C. (2014). Police have a much bigger domestic abuse problem than the NFL does. Retrieved from https://www.theatlantic.com/national/archive/2014/09/police-officers-who-hit-their-wives-or-girlfriends/380329/.

Galtung, J. (1990). Cultural violence. *Journal of Peace Research, 27*(3), 291–305. Retrieved from https://www.galtung-institut.de/wp-content/uploads/2015/12/Cultural-Violence-Galtung.pdf.

Gomez, O.A., & Gasper, D. (2013). Human security: A thematic guidance note for regional and national human development report team. United Nations Development Fund. Retrieved from http://hdr.undp.org/sites/default/files/human_security_guidance_note_r-nhdrs.pdf.

Hakura, D., Mumtaz, H., Newiak, M., Thakoor, V., & Yang, F. (2016). *Inequality, gender gaps and economic growth: Comparative evidence for sub-Saharan Africa*. Washington, DC: International Monetary Fund. Retrieved from https://www.imf.org/external/pubs/ft/wp/2016/wp16111.pdf.

Hindin, Z., & Ariza, M. (2016). When nativism becomes normal. *The Atlantic*. Retrieved from https://www.theatlantic.com/international/archive/2016/05/dominican-republic-la-sentencia/483998/.

Hudson, V. M., Caprioli, M., Ballif-Spanvill, B., McDermott, R., & Emmett, C. F. (2008). The heart of the matter: The security of women and the security of states. *Quarterly Journal: International Security, 33*(3), 7–45.

Human Rights Watch. (2015). We are Dominican. Retrieved from https://www.hrw.org/report/2015/07/01/we-are-dominican/arbitrary-deprivation-nationality-dominican-republic.

Human Rights Watch. (2016). Haiti: Stateless people trapped in poverty. Retrieved from https://www.hrw.org/news/2016/11/29/haiti-stateless-people-trapped-poverty.

Hunte, C. (2016, December 6). Domestic violence 'epidemic' in T&T. *Trinidad Express*. Retrieved from http://www.trinidadexpress.com/20161206/news/domestic-violence-8216epidemic8217-in-tt.

International Labour Organisation (ILO). (2012). Global employment trends for women. Geneva: ILO. http://www.ilo.org/wcmsp5/groups/public/%2D%2D-dgreports/%2D%2D-dcomm/documents/publication/wcms_195447.pdf.

International Labour Organisation (ILO). (2016). Snapshot ILO in action: Domestic workers. Retrieved from http://www.ilo.org/wcmsp5/groups/public/@ed_protect/@protrav/@travail/documents/publication/wcms_214499.pdf.

Johnson, D., & Kochel, T. R. (2012). Race, ethnicity, crime and criminal justice in Trinidad and Tobago. In A. Kalunta-Crumpton (Ed.), *Race, ethnicity, crime and criminal justice in the Americas*. London, UK: Palgrave Macmillan.

Kong Soo, C. (2018, February 4). Venezuelan crisis fuels exploitation in T&T. *Trinidad and Tobago Guardian*. Retrieved from http://www.guardian.co.tt/news/2018-02-04/venezuela-crisis-fuels-exploitation-tt.

Melamed, C. (2012, March 9). Gender is just one of many inequalities that generate poverty and exclusion. *The Guardian*. Retrieved from https://www.theguardian.com/global-development/poverty-matters/2012/mar/09/gender-inequality-poverty-exclusion

Miller, B. D. (Ed.). (1993). *Sex and Gender Hierarchies*. New York, NY: Cambridge University Press.

Otto, D. (2011). Remapping crisis through a feminist Lens. In S. Kouvo & Z. Pearson (Eds.), *Feminist perspectives on contemporary international law: Between resistance and compliance* (pp. 75–97). Portland, OR: Hart Publishing.

Pan American Health Organisation (PAHO). (2018). No direct maternal deaths reported in Trinidad and Tobago in 2018. Retrieved from https://www.paho.org/hq/index.php?option=com_content&view=article&id=14503&Itemid=39620&lang=en.

Ramdass, A. (2017, January 11). 3404 child brides in last two decades. *Trinidad Express*. Retrieved from http://www.trinidadexpress.com/20170111/news/82163404-child-brides-in-last-two-decades8217.

Ryan, A.H. (1994). The Prevalence of domestic violence in police families. Retrieved from http://webapp1.dlib.indiana.edu/virtual_disk_library/index.cgi/4951188/FID707/Root/New/030PG297.PDF.

Sant, R. (2017, January 18). Marriage Bill moves to Lower House, UNC abstained in protest–Mark. *Trinidad and Tobago Guardian*. Retrieved from http://www.guardian.co.tt/news/2017-01-18/marriage-bill-moves-lower-house-unc-abstained-protest%E2%80%94mark.

Sen, A. (1999). Introduction. In *Development as freedom*. Oxford, UK: Oxford Press Retrieved from http://www.c3l.uni-oldenburg.de/cde/OMDE625/Sen/Sen-intro.pdf.

Slaughter, A. (2012, November 26). Why family is a foreign policy issue. *Foreign Policy*. Retrieved from https://foreignpolicy.com/2012/11/26/why-family-is-a-foreign-policy-issue/.

Tickner, J. A. (1992). Engendered insecurities: Feminist perspectives on international relations. In *Gender in international relations: Feminist perspectives on achieving global security*. New York, NY: Columbia University Press Retrieved from http://www.ces.uc.pt/ficheiros2/files/Short.pdf.

Tiessen, R. (2015). Gender essentialism in Canadian, foreign aid commitments to women, peace and security. *International Journal, 70*(1), 84–100.

United Nations (UN). (2010, May 18). Our challenges are shared; so, too, is our commitment to enhance freedom from fear, freedom from want, Freedom to Live in Dignity. [Press release]. Retrieved from https://www.un.org/press/en/2010/ga10942.doc.htm.

United Nations (UN). (2015, December 30). *Sustainable Development Goals kick off with start of new year*. Retrieved from https://www.un.org/sustainabledevelopment/blog/2015/12/sustainable-development-goals-kick-off-with-start-of-new-year/

United Nations Children's Fund (UNICEF). (2016). *The state of the World's children 2016: A fair chance for every child*. New York, NY: UNICEF. Retrieved from https://www.unicef.org/sowc2016/.

United Nations Department of Economic and Social Affairs (UNDESA). (2002). Developing a Vulnerability Index for SIDS. Retrieved from https://sustainabledevelopment.un.org/index.php?page=view&type=13&nr=380&menu=1634.

United Nations Development Fund for Women (UNIFEM). (2010). Gender justice: Key to achieving the millennium development goals. Retrieved from https://reliefweb.int/sites/reliefweb.int/files/resources/313E783E66A28DBB852577AC0073ACA4-UNIFEM-MDGBrief-English.pdf.

United Nations Development Programme (UNDP). (1994). *Human development report* (p. 1994). New York, NY: Oxford University Press.

United Nations General Assembly (UNGA, 2012). *Follow-up to paragraph 143 on human security of the 2005 World Summit Outcome*, UNGA, 66th Session, Agenda Items 14 and 117, A/RES/66/290 (25 October 2012). Retrieved from http://www.un.org/en/ga/search/view_doc.asp?symbol=%20A/RES/66/290.

United Nations High Commissioner for Refugees (UNHCR). (2017). *UN Conventions on Statelessness*. Retrieved from https://www.unhcr.org/en-us/un-conventions-on-statelessness.html

United Nations Information Center (UNIC). (2017). *The United Nations System in Trinidad and Tobago supports efforts to end Child Marriage*. United Nations Information Center for the Caribbean Area. Retrieved from http://portofspain.unicnetwork.org/index.php/component/k2/item/293-untt-endchildmarriage.

Verveer, M. (2012, April 23). Why women are a foreign policy issue. *Foreign Policy*. Retrieved from http://foreignpolicy.com/2012/04/23/why-women-are-a-foreign-policy-issue/.

Woetzel,J.,Madgavkar,A.,Ellingrud,K.,Labaye,E.,Devillard,S.,Kutcher,E.,...Krishnan,M.(2015). *How advancing women's equality can add $12 trillion growth*. New York, NY: McKinsey Global Institute. Retrieved from http://www.mckinsey.com/global-themes/employment-and-growth/how-advancing-womens-equality-can-add-12-trillion-to-global-growth.

World Health Organization (WHO). (2001b). *The world health report: Mental health: New understanding, new hope*. Retrieved from http://www.who.int/whr/2001/en/whr01_en.pdf. 20 April 2018.

World Health Organization (WHO). (2015). *The SDGs: Reflections on the Implications and Challenges for Health*. Retrieved from http://www.who.int/gho/publications/mdgs-sdgs/MDGs-SDGs2015_chapter9.pdf

World Health Organization (WHO). (2017a). *Leading the Realization of Human Rights to Health and through Health*. Retrieved from https://www.ohchr.org/Documents/Issues/Women/WRGS/Health/ReportHLWG-humanrights-health.pdf

World Health Organization (WHO). (2017b). *The pilot project: Adolescent sexual and reproductive health programme to address equity, Social Determinants, Gender and Human Rights in Nepal*. Retrieved from http://www.searo.who.int/entity/gender/documents/national-asrh-programme.pdf?ua=1.

Wrangham, R., & Peterson, D. (1996). *Demonic males: Apes and the origins of human violence*. Boston, MA: Harcourt Mifflin Harcourt.

Wucker, M. (2015). The Dominican Republic's shameful deportation legacy. Retrieved from http://foreignpolicy.com/2015/10/08/dominican-republic-haiti-trujillo-immigration-deportation/.

Young, S. (2017a). In our backyard: The Caribbean's statelessness and refugee crisis. Retrieved from https://www.brookings.edu/blog/order-from-chaos/2017/06/20/in-our-backyard-the-caribbeans-statelessness-and-refugee-crisis/. Washington, DC: The Brookings Institution.

Young, S. (2017b). Why human security is national security for Small Island Developing States. Retrieved from https://www.brookings.edu/blog/order-from-chaos/2017/06/12/why-human-security-is-national-security-for-small-island-developing-states/. Washington, DC: The Brookings Institution.

Chapter 8
Drawing in or Ruling Out "Family?" The Evolution of the Family Systems Approach in Sri Lanka

Evangeline S. Ekanayake and Nilanga Abeysinghe

Introduction

A few months ago, an old colleague contacted with a request to conduct a day training for her newly appointed counselling assistants. We had several discussions about the type and level of training they already had and what sort of training needs they were pressed for. These discussions confirmed the understanding we already had about the limitations of their overall training and the complex nature of the cases they deal with. She mentioned that these counsellors were not only working with limited training and supervision but dealt with a clientele with minimum support in their home and work environments. We had seen this pattern with other diverse client groups too. For example, in the area of labour migration, lesbian-gay-bi-transgender (LGBT) groups and people struggling with addictions are a few.

We tried to answer the big question: "What might be the most beneficial topic for this training?" By this time, Evan, who is co-authoring this chapter, had trained some government staff involved in counselling services and field staff of few community-based organisations on family systems therapy (FST) and was engaged in follow-up programmes. We discussed the challenges of these newly trained counsellors in comparison to the ones that Evan had already worked with. It was immediately apparent that a common factor loomed large in all groups and this was the significant and powerful "family factor" that compounded the nature of people's problems in current Sri Lankan society. It was obvious then that this demanded a robust and creative methodology that would enable the Sri Lankan counsellor to skilfully navigate the factor of family to therapeutic advantage. Thus, we offered FST as a topic worth considering for this training among a few other topics, which they readily accepted.

E. S. Ekanayake · N. Abeysinghe (✉)
Faculty of Graduate Studies, University of Colombo, Colombo, Sri Lanka

© Springer Nature Switzerland AG 2019
L. L. Charlés, G. Samarasinghe (eds.), *Family Systems and Global Humanitarian Mental Health*, https://doi.org/10.1007/978-3-030-03216-6_8

On the one hand, there was relief in finding a means by which the visibly powerful influence of family could be addressed; on the other, trainees were keen to explore how family systems approaches (FSA) could (or not) work with the real-life cases that they had faced recently.

How would the concepts of FSA translate into practice in the absence of a clearly identifiable family or a system that was willing to collaborate? Can we practise FSA in the absence of key family members, who were sometimes perceived to be the cause of problems?

Is FSA supposed to replace the way we used to work with individuals?

Should we seek assistance from other officials (such as the police department) to ensure the compliance of families? Would FSA complicate our already complex case load?

These were some of the questions and concerns raised by our trainees. Interestingly some of the very same questions had been raised by trainees in the groups that Evan worked with. We knew we were on to something significant. Perhaps a strategic change in the way people understood their problems and their significant relationships was perhaps been drawn together in these therapeutic spaces.

Apart from this group of counsellors, we have had the opportunity to introduce FST to other groups of counsellors and others working in the psychosocial sector. Hence, in addition to the above concerns of the trainees, we, as trainers, had a few questions ourselves in terms of making FST relevant to each of the different groups we worked with. One predominant concern we constantly struggle with is language. How could we best translate the concepts of FST (or any other approach in psycho-social work for that matter) into our local languages, Sinhalese or Tamil,[1] preserving its meaning in the sociocultural contexts where it will be used? Some of the trainings were conducted in Sinhalese language, and we attempted to get the feedback of the trainees as to what it meant to them and their clients. However, some groups were trained in the English language, and we had trainees from both groups who worked in Sinhalese and Tamil. Thus, it was of significant concern to us that the concepts are translated accurately and effectively into both local languages and that they made real sense.

Why FST in Sri Lanka?

Why are we (or for that matter counsellors practising in Sri Lanka) interested in working through an FSA than to work with the individual who is faced with the problem? Though Sri Lanka has seen many rapid changes in this sociocultural milieu, the family remains a dominant social construct shaping, reshaping and giving meaning to people. The Sri Lankan family-social system has however been

---

[1] Sri Lanka is considered a bilingual country where Sinhalese and both Indian and Sri Lankan Tamil dialects are spoken.

taking different forms and shapes during the last few decades. We see almost revolutionary changes in the way family members relate to each other. Twenty years ago, a family member who worked in one part of the county would hear from his/her family mainly through the "postal system" (snail mail), while he/she would be able to see them once in several months depending on transport and their financial status. However, with the technological advances, communication through phone and social media has become so common that families are connected to each other via video calls and many different ways on a daily and sometimes hourly basis. This has in fact extended to establish much more communication with overseas members. There are views that blame social media "taking over" of face-to-face communication. IT advancements are blamed for the deteriorating bonds between immediate family members as people tend to spend less time talking to each other. Yet, there are other positive factors such as how IT advances have connected people within families who would not have been in touch if not for the facilities available. The impact of the technological advancements on the family systems and dynamics has to be addressed in any effective form of systemic therapy.

In this milieu of the twenty-first century, the functionality of the family seems to have changed overtime, and it keeps on changing in all social strata. However, as a clinician or a lay person, you may agree that in whatever its state, each member of a family has a notable influence on the others. This influence may be positive in some instances while being negative in others. Thus, irrespective of the nature of "how" one relates to the other members in a family unit, we emphasise on the fact that one does "relate" to the family, one does influence and one ends up being influenced in return.

Just as it is in the family unit, there are also other units that we are part of. These include schools, work places, religious institutions, clubs, societies at grassroots level and much more. These organisations that are at the micro-system and meso-system (Bronfenbrenner, 1994) have a significant effect on the quality of one's life. That is, there is reciprocal influence between us and others beyond our primary unit, which is the family. If so, is it possible and worthwhile for a clinician to use these connections or these other systems which sometimes evolve in to "family of choice", rather than biological family to support a client in his/her journey towards recovery?

Mental Health and Psychosocial Support (MHPSS) in the Sri Lankan Context

As mentioned above, Sri Lanka has gone through many social and cultural changes as a result of the sociopolitical and economical changes (and challenges) it underwent since the 1950s. The development of the field of counselling and the broader MHPSS sector also had its genesis in the latter part of this period as a response to the demands of the said transformations. Wolfe (2012) discussing the historical development of the counselling sector in Britain attributes the developmental turning points of the sector to the socio, economic and political changes that influenced the society, especially in the aftermath of World War II. He further compared this with the United States and points out how the same factors contributed to the development of the field and how the aftermath of the Vietnam War specifically contributed. The examples from these countries point out not only the impact of the larger society on the development of the field of MHPSS but also the role of the professionals in determining the standards, values and the best suited directions to respond to the inevitable changing process of the society.

In the case of Sri Lanka, the last decade is marked with a significant increase in the number of state and non-state sector mental health professionals as evident in the Sri Lanka Medical Council (SLMC) records for psychiatrists and clinical psychologists throughout 2007–2017. The same upward trend can be observed for counsellors too and in the state sector alone this was over 300 by 2015 (The Asia Foundation, 2015a, 2015b). At present it is estimated that the country has about 400 state sector counsellors attached to a couple of ministries (with the designations "counsellor" or "counselling assistant"). The level of training and knowledge of these counsellors varies from master's-level (MA/MSc/MPhil in Clinical Psychology) qualifications to 1-year diplomas in counselling.

Along with few other colleagues, in 2012–2013 we conducted two island-wide surveys on the counselling services. Among many other research questions, we were particularly interested in finding out the most common problems that clients presented in counselling. These studies pointed out that "family problems" and "problems related to school education plus exam-related issues" are the commonest (Good Practice Group, 2013; The Institute for Health Policy, 2013). In addition to our findings, Sri Lanka has continued to have a high suicide rate since the 1990s. In 2014 it was indicated as 28.8 per 100,000 individuals by the WHO. There are arguments that these statistical data are somewhat overestimated due to the lack of actual data while acknowledging that suicide attempts or deliberate self-harm rates in Sri Lanka are one of the highest in the world (Knipe, Metcalfe, & Gunnell, 2015). A significant proportion of these attempts are linked to family conflicts. In addition, population projections for Sri Lanka indicate that there will be an increase in the population over 60 years of age over the next decades (De Silva, 2007). Furthermore, WHO projects that by 2030 the global carer burden of mental illnesses will be the highest among all other health issues and Sri Lanka is no exception. The impact of an ageing population on the construct of family is likewise profound, as elders are still largely looked after within the family. This is because there is still no adequate social support system to take care of the growing ageing population and its expansion. Additionally this is not complemented by increased services or facilities for elderly populations. This means that Sri Lankan family systems are going to be further impacted with its ageing population.

In the backdrop of these current and projected mental health-related issues, Sri Lanka is yet struggling to recover from the aftermath of the three-decade-long civil war. Thus, it is important to understand that the MHPSS sector in Sri Lanka is still short staffed to deal with the demand despite the increase in numbers during the past decade. At the moment there are a few state and non-state sector institutions and universities that train counsellors. Nevertheless, it is unlikely that this process will be able to train sufficient numbers of counsellors who could cater to the increasing demand. Thus, we as professionals in the field of MHPSS at present are challenged with making necessary decisions to figure out ways of overcoming this issue.

Inevitable Challenges: A Different Approach and Chances of Success

Clinicians should ideally focus on many factors that affect their therapeutic success. These factors may range from characteristics of the therapist, the type and quality of therapy session, client's problem situation or diagnosis (if there is one), willingness to take part in therapy, etc. These can be broadly categorised as follows:

1. Characteristics related to the therapist
2. Characteristics related to the therapeutic environment
3. Characteristics related to the client

In the light of the available resources in the MHPSS sector, the limitations related to realistically increasing the number of counsellors and the facilities for therapy are apparent. Therefore it has become imperative that we consider using the limited time that could be allocated for a single client more efficiently by introducing a therapeutic model that draws in and utilises those people who are immediately around the client as a system that facilitates the recovery and better management of the client's condition. Those in the closest proximity to the client may be a conventional family or a family system of choice, which incorporates neighbours unrelated family friends, faith families (groups of religious worshippers who take care of each other) or an institution in which the client is positioned, such as a home for elders, a school, some form of a care home or any other institution. And so, we have been challenged to consider whether it would make sense to understand, reinterpret and utilise FST in a way that best fits a rapidly changing social context of Sri Lanka.

We will share our experiences and our dilemmas in introducing and training existing and novice counsellors in FST. Thus, the rest of this chapter will be a reflection of how we have proceeded so far and our thoughts on possible causes.

Family Systems Approach in Sri Lanka

An FSA Class on a Saturday Afternoon

The scenario is an air-conditioned classroom where 25 adult postgraduate students gather on a hot Saturday afternoon. The group is a mixed bunch of professionals from a wide and wild range of professions from teachers, media people, the military, religious orders, state-employed counsellors and development workers. The topic of the day is working with families. There's a keenness in the air. Almost all in the class, regardless of their field of work, are required to deal with families in difficulties or conflict. Almost all share a sense of frustration in finding adequate and effective means of navigating the complexity of such work. In the first 3 h, we have gone through the theory of FSA. Something makes the afternoon seem hotter and wills battle with eyelids to keep alert. Then we shift gear.

The class changes position to make a circle and every one gathers round. Five volunteers are invited to step forward in to the space in the middle. The case of a family which was presented earlier is about to be brought to life. The FS approach is about to be tested. The moment of truth is here. All eyes wide open.

1. The volunteers each take a role as a family member. They are given bits of paper with a brief description of their role in the family and given time to assimilate this role.
2. The problem is presented to the whole class including the volunteer actors and those observing. It is a situation of family conflict.

Case Study

Thiyalini, a 42 year old mother is a returning migrant worker. She finds her family doing financially well, but her relationship with her husband Thileepan is strained and conflictual. He is withdrawn and hardly comes home, from fishing at sea which is his livelihood. Thileepan feels inadequate as his role as a provider is being challenged. Further, his wife's expectations of a man have become more sophisticated. He therefore, withdraws into himself and his fishing. Thiyalini is disappointed and is frustrated as despite her years of hard labour for the family and faithfulness to Thileepan, he is still not happy with her and even accuses her falsely. There's conflict in the family on so many little things that their son Thangesh has started to vanish into his virtual world on his smart phone and doesn't connect with anyone. Their daughter Sutha loudly expresses her disappointment in her parents, says that things were much better before mother left even if they were poor and declares that she will never marry which is a terrible shock to her grandmother (Thileepan's mother) who looked after the children in Thiyalini's absence. She now lives to see Sutha become a bride one day. The family is distraught and cannot figure out how their bonds have splintered.

3. The facilitator invites the family members to assume their roles and take their seats where ever they are comfortable.
4. The facilitator asks the observers what possible therapeutic goals can be made realistically for a first session. It is established that the first goal could be that of allowing the family to articulate their difficulties and the second might be to help them see that the difficulty is not merely personal but is systemic in that it involves them all and their pattern of relationship to each other.

5. The facilitator next asks the observers if they were to intervene with this family whom they might want to start with in order to move towards the first two goals. They select the grandmother (Thileepan's mother) and, for purposes of a case, assume she has sought assistance in helping to convince her granddaughter that she should consider marriage despite her disappointment with her parents' marriage.

6. The facilitator first models engagement with the grandmother and how the conversation moves from the stated (felt) problem (wanting to convince her granddaughter of marriage) to the wider context of the systemic issues in their family.

7. At this point the role play is paused, and a very brief discussion of the use of different tools and strategies used ensues between the observers and the facilitator. The observers are now taking the role of a "reflection team" which watches the process and gives feedback. The next goal is outlined. This goal is to explain the FSA and encourage the family member (in this case the grandmother) to invite the rest of the family to participate in a few sessions.

8. This step is attempted by one of the "reflecting teams" (observers) who assumes the role of the counsellor (taking over from the facilitator). The rest observe how she navigates the conversation and brings the grandmother to a point of recognising that the real issues are broader than getting her granddaughter to agree to marriage and that a systemic approach might be worth considering.

   By this time the class is completely engaged. They group themselves into fours and fives and observe the interaction in the centre of the room closely to pick out the following:

Observations: A Quick Discussion by the Reflecting Team Follows at this Stage
(a) What is the interaction like? How easy or difficult is this conversation for the client and for the counsellor?
(b) What specific FSA strategies or other techniques do you perceive being used? How effective are they?
(c) What are your observations on the use of linear questions and circular questions?
(d) To what extent do you think that conversation was successful in gleaning information, in bringing insight and in motivating client for the next step?
(e) Are there things you might have done/said differently?

9. We proceed even further. This time it's to run the first session with some family members together. We have the mother Thiyalini, the grandmother and the daughter Sutha agreeing to attend. The facilitator once again resumes the counsellor role to model the following:

   (a) Convening a session and explaining the process boundaries and collaborative nature of the exercise.

(b) Facilitating goal setting by the family and assisting their process of agreeing on what they want to achieve among themselves.
(c) Creating a helpful enabling atmosphere.

The Reflection Team and the Learning Process
In this phase of the exercise, the "reflection team" (who are the observers or the rest of the class) is encouraged to pay attention to the process: They are asked to reflect on what way FSA has in common with group therapy facilitation in general and in what ways FSA is unique. They are asked to reflect or watch out for how the facilitator uses the family roles and relationships, the existing dynamics such as the power balance within the family, the patterns of behaviour the beliefs that each has about the other and what strategies the facilitator uses to navigate the presenting family dynamics to therapeutic advantage.

10. The facilitator begins by addressing Thiyalini, her mother and Sutha her daughter; recognising them, their role and contribution within the family; and also raising the issue of their role in the current situation. The facilitator soon begins to use circular questions to create a discussion by drawing the three women in to the conversation and especially strategising to enable them to talking directly to each other. Awkwardly, reluctantly and almost angrily, at first we see Thiyalini, her mother and her daughter begin to respond to the circular questioning. The facilitator steps back slightly enabling them to speak and watches their dynamics play its self out while remaining the voice that draws everyone's attention to specific qualities, significant moments, tones, words or exchanges in the interactions. In this way the facilitator enables insight within the family to recognise the unique qualities and characteristics of their family system.

Observations
The observers are encouraged to pay attention in their groups to the following.

What are the most prominent features of the facilitator's role in this interaction? What are the most important things she does to enable the process?
How effective was this enabling?
What are the visible dynamics between the members of the family present at this session?
How well does the facilitator recognise and draw on these dynamics to therapeutic advantage?
What were the significant points in the conversation? What was useful to bring about those significant moves?

The role plays up to this point have been both educative and entertaining. The class is now buzzing. Some want to see more and go to the next exercise, some want to discuss their questions and yet others want to try it out for themselves. Many voices are heard together. (This is common in Sri Lanka for many people to talk at once!) The facilitator decides to strike while the iron is hot and take a quick Q&A break! Questions are recorded on the board so the next hour can work towards getting some realistic answers:

Key Questions Raised by the Reflection Team
"How do you decide when to use FSA? What are the indicators that this would be the best approach?"
"How can it be combined with other therapies?"
"It's complicated enough to manage one client, but isn't it just unnecessarily complex to manage many?"
"What if there are competing priorities and/or the family cannot agree on what the goals ought to be?"
"What if some family members are not cooperative? Or disruptive?"
"Many families are fragmented these days? Can FSA work in the context of fragmented families with one or more members unable to or not willing to join?"

These questions were noted, and since the class time was insufficient to go into them all, it was agreed that we would all watch out for answers to these questions in the ensuing exercises. For the purpose of this document however, we will use some further examples of working with FSA both in the classroom and in the field to illustrate how we have responded to these questions. But before we leave the postgraduate class and their Saturday afternoon reveries, we do one last exercise. This was a burning issue, the one that demanded immediate answers.

"Many families are fragmented these days. How will FSA work in the context of fragmented families where one or more members are unable to or unwilling to join?"

11. The facilitator invites the volunteer actors once again to take their roles and places, and we all return to the story of Thiyalini and Thileepan. She addresses the reflection team asking if we could all reflect on why two members of this family are estranged or disconnected. She asks the team to have a think about how they each might engage the present family members on the issue of the absent family members and how they might think of strategies to enable Thiyalini, grandmother and Sutha to think about, understand and find a way to reconnect with Thileepan and son Thangesh. She next engages each family member on this issue.

"One of the things that strikes me strongly is how committed your family is to each other. I see this in how you have set time apart to come and meet like this and to be together. You seem to have a very strong desire to be together as a family. (Pause. Watch. Wait for response.) She proceeds noting their uncomfortable silence. "Yet, there seems to be a gap. You are talking about, and, in fact, our whole conversation before this has been referring to two people, two beloved people (she smiles) who are not even here" (waits, looking around).

Sutha: "I told my grandmother. I told her this is not going to work they will never come. They don't even come to eat, how will they come to talk about problems? I told you (looking at grandmother)".

Facilitator: "Yes Sutha, but let's look at this again. They are not physically here. Yes we know that. But that is one of our goals. To help you all reach each other as a family. So let's start by accepting that they are not here. Do you think it will be useful for us to take some time to really go in to 'why' they are not here?"

Thiyalini: "Why?" We all know why! He is just not bothered about us. He cares more about his net and boat than about if we are living or dead. That's why! And the boy, of course the boy is following right after the father! For him that phone is everything. Oh why, why did I ever give him an expensive phone like that!

Grandmother: "Aiyo children, men are like that! We know this. Why are we expecting that these two will be any different? I think we should talk about this girl's future and..."

Sutha: Please grandmother! If you say men are like that, then why would I want to marry a man like that?

Facilitator: Ok so, we each have these beliefs about why the two men in your family are so distant, we have some explanations for this in our own minds. But my question to you now is, can we look at what Thileepan and Thangesh must also be thinking and feeling at this time?

Sutha: But how they are not here!

Dealing with Absent Family

Facilitator: "OK. Let's try something like this (She places a chair in the circle. Yes! An empty chair.). This chair represents Thileepan! For the next few minutes let's all try and bring Thileepan into this room through our knowledge of him. For the purpose of our goals, let's try and honestly and as accurately as possible try and understand and articulate his feelings, his thoughts and why he is staying away from home".

(There is a pause. It is as if everyone is almost recognising another person in the room and trying to connect with his thoughts and feelings. The facilitator entertains the silence.) Then she repeats.

"We are all going to honestly and accurately try to focus on what Thileepan must be feeling and thinking. This is how we will do it. It is as if we will each get in to his head and bring out what we think is in there. But of course this must not be what we want to say but what we honestly think he is feeling or thinking even if we are uncomfortable with what we find, in his mind.

When we are ready with what we think Thileepan is feeling and thinking, each of us will get a chance to slip in to this chair and simply say in his words. What we think he is feeling, thinking and why he is doing what he is doing. It's as if we become him for a minute. Who likes to…"

(Sutha is already on her feet and headed for the chair. Her mother and grandmother are wide eyed. Meanwhile, the reflection teams are watching in rapt attention. Those who were scribbling notes have forgotten this altogether! The scene unfolds.)

In a surprisingly authentic way each member of the family takes turns at siting in the empty chair and guided by the facilitator they first do around of what Thileepan must be feeling. They have to be helped to make the distinction between feelings and thoughts, but they catch on. They bring up feelings such as:

"Things have changed so much around this house. I'm not comfortable".

"It's more peaceful out at sea. Let them do what the hell they want".

"We were all happy and content before she left".

"I'm not sure if my wife is happy with our home since she came back".

"I'm not sure if she is happy with me. I worry that she will leave us again".

The facilitator next summarises and checks for accuracy and clarity. The facilitator checks if everyone feels they can agree with what the others mentioned as Thileepan's feelings and thoughts and if there is any discrepancy, they mention it now.

"Do you really think Thileepan is feeling like that? Thinking those thoughts? How realistic is this?"

Once general concurrence is established, we realise it has led to a remarkable simulation of Thileepan's feelings and thoughts which is making everyone consider the perspective of the absent family member. This is then helping the family to gain insight in to why this family member is responding as he does and reconsider the way they each need to respond to him, leading to a recognition and reconsidering of unhelpful dynamics. All this emerges in a brief discussion. The facilitator next guides towards the next exercise.

Facilitator: "In this step having heard what Thileepan has said to us, we each take turns to respond to him and tell him something in response to the things we heard as his thoughts and feelings. What do you wish to say to Thileepan in response to his thoughts and feelings? Once again it must be honest but helpful too. Helpful towards reaching the goals we have decided for ourselves".

Each member gradually speaks up.

"Why didn't you ever tell me?"

"I'm making raal (prawn) curry on Wednesday OK? Come early".

"If you stayed home, you would know better than to think like this".

"Running away won't help".

"Sorry".

"Would I go through all this if I wasn't thinking of you and the family?"

The facilitator draws the exercise to a close, asking each one how they felt and what they had experienced and what they were taking away with them. She also explains what will happen in future sessions. The exercise is ended.

The class breaks into a round of applause which is very welcome to break from the intensity of the roles that each one had gotten in to. The reflection teams (each with 4–5 members) are given time to discuss their observations and learnings. After a break, they will share their observations of the whole process. Here's a peek at some excerpts:

"What I found useful was to know that you can start with just one family member and you don't necessarily need all".

"It's not as complicated as I thought! I really had no idea of how to get about this, but it's much clearer what can be done with FSA".

"It's very entertaining to watch our classmates, but I'm still worried if real-life things may not go so smoothly".

"I always wondered if it might be unrealistic and too contrived to just imagine what an absent family member will be thinking, but I see that borrowing the Gestalt empty chair within this exercise and creating the right atmosphere can make something of an authentic setting which helps people be real".

The Final Exercise of the Day
The reflection groups which all have around 4–5 members are asked to select a space for themselves and regroup. They are each given a small and relatively uncomplicated scenario which they will use to practise with. One member at a time in each group takes one aspect of therapy (as practised above) and facilitates the conversation, while the others take on the roles of family members. The different aspects they practise are:

(a) Helping a family or an individual seeking help to consider FSA and making a case for FSA
(b) Negotiating the first conversation by bringing a few members of a family together introducing FSA and its process
(c) Setting goals
(d) Using linear and circular questions for their different purposes
(e) Navigating the issue of absent family members
(f) Recapping and summarising learnings with a family

The class is abuzz with many intense pockets of conversation taking place together; every member is now immersed hands on in grappling with FSA; as the sun slowly slides down on our class, we leave them to the lengthening shadows.

FSA and the Evolving Concept of "Family"

As in much of the world, the concept of family in Sri Lanka too is an evolving one. Not only has this change meant that just a generation ago our parents had six, seven or even ten siblings but now we only have one or at the most two other siblings. It's also true that our families tend to move apart sooner and more often with children leaving home and parents far more often than earlier. Almost every family in the country now has someone who has left to either go to a major city or to other countries for work or migrate for safety reasons due to ethnic conflict, political unrest or in pursuit of international education. The 30-year-old armed conflict has left its own bloodstained mark on family systems. The 40,000 lives lost to this war each leave behind a shattered family and a fragmented family system which has had to evolve in to what we have today in female-headed households and a thriving diaspora across the globe which nurtures fragile connections with a splintered motherland. Psychosocial practitioners are now picking up the pieces of a wounded family culture.

On the economic front, the open-market economy threw open doors. A bloating job market for cheap Sri Lankan labour has meant that the stronger, healthier and younger family members often have had to leave their elderly and children in the care of each other to earn a living away from home. More women in Sri Lanka engage in labour migration, making them principal breadwinners and turning family power structures on their head. With the absence of fathers and sons due to war and the absence of mothers and daughters due to labour migration and education, families have had to co-opt members. Grandmothers and grandfathers, single "aunts" or other distant relatives and even neighbours and friends have joined the remaining family to help sustain it. Though the current laws are unfavourable towards LGBT communities and families, there are signs that evolving family structures in Sri Lanka will eventually include LGBT families as well.

This is all in sharp contrast to our parents' generation when it was common for families to be large, for children to marry and stay in the same house with their parents or in an adjoining house in the same compound, for communication to be face to face, for males to be the sole breadwinners and for a patriarchal hierarchy to be maintained.

With current trends, the geographic and emotional distance between family members has profoundly affected family dynamics. This we already saw played out in the "family systems" classroom learning activity. And yet there are many more ways that evolving concept of family impinges on the way families now live, love and link.

FSA in the Community

I pour myself a cup of tea, freshly brewed with unblended leaf tea straight from the hills of central Sri Lanka. The aroma takes me back to the green slopes where this tea came from and where we met the amazing community workers and psychosocial practitioners belonging to a local community-based organisation. They work with preschool children and their families to provide psychosocial services to troubled households "at risk". We would visit them each quarter to share learning experiences, methods and tools to make their engagement with families more effective. Those recollections are as warm, pungent and stimulating as this steaming tea.

The group is a mix of young female preschool teachers and a smaller more senior group of "counsellors" with some basic diploma level counselling qualifications with years of field experience. Together they work as community mobilisers visiting and working with families of migrant workers. The preschool teachers have no formal training in counselling but are supervised by the "counsellors" with the diplomas. They work by identifying children of migrant workers who attend the preschool and exhibit some form of distress or family dysfunction. This is very common in these communities. Once identified preschool teachers do home visits and usually work with the grandmother or aunt at home. We listen to them review their work – mostly frustrating encounters.

"I used to love home visits, but now I feel my stomach tighten as I go down the road. It's going to be another useless visit".

We ask about specific problems they encounter and what is most difficult about working with families. Then we slowly explain some basic ideas of FSA. We are met with blank faces. We doggedly keep going trying to make it as basic as possible. "It's an approach that acknowledges that family members affect each other and that their dynamics or relationships can be used to bring insight and change", we assert trying to be enthusiastic. The blank faces now register creased foreheads.

"How to do that?"

"Well", we plod on, "We have the family talk to each other, and we show them how we use linear and circular questions to get the members to pay attention to each other's thoughts feelings and words".

Silence. Blank looks. Creased foreheads. No progress.

"Do you think it will help you to try some of these?" we ask tentatively.

"But we can't get everyone to sit together like this. They will never come!"

The silence is broken. The politeness of our trainees which prevented them from disagreeing with their trainers is now giving way to useful honest talk. All start talking together and exchanging their frustrations.

"OK, OK let's try and put down some of the most difficult challenges you are facing in working with these families shall we? Shall we write them down so we can take each on and explore ways to deal with them?" Now the trainees quickly group themselves into four small clusters and pen down their daily demons.

- *We just go to inquire about the child we teach. Why they didn't come to school or why they are crying in class all the time or something, and from the time we walk in the door way, it's a load of problem after problem. It's just so vast and overwhelming. We don't know where to start.*
- *Most often when we learn of problems of the family, it looks like it can be improved with a good talk together as a family. Usually there is one person responsible who can make a huge difference in the situation, and most often that's the one person who is not at home and who will not come for our conversations!*

(continued)

(continued)

> - *It is hard to meet family members. They are out plucking tea or gone for their daily labour. They earn by the day so they are hardly home. When one is home the other isn't. We cannot get them to all stay home together.*
> - *It is very hard to get them to talk to each other and listen to each other. It's not done much, and it's like part of the family culture that many fathers don't talk to their kids except about essential things. No one talks about feelings and fears, and few know how to comfort each other in the family. When a migrant mother leaves the family, they assign someone to feed the child and take her to school, but no one thinks that it's important to talk to the child and help to comfort her for the loss of her mother. We don't know how to get families to focus on emotional needs.*

Everyone feels better after the real issues are put down. Now they are all keen to know the following:

"What is this family systems approach about? Can it really help us in addressing the above issues? Would it still be robust and flexible to fit in to the ground realities of the families we work with?"

I quickly readjust our training targets for the day. "Shall we look at the four problems you have mentioned here and see if FSA can be used in these situations"

- **Difficulty focussing on one single problem** as there are so many in a family. We take some time briefly role playing a conversation between family members and the counsellor/preschool teacher about selecting one issue that most of the family would agree on as priority. The key factor in deciding on this or anything else is that the views/feelings of all are considered even if they are not physically there.

- Questions like the following are used:

- "What do you think would be the most important thing or the first thing appa (dad) would like to get sorted?"

- "Do you really think this would be the most important thing for him?"
- **Dealing with absent family members.** Here we share our role plays combining the empty chair technique together with the circular questions to get as close as possible to understanding perspectives of an absent family member and to practise how to engage this family member from a distance. We share with these trainees our other experiences of using this technique on other villages and in the Saturday afternoon class. Our tea country group is now really engaging! We role play a couple of short scenarios, the first done by us the trainers and the second by them.

We take the next two issues together and combine them in the next discussion and round of exercises.

- **Inability to sit and talk due to work commitments and the lack of a culture of talking openly about feelings and thoughts among older family members and younger ones.**

"So do we all agree that these are issues and that we need to work out a method of helping our families through these difficulties?"

"Well if you say it's possible, let's see!"

"OK. Would it help if we took a particular case to help us discuss this? Any one has a story we can work with?" One of the counsellors offers us a case she is currently working on:

"I'm working with a family who is on the verge of having their mother leave the country for employment… I have been trying to help them prepare well before the departure. They prepare for the physical needs, but I just can't get them to recognise the emotional needs".

Kanthi 34 and her husband Ranjan 37 are in agreement about her leaving for 4 years. They want to get out of years of strangulating in financial debt. They have brought Kanthi's mom to live with them so she can look after the children for the next 4 years. Ranjan has agreed to come home early from his three-wheel driving job. They have opened an account for the new money she will earn. They feel that they have prepared well. However, from the day they started to talk about her leaving, their daughter of 7 years has been sick. She has been vomiting, refusing food and was even taken to hospital for a saline drip. Their son of 11 has been reported fighting in school, and Ranjan hasn't been able to sleep at night. He feels sleepy during the day and nearly had an accident while driving. There's constant tension and bickering in the house as never before".

Me (the trainer): Which of the family members do you think will agree to sit down and talk or work in collaboration with you?

The counsellor/trainee: I think Ranjan and Kanthi's mother are too caught up in work. They consider it a waste of time.

Me : What about the children?

The counsellor/trainee: Yes, I think I can engage them both in some activity which will help them talk.

Me: Can you help them understand the concepts of feelings and thoughts? And then the concept of fear and hope?

The counsellor/trainee: *Yes, I think we have done something similar about emotions before but why? What can this achieve?*

Me: *Do you think it will help this family recognise their distress and tension and each other's distress and tension and how it shows up (is manifest) in our physical health and our interactions? Would it be possible to have them share their feelings* *with each other some way? I'm hoping this will help them all feel more relieved and more aware of how they can and need to support each other at this time?*

The counsellor/trainee: *Yes, actually I think half the distress these children face is because they can't speak about the mother's leaving. It is not discussed. It is just happening. They are old enough to know she will leave and what that may feel like. But no one even asks them what they feel. I think the whole family might really feel better if they talk, but that will not happen.*

Me: Why?

The counsellor/trainee: *See I can never meet them all together anyways, and even if I did meet individually am not sure they will speak openly about feelings.*

Me: *Ok I see your difficulty. Is there a time in the day that they are all together? Any time? Is there a place in which they all meet at any point in the day or night?*

The counsellor/trainee: *Yes, I can find that out for sure. I think they all meet for dinner, and though they don't talk much, they serve their food and then eat and listen to the news on the radio at 9:00 then they go to bed. There's no way I can access them then.*

Me: *Yes, that is clear but I have another idea. You guys need to tell me if it will work. I have seen it work in other places. Here it is* (everyone draws closer):

So we have the two children who are accessible and who will work with us, may be after school. Can we start by making a suitable space (occasion) for them to talk freely about their feelings about their mother going away?

Several counsellors: *Yes, yes we have done things like that; we can use some toys and materials and help them to talk.*

Me: *Oh great. Can you also help them to talk about specific emotions they feel in relation to the impending departure? Like fears? And hopes/desire?*

Several counsellors: *Yes, we are familiar with talking to children about their emotions. It really helps them to understand themselves and even other children better.*

Me: *Wonderful! Now that we have that step also possible, here comes the tough part. What we want to try is to see if this whole family can be encouraged to speak about their true feelings and to hear each other and recognise each other's distress. This will then help each one perhaps realise that they can relate to the other family members in a more sensitive way, when recognising the distress and hearing each other.*

One of the counsellors: That sounds great if we can do this for a family, but we can only do this with the children as we only have access to them. That's the whole problem!

Me: (Pushing my luck a little further) Okay so here's the thing! If we can talk to our children about their feelings related to their mother leaving, do you think we can do these next three steps as well?

1. Can we help them see a connection between talking about feelings and living more successfully? Talking about feelings and being able to be healthily and not get in to trouble so much? Talking about feelings and preparing for mom's departure in a better way?

2. Can we help the children to see that if they do better after talking about their feelings, then their dad and grandmother also will probably do much better if they too get a chance to talk? Can we get them to see that dad and grandma might need a bit of encouragement or help because sometimes big people also need help to do this?
3. Can we challenge the children to try and actively help their dad by talking to him about their own feelings and asking him about his? Can we challenge/motivate them to do this also with their grandmother? We could make it a lot easier by giving them a tool to help them do this for themselves and for their parents as well?

At this point this chart is presented to them as a tool to help the children articulate their feelings and then also to at least try and have a simple conversation with their parents and fill in the chart for or with them.

The family fears and hopes chart

The family member	My biggest fear (about mom/wife/daughter leaving)	What can I do to prevent it?	My greatest desire (hope)	What can be done to achieve it
Migrating mother/father	My children will cry for me and not go to school My husband will waste our money	Call regularly and encourage them, giving them motivation Make a plan on how to manage the money with husband Send only what he can manage	See our house completed See my daughter to her O/Ls well	Ask my brother to help my husband to regularly finish the unfinished bits of the house. Call regularly and encourage my husband Keep in touch with the school teacher through my mother, and monitor her progress. Get extra help when she needs
Spouse	My wife will not send money on time My wife will not return	Discuss and set up bank instructions for regular debits Keep regularly in touch and build a close and loving bond by talking often and sharing feelings	To finish the house and buy a van for business To have wife home again and plan daughter's wedding	Regularly keep working at the unfinished house Save money so wife can return Keep close relationship so she will want to return, and work on how to maintain intimacy with wife in regular phone conversations

The family member	My biggest fear (about mom/wife/daughter leaving)	What can I do to prevent it?	My greatest desire (hope)	What can be done to achieve it
Children	No one will come to the school play to watch me Everyone in school will get to know my mother is doing housework in the Middle East	Discuss with family and ask grandmother or father to come for school functions Learn to tell them how brave mother is to go alone and work How much she loves us to do such a thing for us What great plans we have when she comes back	To have my own laptop To see mother at home when I come back from school	Trying to save money towards buying a laptop Finding ways to earn this money Keeping in touch with mother by talking to her and helping her decide to want to come back
Grandparent/ family member stepping in to assist	That I will be helpless if the children fall sick or if I fall sick If the money delays, I will be stuck	Discussing and making plans who will take over or give relief when grandmother needs a break Talking about options in case money is late Making spouse take responsibility to find options for money if the regular income is late	For my daughter to have a safe place to work To go on a pilgrimage to India	Discuss and find out what is possible about daughter's working conditions and what options she has to get help, who she can contact and who we can contact if we need help for her Tell the family about this, and tell migrant daughter to contribute a bit regularly and save for this trip

The trainees irrupt in a chorus of words all talking on top of each other. Some say it's possible, others say it's not and others say let's try. And there's only one way to find out!

Yes! We run a couple of rounds of role plays to get the dialogues right. We get back to working in the four small groups. The observer group gives insightful comment on the process.

Groups 1 and 2: Practise role a role play on how we could help the children to do this exercise themselves. How we would introduce the exercise and its purpose to the child, show them the steps and go through it with them answering a child's questions.

Groups 3 and 4: Work on how the counsellor could take the child a step further in talking about this exercise at home while doing normal day-to-day things. How a child can make the father and grandmother interested in slowly talking about their own feelings related to their mothers leaving the country for work. They practise responding to different negative responses the adult may give the child and help the child understand why it's important to draw the adult in to the conversation and how they might be able to do this during their different snatches of time together while cooking or while being bathed or being taken to school or doing the marketing. The possible conversations are rehearsed till the child feels confident. The counsellors often remind the child of the purpose:

"We need to listen to each other as family members to see what each one is feeling and thinking about something big that affects us all. Then we can help each other feel better, and if we all feel better, we can all live a much more happy life without getting in to so much trouble, without fighting all the time, falling ill and being very unhappy generally".

"Some people are not used to talking, so we need to help them slowly to feel OK about talking. We don't rush them, but by talking ourselves, we encourage them; we can also share with them what we have learned about sharing feelings and doing better"

"How can the child ask the parent about their feelings? Is that realistic?"

Will parents really respond?

Some snippets of those role play conversations cut through time and the aroma of my 2nd cup of tea as I recall and make notes.

Child: Appa, look what we did with my teacher today. She asked about amma and when amma is going and how I feel about it. I write here that I hope amma will send me a new school bag but that I cry every night, see?

Appa: What? What rubbish is this? What are you doing in school wasting your time like this? Don't you learn anything?

Child: No, no appa. Teacher said that it's good to talk about feelings because if you do you may not get so sick so often. Teacher showed me that when we don't realise what we feel, we can't even study properly. See appa, sister has been so sick lately no? Appa? Is this true?

Appa: (Thoughtfully) hmm... Anyways have you done your homework?

Child: I will do it appa, but I wanted to ask you first, what do you feel about amma leaving? Do you also get scared? What makes you most scared appa?

The observer group takes over and another active discussion and summary end the day:

"Can this work? Shall we try? It will! It may! Why not?"

"This method isn't limited or confined to sitting face to face in a room and having to talk about one's feelings. I think it can work!"

"But it demands too much from the children!"

"Well sometimes children are so honest, adults reciprocate very well to this. It may work if we work well with the children first!"

"We could also start with directly approaching the grandmother or someone else in the family if the children find it to difficult".

"Anyways, we have something now at least that we can use to work with families who don't necessarily sit together. Some of our biggest hurdles are overcome with this! I'm going to try it for sure!"

"I think this exercise helps to modify our work to fit in to the ground realities of the families we work with".

A mix of trepidation, anticipation and excitement filled the air in those closing moments of a day's work with counsellors in that lush tea country.

I close my notebook. It had been good remembering. I pour myself one last cuppa and sit back relishing that familiar clink of china and the unmistakable aroma and taste of unblended leaf tea and gently fold away the rich memories of FSA in the hills.

Conclusion

Having discussed our experiences of introducing and promoting FST to the MHPSS sector in Sri Lanka, we would like to draw a parallel between the MHPSS sector and FST. A closer examination of the MHPSS sector reveals the diversity and interdependence within the field. Our field of work and our co-workers in this field are themselves analogous to a family system. Each actor in this sector contributes to and influences the others. The sound functioning of the others play a major part in the success of one actor or one set of actors to make the maximum contribution to the field.

The problem in one group of actors, such as lack of referral pathways or poor communication, eventually affects the other stakeholders and the overall functioning of the MHPSS system. Thus, any administrator attempting to uplift the MHPSS services will have to study the connections, communication pathways and their current status to enable the system to function better. This is pretty much like an FSA itself! These common principles and steps are vital in ensuring the smooth functioning of any system.

Thus, when using FSA as a therapeutic tool, it is important for the clinician to help the client and the members of the system who are involved to understand how the system operates at the moment and how it impacts each other. Who else in the system can contribute to a positive outcome and what strategies could be used to draw them in?

In the same way, we present this parallel as an example for trainers to explain the concept. In our experience this has been a practical and easy way of explaining to the trainees the concepts of FSA using an interactive discussion on how we all in this sector function as a system.

Recommendations

Our experience with using and training counsellors in FSA made us see the need to adapt it to fit the socio-economic and cultural realities we work within here in Sri Lanka. We present the following as some key learnings based on our reflective discussions on what was successful or what seemed to put us on a track towards success.

- There is much diversity in the community of psychosocial practitioners, with varied levels and depths of training, exposure and skill. FSA can be and needs to be presented in a way that is comprehensible and practically applicable to the different levels of practitioners.
- It's very important to try and get the right balance of being faithful to the theoretical foundations and basic principles of FSA while creatively modifying its presentation to address field-level realities. This is particularly true in the case of dealing with "absent family members" and family members who can't for some reason do "sit-down", "face-to-face" conventional sessions.
- A key factor contributing to successful results is the skilful blending of FSA theory and techniques with other tools and approaches in practice so that practitioners are flexible enough to be relevant and successful without compromising FSA principles.
- Practitioners of FSA must keep in mind the evolving nature of the family system and not be constrained or limited merely to the biological family but to those who may form an inner "family of choice" of the client or the other networks that exert a greater influence than family in the life of client/s.

- We co-authors do have our own hesitations and worries that lead to continued reflections about being faithful to the FSA theories and principles. Yet, we still find that flexibility of style is powerful and creates FSA model(s) that is practically applicable in the local context.

Embarking on this journey of using FSA and also training diverse groups to use FSA in continuously changing family and social systems has been an exciting and challenging adventure. The experiences we shared in this chapter are some that we thought will benefit practitioners and reviewers of FSA attempting to draw out practical ways of enhancing and promoting the use of FSA in different contexts. We look for other experiences eagerly to draw out and strengthen our own approaches while hoping our experiences will contribute to your endeavours in teaching, learning and practising FSA in this varied and wonderful global social system we are all a part of.

References

Bronfenbrenner, U. (1994). Ecological models of human development. In *International encyclopedia of education* (Vol. 3, 2nd ed.). Oxford, UK: Elsevier Reprinted in: Gauvain, M. & Cole, M. (Eds.), *Readings on the development of children*, 2nd Ed. (1193, pp. 37-43). NY: Freeman.
De Silva, W. I. (2007). *A population projection of Sri Lanka for the new millennium, 2001–2101: Trends and implications*. Colombo, Srilanka: Institute for Health Policy.
Kinpe, D. W., Metcalfe, C., & Gunnell, D. (2015). WHO suicide statistics - a cautionary tale. *Ceylon Medical Journal*, 60 (1): 35.

The Asia Foundation (2015a). *Mapping Study of the Work and Capacity of Counselling Assistants of the Ministry of Child Development and Women's Affairs*. Colombo: The Asia Foundation.

The Asia Foundation (2015b). *Mapping Study of the Work and Capacity of Counselling Assistants of the Ministry of Social Services and Counselling Officers of the Ministry of Child Development and Women's Affairs*. Colombo: The Asia Foundation

Woolfe, R. (2012). Risorgimento: A history of counselling psychology in Britain. *Counselling Psychology Review*, 27(4), 72–78.

Chapter 9
Transvision: Unknotting Double Binds in the Fog of War

Douglas Flemons and Laurie L. Charlés

> …
> I was told once, only,
> in a whisper,
> "The blade is so sharp—
> It cuts things together
> —not apart."…—*David Whyte* (2012, p. 131)

> War is the realm of uncertainty; three quarters of the factors on which action in war is based are wrapped in a fog of greater or lesser uncertainty. A sensitive and discriminating judgment is called for; a skilled intelligence to scent out the truth.—*Carl von Clausewitz* (1989, p. 101)

Laurie: Wait. You want to start this article straight off as a conversation?

Douglas: You just did. Excellent! Why not? A conversation about the conversations we were having in 2014.

L: A meta-conversation.

D: Gregory Bateson (as you know, the philosophy-inclined social scientist who established most of the theoretical underpinnings of family therapy) would call it a meta-logue or *metalogue*—a dialogue in which the pattern of the interaction reflects, mirrors, or contributes to the topic at hand (Bateson, 2000).

L: Like a poem.

D: Yes. So this is a metalogue about what transpired when you reached out to me, distraught and disoriented. You were back in the States, following a family therapy training you did in Beirut with mental health folks in Syria.

L: My Syrian trainees were themselves all mental health practitioners. I was contracted by the World Health Organization (WHO) to help them

D. Flemons (✉)
Nova Southeastern University, Fort Lauderdale, FL, USA
e-mail: douglas@nova.edu

L. L. Charlés
Family Therapist, Independent Researcher, Boston, MA, USA

© Springer Nature Switzerland AG 2019
L. L. Charlés, G. Samarasinghe (eds.), *Family Systems and Global Humanitarian Mental Health*, https://doi.org/10.1007/978-3-030-03216-6_9

learn to think and work systemically with families at the same time they began to supervise other Syrian clinicians working in the midst of the conflict. I met them in Beirut for the in-person training because it was less dangerous than doing it in Syria at that time.

D: How long was that initial seminar?

L: They were in Beirut for 3 weeks; my teaching was concentrated in the third week. But in that short time, a remarkable bond was formed. I met them in the third year of the war; our conversation here is taking place in the war's eighth year.

D: Is that common for you? You've done similar seminars in other hot spots.

L: I typically form close bonds with my students and trainees, but never like this. Maybe the real-time, conflict-affected nature of the situation, its urgency, contributed. For example, one of the trainees' family members was kidnapped by an armed group at the time of the training. Such things have been a defining aspect of the Syrian war, and the training group stayed on high alert, monitoring and vicariously experiencing one of their colleagues going through such a traumatic event in real time, right there in front of them. I watched them closely, as I had never seen a group like this. To this day, they remain apart, unique.

D: If you had nothing of significance to offer, they would have seen through you in a second.

L: Absolutely. There can be no posturing in an environment like that.

D: And then, as part of the same contract, you signed on for providing ongoing supervision of supervision, using Skype and other means of contact, for four of them.

L: Yes. I worked with about 40 that first training and concentrated supervision of supervision with four of them. Our connection, it just crystallized. And was it ever intense! Much passed between us without ever having to be spoken; it still does. It is safer that way, in war, perhaps, especially given the nature of the Syrian conflict. In my face-to-face training, their eyes said it. And then in the subsequent distance-support part of the project, our connection was deepened via tone of voice, texts, pictures, stories, poems, and art sent back and forth. I can still see and feel their courage in the face of violence, their quiet dignity in the face of uncertainty. And at the time, it was tearing me apart, for reasons I couldn't fathom. I felt silenced by the war and unable to breathe. You know that sensation of drowning? I couldn't get enough air.

D: It was your wordlessness and breathlessness that prompted you to reach out to me.

L: Yes. And my contacting *you* wasn't a random choice. In both the Syrian training and the virtual supervision, Douglas, as part of both of them, I had introduced them to your work, your way of thinking, your writings (e.g., Flemons, 2002; Flemons & Gralnik, 2013). Your ideas and clinical approach continue to influence and guide me, wherever I'm teaching.

So you were already there with me, a little; it made sense, then, somehow, to turn to you when I felt so messed up.

D: You didn't ask me for supervision of supervision of supervision.

L: Hell no! Is there such a thing?!?!

D: Too many damn levels.

L: Supervision (<Latin *super*, "over" + *videre*, "to see") entails a "looking over." I didn't want "over-over-sight." But I needed to talk with you. I was desperate.

D: You were experiencing an existential crisis.

L: Yes—and I'm just a drop in the bucket. All of Syria was, and still is, experiencing an existential crisis. Struggling to hold themselves, their families, and their country together. The World Bank Group (2017) recently published "The Toll Of War: The Economic And Social Consequences Of The Conflict In Syria," a study assessing the economic and social consequences of the Syrian conflict as of early 2017. According to the report,

the conflict has inflicted significant damage to the Syrian Arab Republic's physical capital stock (7 percent housing stock destroyed and 20 percent partially damaged), led to large numbers of casualties and forced displacement (between 400,000 and 470,000 estimated deaths and more than half of Syria's 2010 population forcibly displaced), while depressing and disrupting economic activity. From 2011 until the end of 2016, the cumulative losses in gross domestic product (GDP) have been estimated at $226 billion, about four times the Syrian GDP in 2010. (p. 14)

D: Pervasive, insidious destruction.

L: Yes. It was so insidious even then, that time when I first emailed you, asking if we could talk. I was just a drop you see, but still, I was reeling in confusion and in pain. It was years ago, already, and although things are still unclear for Syria today, as we write these words, back then I was a blank; I had never encountered such an experience. I couldn't see what was wrong; I felt I wasn't being helpful with the Syrians, despite what they were telling me. I thought I was unable to continue, wasn't sure I could finish the project well. Not just finish it, but finish it *well*. I didn't want to phone it in. All of it was too important to me. I needed to talk to someone who could understand without having to know everything, without my having to get you up to speed on Syria.

D: We've known each other for a long time.

L: Ever since the early 90s, when I came into the doctoral program at NSU (Nova Southeastern University). You were one of my first teachers and, later on, became my clinical supervisor and my dissertation chair.

D: I have many fond memories of our working together.

L: So do I. Although all my friends thought I was crazy to work with you!

D: Unlike them, you weren't afraid of me.

L: Many times while working on my dissertation, I found myself exceeding my own expectations for what was possible. You had that effect on me. And you got me. To my bones.

D: You were driven: hungry to learn, fired up to make a difference in the world. A passionate thinker and researcher and a compassionate therapist—you had it all. And what? Two weeks after you graduated with your Ph.D., you were off to Togo for 2 years with the Peace Corps (Charlés, 2007). Such a badass. No swanky private practice for you. And in that, you haven't changed a bit. A far-flung family therapist.

L: That's hilarious, Douglas. You're a bit far-flung yourself. A Canadian expat, living in Florida.

D: Yep, I moved catty-corner on the continent—from Vancouver to Fort Lauderdale (with a stopover in Texas for a few years). I know a little about physical dislocation, but nothing like what you've gone through.

L: You're too humble, Douglas.

D: Just stereotypically Canadian. So sure, my emigration also gave me visceral knowledge of identity disorientation, but coming to the States didn't entail learning a new language.

L: I very much wanted to be disoriented inside another language—to be made to live and work in it. I knew it would be tiring but in a way completely different than my dissertation had been. This wasn't about being a badass: I just wanted a break after my dissertation. My 3-year study of a hostage negotiation (Charlés, 2008)—with you as my chair and involving experts from the FBI—drained me. I was spent. I needed to rest my brain. Going to the Peace Corps was a way to let go of all of that and energize my physical muscles and regain a sense of who I was without any labels.

D: Okay, but note that your method of resting your brain didn't involve sleeping on a beach for a month. You *sought out* disorientation. That's the badass part. Knowing about this quality of yours helped inform my response to you when you contacted me inside the swirl of the Syrian crisis. But back when you were freshly graduated, you passionately threw yourself into a different world: a first step into what has become a career as a peripatetic teacher, trainer, researcher, writer, therapist, and supervisor. When I get an email from you and respond with "where in the world are you?" and "what in the world are you doing?," I'm not just using turns of phrase. I'm asking real questions for which I'm sure to get surprising answers.

L: One night in a bar in Europe after too many beers, an American colleague, someone I thought of as a friend, accused me of being a colonialist.

D: So edifying to be schooled by a self-righteous indignantary.

L: Ha! An apt description.

D: Alcohol limits the ability to think clearly. The Enlightenment came about at a time when people in Europe started drinking coffee rather than alcohol as a way of not dying from the bad water. So there's that.

L: Sure. If we'd been sipping espressos, he might not gone off in quite so dramatic a way. But he's probably not the only one to have voiced that opinion.

D: Always a good idea when offering something to another to be sensitive to how it defines the relationship between the giver and the receiver. Does the receiver have the freedom to refuse? To walk away? To accept without strings?

L: We do this as systemic therapists all the time. We never rush in with the answers, anxious to be "helpful."

D: Right. With ongoing self-of-the-therapist reflection, with information gleaned from what our clients do and say, and with the thoughtful input of supervisors and colleagues, we can, I think, effectively distinguish between colonial transgressions and collaborative transformations.

L: Colonialists overwhelm and undermine those they dominate.

D: You're a collaborationist, not a colonialist. You inspire those with whom you innovate.

L: They inspire me! Today I am writing from my lovely flat in Colombo 02, in Sri Lanka. I am working on a project to develop a manual for use in systemic group work within the country. After a 26-year civil war, they are in a process of reconciliation, implementing various transitional justice initiatives.

D: Yep, exactly my point. Cross-cultural transformations are possible through invitations for innovative collaborations. You live that.

L: I try to. I was in Libya after the 2011 revolution and in the bush of both the Democratic Republic of Congo and the Central African Republic (Charlés, 2010)—all conflict-affected states with citizens facing extreme adversity and violence. In the midst of the Syria work, I began serving as a technical consultant during the Ebola Virus Disease Outbreak in West Africa. Each presents different, challenging, and scary moments. But Syria is, of course, different. The war in Syria is precedent setting in so many ways. It has broken every rule; everything we thought we understood about warfare has had to be reconceptualized because of Syria.

D: It obviously threw your approach to teaching and supervising into disarray.

L: Absolutely. Which has led me to rethink family therapy and what I bring to it. At the time (and still now) I was inspired and influenced by the theoretical clarity informing your therapeutic sensibility. You say very specific things in your book *Of One Mind* (Flemons, 2002) that I often repeat in my trainings across the globe—for example, the idea that we need to adjust to clients and not the other way around. This comes from you.

D: Right, it's not the client's job to make us comfortable.

L: And also, the importance of therapeutic curiosity.

D: The posture of curiosity is critical in shifting the client's relationship to the problem.

L: But you're very careful to distinguish *professional* curiosity—making sense of the intra- and interpersonal patterns of the problem and exceptions to the problem—from *personal* curiosity, which has no place in therapy. In conflict-affected states, curiosity can be deadly. You'd better have a good therapeutic reason for the questions you ask.

D: Yes! And stay sensitive to life-and-death cultural and contextual complexities before, during, and after you pose them.

L: These ideas are very, very relevant to the work I do, especially so in conflict areas.

D: But ideas alone were not enough to help you sort through what was going on for you. Something definitely felt off kilter.

L: Back then, in 2014, after I'd first met those Syrian colleagues, I was home, back in my own safe and sweet world again, and I couldn't think straight. I couldn't talk…to anyone. Actually, it was the first time I stopped talking about my work to my loved ones. Never before, neither as a supervisor nor as a supervisor of supervision, had I been in the position of having to think about the possible death of people I was training. The worst thing, the thing that pushed me to call you, was that I couldn't seem to stop crying. As soon as I'd send off a communication to someone in Syria, and then get a surprising message back from one of them—sometimes immediately and sometimes days later—I'd find myself completely undone. Their silence communicated as much as the messages they tapped out on their smartphones. Often out of the blue, I'd start weeping; sometimes outright sobs came deep from my gut. Actually, I had every kind of crying happening! It scared me to feel so intensely *about* them and *with* them.

D: You were in a fog.

L: Seriously fucked up.

D: Seriously fogged up.

L: Yes, as in our von Clausewitz epigraph. Back in the early 1800s, he characterized the "fog of war" as a condition of maximum ambiguity, making everything suspect.

D: Finding your way through fog is damn near impossible. When you're driving in it, you want to see as far in front of you as possible, but if you flip on your brights with this in mind, you see only a well-lit wall. So rather than attempting to see farther or more expansively, you need to shift your focus and your goal.

L: If you're smart, you flip on your dims. And inch forward.

D: Refocusing on what's right in front of you, what was a wall then becomes a terrain to enter and explore.

L: Which is what you had in mind when talking with me?

D: Something like that. I wasn't exactly sure what you were wanting from our conversations.

L: We had four of them, all on Skype, over 6 months. I was working in Texas at the time, using Skype also for my ongoing supervision of the Syrian trainees.

D: During our first conversation, you spilled out so many details all in a rush, and I found it fascinating—you got me up to speed by pulling me straight into the middle of your heart-wrenching, gut-wrenching impossibilities. Often with my trainees, I'll ask them to back up and provide some orienting details. I didn't do that with you. I assumed that as a seasoned clinician and globe-trotting supervisor, you knew how to do that, and so you would be laying things out that way if you could. Somehow you couldn't.

L: No.

D: Also, I was influenced by my approach to hypnotherapy. When I'm facilitating trance learning with clients, they may assume I know what they are experiencing at that moment, even though I have no clue. Sometimes I bring them out of hypnosis so I can check in and get an overview, but at other times I'll just go with whatever is unfolding, picking up enough details along the way to be there with them. I attempt to get a feel for what's important, to get a sense of it. That's what I did with you. I figured I would, with time, be able to make out the outlines of whatever hell you were inside of.

L: Yes, exactly. I was inside something that I couldn't name. "Hell" is a good approximation.

D: When we started writing this chapter, we circled back to this hell, making sense of what you were going through.

L: And how you responded to it.

D: We came to understand the shape of our 2014 dialogues not as *supervi*sion but as *trans*vision (<L. *tere-*, "cross over, pass through" + *videre*, "to see")—a "looking or seeing *through*."

L: Right. Flipping from brights to dims with the intent of developing a felt sense of the fog I was lost inside.

D: In the beginning, I could detect only vague shapes and shadings and movements.

L: It was a relief to talk to you that first time. I had a witness. I knew you would do everything that was required in terms of professional discretion; nevertheless, I was very shaken talking to you. I remember giving you a brief report about the situation in Syria at that time, assuming you knew very little about what was going on for the people living there. At the time I first met the Syrian clinicians in Beirut, mid-2014, the war didn't often make it into the US headlines. That changed later in the summer, with the beheading of the US journalist James Foley by ISIS.

D: You were right. I didn't know anything beyond what I'd heard on National Public Radio and had read in the New York Times.

L: But that didn't matter to me. I had tried talking with clinicians who were seasoned by war and conflict about what I was going through, but they had nothing to offer me, save for a knowing, sincere, shrug. As a therapist and supervisor, you pay attention to process much more than content. That's what I craved. It matters, your attention to process.

D: Details are important to me but only because they bring into relief patterns of interaction. I'm after a visceral sense, an embodied knowing of communicational complexities—I want to get my hands on relational, rather than rational, truths.

L: A heartfelt grasp of the heart of the matter. That's exactly what I needed. At least as a starting point. The Syrians always talk about heart, actually. It's one of the most amazing things about having worked so closely with them—their deep sense of compassion, love, and warmth: towards me and towards each other.

D: I was stunned that it was even possible, never mind safe enough, for you to have travelled into, or next to, a war zone to offer something as ordinary, as prosaic, as family therapy supervision. And now you were continuing that work from a distance, from the States.

L: Yes. I was communicating with the group of four in a variety of ways, sometimes multiple times per day. The extreme nature of our communication—intense, vivid, practical, philosophical, delightful, painful at times—all occurred in the midst of their own experience of the fog of war. Their communications to me grew in range as they became more proficient as family therapy practitioners and more curious as family therapy supervisors, themselves. That initial project ended in 6 months, as per my first contractual obligation. But the war didn't end. They continue to implement family therapy and do their work in the midst of what is still a never-ending war. And, because I'd promised them my support the first time I met them, and because it was the right thing to do, I, too, continued.

D: You had immense respect for them.

L: Absolutely. They are so sharp, so intelligent, so *present*. Perhaps because they look death in the eye every day, they were willing to look me in the eye, asking direct, soul-searching questions. I think they are fearless. And so creative! With such unrelenting curiosity about family therapy and supervision. And, in the midst of everything, full of good humor.

D: Go figure.

L: Meanwhile, in the safety and comfort of the US, or wherever I was on the globe, I was truly a mess.

D: I sure sensed that this profound difference in circumstance was contributing a lot to your vomit-worthy distress.

L: I wasn't throwing up!

D: Oh, good!

L: But I did have trouble eating. And I lost about 20 lbs.

D: Helluva diet. Your high regard for your Syrian trainees bordered on awe. The bright light illuminating them eclipsed in importance, in relevance, anything happening in your life in the States. As learners, they outshone your students here.

L: No kidding! Their depth of commitment and interest in helping families in Syria forged a bond between us. They embodied the spirit of so many trainees I've had over the years, but all at once, rapidly, and in combination.

D: I remember saying to you at the time that given the Syrians' grit and fierce intelligence, I'd have hated to be your student in the US, referencing some personal challenge to explain why I was turning my paper in late or failing to show up for your practicum. You couldn't possibly have taken me seriously.

L: Right! It was a deep privilege to be working with this group of Syrians. My US students were captivating in their own way, definitely!

D: Yeah, but they inhabited a very different world. I sensed you were struggling to feel worthy as a supervisor for the Syrians.

L: I don't even know what that means. I was confident about the work I was doing with them, and the work they were doing with their supervisees, but I didn't feel like their supervisor. Sometimes I felt that what I was doing involved so much more than teaching, or training.

D: It felt to me like your life in the US, along with the life of your students and family here, seemed drained of significance when juxtaposed with the lives of the Syrians.

L: We didn't have to worry routinely about one of our loved ones disappearing without a trace, or what we might do to support client families who have been exposed to shelling, snipers, incendiary weapons, bomb blasts.

D: Yep, that's the point. Your life here was, and is, easy by comparison. Along with your feeling a lack of relative usefulness, I sensed your life felt drained of legitimacy.

L: Everything was drained of legitimacy. What right did any of us have to complain, given the horrors of what families there were facing? I've long been intolerant of complacency, but my experience with the Syrians put that sensibility on steroids. I felt so angry at the world for turning their back. And I couldn't talk about what I was going through; it didn't feel safe for me or for my Syrian colleagues. My insides were all twisted up with secrets and fear, anger and grief.

D: Exactly! That alone would be enough to tie anyone in knots. But, given *your* physical safety and *their* ever-present, overwhelming danger, you considered your pain completely illegitimate! That's got the makings of a double bind.

L: Gregory Bateson was the one responsible for the double bind theory of schizophrenia.

D: Yes. Along with the research team he put together in the 1950s to study levels of abstraction and paradox in communication.

L: The article they wrote, "Toward a Theory of Schizophrenia" (Bateson, Jackson, Haley, & Weakland, 2000), has been much criticized and widely misunderstood.

D: Yes. And Bateson later said that they published it prematurely. They were inventing a new epistemology, a circular, layered way of making sense of the circular, layered phenomenon of making sense. They didn't yet have the recursive grammar necessary for articulating it clearly.

L: Recursive grammar? You mean a cybernetic vocabulary?

D: Yes, but also an architecture or chord structure for characterizing the recursive, self-referential nature of mind—the implicit structure that shapes our talk about it. Bateson later used both stories and metalogues to get some of it said.

L: Self-reference generates paradox.

D: Good point. A double bind can perhaps best be described as a Batesonian paradox, an ironic tangle in a relationship with oneself or with significant others. Such knots couldn't and wouldn't take shape if it weren't for the multi-level nature of mind, meaning, and communication, or for the relational nature of the self.

L: As in communication *about* communication, right? *Meta-*communication.

D: Exactly.

L: So when I said a few minutes ago that you are too humble, and you replied, "just stereotypically Canadian," then that was being humble about being humble. Meta-humility.

D: Good ear. As we experience and communicate intra- and interpersonally, we are also continually meta-communicating—verbally, nonverbally, and paralinguistically—about what we're making, or wanting to be made, of these experiences and communications. A quizzical frown; a belly laugh; a dismissive gesture, tone of voice, or criticism: All such meta-communications contextualize the experiences and communications they're *about*—they make sense of them, they ascribe a sensibility, they define an orientation.

L: Complexity ensues.

D: Yep. So a person might tear up *in reaction* to a thought, then have a thought *about* the tears, which inspires new tears *about* the new thought, which give rise to yet another thought *about these* tears. Or the person might tear up *in reaction* to a partner's comment, inspiring a follow-up comment from the partner *about* the tears, giving rise to new tears *about* the new comment, and so on. In both intra- and interpersonal relationships, such interactive patterns don't play out as a simple back-and-forth exchange; rather, they unfold in an elaborate, mostly implicit, layering of understanding. Each response can be *meta-* to, and thus context-defining for, both preceding and subsequent communications and experiences. This imbricated spiraling of perceptions and messages, whether within the self or between people, spins meanings that can weave—but also unravel—a sense of identity.

L: Sounds like a double bind to me.

D: When we ourselves or someone who matters to us questions or dismisses the legitimacy or meaning of one (or more) of our perceptions, emotions, thoughts, or actions, the negation is often not restricted just to the particular item of experience. Through reflexive cycling, it can also pervasively undermine the integrity of, or the available options for, the self as a whole.

L: This is what it means to be caught—knotted up—in a double bind.

D: Yes. Unable to get outside the self-defining parameters of a context-setting negation, a person can become helplessly ensnared, such that any and every considered choice or attempted option for reacting or responding to it proves to be wrong or impossible.

L: Sounds like a recipe for agony.

D: Yes. Suffering ensues.

L: Something like that was going on for me.

D: The combination of your aching worry about the Syrians and your having access to physical safety not remotely possible for them meant that your emotional response, your tears, were for you an indulgence, a luxury they couldn't afford, rather than a legitimate expression of your helplessness. The more you cared and fretted about their safety, the less you could forgive yourself for not following the emotional example of these amazing people. An ironic tangle, for sure.

L: I tried my best to follow their example. You talked to me about keeping my heart warm, my feet on the ground, and my hands open, ready to offer and ready to accept. I wanted to do this, but I struggled with it, between my tears, my fear, and my anger. Which left me feeling more in a fog. Worse, I had helped them feel excited about bringing family therapy to their work in Syria. But then it seemed that this made them more exposed, risking their lives to do the work I had trained them to do. I was horrified!

D: And then on top of that, you were afraid to talk to me about it. You were never clear about it, but I suspected that their being in ongoing contact with you, someone holding a US passport, even though you had been contracted to work under the auspices of WHO, posed complications for you and your trainees.

L: Yes and no. But better if I refrain from going into any part of that, Douglas.

D: The war rages on, and the danger, at multiple levels, continues unabated.

L: Yes.

D: At the time, I heard you flailing, grasping for a life-line, or at least a sanity line.

L: You thought I was crazy?

D: Your trainees' lives were in danger, you didn't feel emotionally safe to think or talk about their situation, and it didn't feel legitimate for you to be more upset than they were. Enough to make anyone bat*shit* crazy.

L: Imagine, Douglas, if every single person you are training right now in your program was overnight at risk of immediate and violent death, disappearance, or torture. So are their clients, colleagues, family members. And yet, you still have to supervise trainees, you still have to do the business of living, of working, of supervising. How does one do that without going crazy?

D: No wonder you were wrapped so tight. It was hard for you to breathe, never mind think. You wanted to talk, but you kept hesitating, redacting, alluding to conditions and complexities. You kept circling, never quite landing.

L: I was so afraid, Douglas. I didn't know what I could tell you. Not because I couldn't trust you. I knew I could. It wasn't that. I was afraid to say anything that might risk their safety or reveal too much about their personal lives.

D: You can't get unknotted from a double bind if being in it keeps you from adopting a meta-perspective.

L: I couldn't get meta. I couldn't "zoom out," as the Syrians would put it.

D: Getting free requires a kind of judo logic, a context-transforming engagement capable of unraveling the perseverating pattern of the suffering. One way to achieve such an extrication is to recognize the nature of the double bind and then to address or comment on it.

L: But that requires being able to speak, and when speaking out risks death, then not-seeing and not-saying become pervasive and oppressive.

D: Right. You have to be able to notice it *and* make note of it. Your reaching out to me I took as a valiant effort to find a safe purchase from which to observe and recognize how you were caught and then to breathe and to discover the freedom to move.

L: Yes. I was frozen in place. You felt safe to talk to, and I needed to feel safe myself. Feeling safe didn't feel wrong, but it did feel wrong to exclude the Syrians. They needed to feel safe, too. So did their clients— in fact, that was often a presenting problem in their trainees' cases. So safety took on a different meaning. They were *all* that mattered to me at the time. I think that's why I couldn't quite land. I was with them, virtually, in a world I could neither name nor share.

D: I saw the need for safety as the organizing principle of your supervision with the Syrians *and* with your work with me.

L: Safety was critical but elusive.

D: So you welcomed me into your fog. Into your fucking fog. I was honored.

L: I could tell you weren't afraid. That helped.

D: I hoped I could get my bearings, to get a sense of what you were going through, without, in the process, contributing to, or myself getting caught in, the double binds knotting you up.

L: I knew I didn't have to worry you'd label my tears as evidence of vicarious trauma or compassion fatigue—as evidence of a liability.

D: Someone so inclined could have accurately told you that you were exhibiting symptoms of these conditions.

L: Fuck that. Maybe I was. I couldn't tell. Later on I learned from friends how common it is to begin weeping out of nowhere when you're displaced by, or are living or working in the middle of, a war. But I knew then I could talk to you and trust that you wouldn't trivialize me or my experience with some tidy answer.

D: Right. You would have taken a rush to certainty, a rush to the removed, self-satisfied safety of an abstraction—a pat diagnosis—as a clumsy *rescue attempt*. Anyone attempting to use a label to pluck you out of the body-based, flesh-and-blood realities of what was unfolding for you and the Syrians would have done a kind of violence to all of you. The last thing you needed was more violence.

L: Exactly! Reaching out to you, I never questioned your ability to handle the intensity of what I had to say. This was critical. No one wants to hear the graphic details about that level of violence; it's human nature to turn away. I didn't think you would be thrown off by that or by my tears. I hoped you could help me stop them, actually. I didn't know how. I didn't know if the tears were going to stop me first.

D: Yeah, well. I'm not a fan of the idea of having to stop something—to stem tears, say—as a precondition for moving forward. That also seems to me an act of violence, and that runs counter to my orientation as a therapist. Hell, I'm a vegetarian!

L: You're a therapeutic pacifist.

D: Or a pacifist-therapist.

L: And obviously a pacifist-supervisor. Or pacifist-transvisor.

D: Ha! Damn. Looks like I need to get new business cards.

L: That brings up a question I've been meaning to ask you.

D: Sure.

L: When I first contacted you, I offered to pay you for our time. You said, and I quote, "Pay? We can talk. Not my motivation."

D: It wasn't.

L: We never came back to it.

D: You didn't get my bill?

L: I'm asking a serious question. I was getting paid for my supervision. Why not get paid for your transvision?

D: Good point.

L: Professionals should be willing to accept payment for their services.

D: Absolutely.

L: So....

D: I'll give you two different answers.

L: Okay.

D: Payment is transactional. One person gives another person a designated amount of money for a designated product or service.

L: There's nothing wrong with that. Isn't that how you run your private practice?

D: Absolutely.

L: So what was the difference here?

D: We had a connection that went way back, and your pain was not transactional. It was stripping your gears. And it was outside or beyond your contract with WHO. Or it suffused it.

L: All of the above.

D: So you didn't say to me, "I have some intriguing supervisory conundrums I'd love to get your input on. Do you have time to spend a few hours chatting with me?" If that had been the entry into our conversations, then, sure, I would have settled on a fee that would've worked for both of us. But when you called, your epistemology was bleeding. Badly. To talk about a fee would have taken us outside the existential request you were making by virtue of contacting me.

L: Okay. And your second answer?

D: It has to do with how I think as a hypnotherapist. As you know, I pay a lot of attention to relationships between clients and therapists—to communicational invitations and responses and what they imply for expectation and possibilities for change. From the first email I received from you, we were inside what I would define as an intense trance experience.

L: Hold on a second. You were doing hypnosis on me?

D: I don't "do hypnosis on" people. Trance is a name for a special mind-body and/or self-other connection, where the normal boundaries of everyday awareness and identity are not relevant. In negative trances, such as what you were experiencing at the time, this results in an inability to rely on the usual orienting cues and thoughts that provide self-organizing stability. In positive trances, such as those that develop inside the kind of safe and absorbing conversations we had, the problematic boundaries can become diffuse, and therapeutic shifts—shifts toward a returned sense of a viable and resourceful self-in-the-world—can be made.

L: Hence your not being troubled by my fog.

D: Exactly. Since you were in crisis, why waste a good fog by talking rationally about something transactional? I was far more interested in putting your blurred boundaries to good use.

L: You told me at one point that I could find a way to *use* my emotional responses to inform what I was doing.

D: Sounds like something I'd say.

L: That was a revelation.

D: I think of it as shifting strategies—from countering to *en*countering. Instead of striving or battling *against* some thread of your experience as a means of achieving relief, you find a way of connecting *with* it.

L: Maybe that's why I could trust you. I trusted what you know. Through your work, through your life, you've come to know about violence, pain, and suffering; you know about change; you know about process. You are fearless about your work, Douglas, just like the Syrians, actually. And of course, you know me. But I also trusted *how* you go about your way of knowing.

D: Bateson quoted Blake, who said, "A tear is an intellectual thing." There was a hell of a lot of embodied intelligence, a lot of relational understanding, being expressed in your tears. I was all in to discover how they *made sense.* I like that way of describing it, a description that has always oriented Shelley's work (i.e., Shelley Green, Douglas's wife and colleague). Sense-making is grounded in sensory experience; it is body-inclusive understanding (Flemons & Green, 2018). This underscores the embodied nature of any kind of relational knowing. No need to discount or contrive to control tears if they are sensible, if they are *sense-able.*

L: I didn't have to protect myself in talking with you. You didn't try to change the subject; didn't want me to provide you with contacts in WHO so you could travel internationally, too; didn't blather on about your political opinions about the war; didn't congratulate me on my bravery; and didn't express pity for the "poor Syrians." I loved that you didn't do any of that, Douglas.

D: Yep, there are lots of ways to fail in such conversations. On the surface, pity seems a heartfelt reaching out, but it is undertaken at arm's length, and the arm is stiff. It asserts the removed superiority of the person expressing it. That is so decidedly not you.

L: This is how I learned to work with the Syrians as well; I didn't try to rescue them; I didn't need to know their political opinions or share mine; I didn't try to change the subject. But I could be with them, fully in every *sense*—as Shelley would put it—as best I could. And they were living in the fog of war. So I went there, too, with them. Virtually. Relationally. And brought you along with me.

D: And it didn't end there, of course. This was the first of several family therapy training projects you've undertaken over the years in the region.

L: Yes. A core group of family therapy-trained practitioners have remained in the country.

D: Gives new meaning to notions of commitment and caring.

L: Yes, they stay despite, as von Clausewitz (1989) noted, the "layers of increasing intensity of danger" (p. 113) that war brings.

D: Their lives are never not in danger.

L: I carry that fact with me, always. But I also carry *them* with me everywhere I go—they're with me in every project and every presentation I do.

D: Like a behind-the-mirror family therapy team?

L: Exactly! They have added so much significance to my life and to my work—"layers of increasing intensity" of systemic meaning.

D: You tell stories about them.

L: Sure. But my learning from our teamwork makes its way into other stories, too.

D: How could it not? Bateson (1979) said, "A story is a little knot or complex of that species of connectedness which we call *relevance*.... Any A is relevant to any B if both A and B are parts or components of the same 'story'" (p. 14). Their relevance to you and how you think and work stays alive in this way. You live that narrative truth.

L: I am known by my trainees in Syria as a storyteller. They joke with me, because I have so often said to them, to give a clinical or supervisory example of some kind, "That reminds me of a story...." Toward the end of my reaching out to you about all this, after we'd had several of our conversations sprinkled over several months, I began to tell them stories about the work I'd done with you. I talked about our supervision of supervision of supervision—about our transvision—though we weren't calling it that yet, not then. I talked to them about these layers of complexity, and about Erickson (e.g., Erickson, 1980; Erickson & Rossi, 1980), and about learning and practice. When they began to talk about clients who were suicidal, I shared your *Relational Suicide Assessment* (Flemons & Gralnik, 2013) work with them. Telling them stories about my seeking supervision in my professional world was also useful, as it was a safe way of communicating. They could take the stories and apply them to their own situation, rather than feel compelled to give me details they were unable to share (because of lack of electricity or internet, or security, or for whatever reason they might have).

D: So, right, after a few months, our Skype conversations came to an end. Over the course of them, the war continued but, I sensed, your fog lifted. Your tears no longer refracted everything you were seeing and thinking.

L: I don't think the fog so much lifted as that I was able to be inside it, enveloped in it, without panic, without a desperate sense of futility. My life, my close relationships with family, friends, and students—I could experience each of them as legitimate again, even while I stayed in contact and continued to work with my Syrian trainees. Interestingly, although the Skype chats with you ended, I remember your presence accompanying me for years, rather than months. Plus the Syrians know you, now, too. And here we all are, together on the page.

D: So how do you account for such a shift? What was the process of it? You got to where you were breathing again. And eating. Living. You were extricated.

L: Released from the double binds. Yes. Initially, my body was back in the States while my heart was still in Syria. It is still there. But it's not a separation, not anymore.

D: Not cut off from yourself.

L: Connected to myself, rather. And to them.

D: In the rawness of it, the pain of it, you came back together.

L: Yes. In the other epigraph for this chapter, in a poem of David Whyte's sent to me by our friend Muriel Singer, there is the image of a blade so sharp, "it cuts things together."

D: I've always loved that the word *cleave* means both "to split" *and* "to adhere." The source of your split, your loss, became the means for the reconnecting to, and the reclaiming of, yourself.

L: Exactly! I started to introduce Syria and the Syrians, without identifying them, inside my life in the US. With their permission, I started to bring their stories and their metaphors to my therapy sessions, their experiences to my family therapy trainees in practicum, their theory questions into my class lessons on various therapy models. They became my colleagues here in the US; they remain so, actually, as I've continued work in other projects and countries. I consult them frequently.

D: Beautiful. Such stories provided you the means of crossing the border between Syria and the States, connecting with clients and students.

L: I did other things as well. I unexpectedly doubled or tripled my typical 5K runs. I traveled a great deal for nonwork reasons—putting myself into different settings while visiting friends who also understood "the fog of war." I upped my monthly massages to weekly ones and did that for 2 straight years. On the downside, for a short but memorable 8 months, I became a smoker. Fortunately, I stopped that habit nearly as quickly as I began it! But my once 2-hour runs are back down to an hour … and my massages, to once a month!

D: Running connects you with your body. As does smoking, in a weird way: It renders your breath visible, tangible.

L: Holy shit. Like fog.

D: Exactly! Maybe it helped to see your fucking fog in front of you. And visiting with sensitive friends connected you to your people, to your mind, before and after Syria knocked on the door.

L: I felt more sane. Complete, whole. Not defined by division, not lost in a fog.

D: My take was that it became safe to be safe.

L: What do you mean?

D: You came to accept your safety as legitimate, no longer a betrayal of your Syrian trainees. You could distinguish yourself from them without feeling you were abandoning them, excluding them, forgetting them. It became emotionally safe to be Laurie, the supervisor with a US passport, somehow still inside Syria but now, also, safely outside.

L: Interesting. They told me more than once I was more Syrian than Syrians. That I became them; they saw me in their world, just like I see them in mine.

D: That doesn't surprise me. Bateson was fond of another Blake proclama-
            tion: "Wise men see outlines and therefore they draw them" (Bateson,
            2000, p. 27). In a fog, it is difficult to distinguish one thing from the
            next, one person from the next. When the lines of perception blur, so
            does identity. Who am I relative to you? Where am I relative to you? We
            slowed down, flipped on the dims, and took the time to make out the
            outlines of what was right in front of you. You developed Blakeian wis-
            dom, Blakeian sanity.

L: Yeah, but didn't Blake also say, "*Mad* men see outlines and therefore
            they draw them"?

D: Yep (Bateson, 2000, p. 27). Outside corroboration helps to distinguish
            wisdom from madness.

L: When you are disoriented and only have yourself as counsel, it is diffi-
            cult if not impossible to tell the difference. You were my outside
            corroborator.

D: I *did* corroborate. I legitimized your experience, made sense of it. I also
            challenged.

L: Your transvision distinguished some outlines I preferred at the time not
            to see. You said things I didn't like, things I still remember *very well*.
            They've stayed with me in a powerful way. You weren't critical of me,
            but you pointed out some things, some critical issues, I hadn't been able
            to face.

D: If I had only agreed with you, we'd have both been lost in the fog. And
            you wouldn't have had the opportunity to distinguish yourself from me,
            either. As Blake would have said, had he been a feminist cybernetician
            living in the late twentieth century, "A wise woman acknowledges dif-
            ferences (and contrasts and disconnects and double binds), and there-
            fore she can draw on them."

L: I no longer felt like I'd lost myself.

D: Welcome back! Such a relief to get regrounded. Reoriented.

L: Tell me about it.

D: You, according to some Syrians I've heard about, are a storyteller. How
            about you tell *me* about it?

L: I just did, I guess! We just did.

D: Well, it's a start.

L: We're missing a few people, though, aren't we?

Douglas: The Syrians? Yes. But if they weren't missing, or if you hadn't been
            missing them, there would have been no chapter. So much of this con-
            versation has been about the presence of their absence.

Laurie: That reminds me of a story....

References

Bateson, G. (1979). *Mind and nature*. New York, NY: Bantam Books.

Bateson, G. (2000). *Steps to an ecology of mind*. Chicago, IL: University of Chicago Press.

Bateson, G., Jackson, D. D., Haley, J., & Weakland, J. H. (2000). Toward a theory of schizophrenia. In *Steps to an ecology of mind* (pp. 201–227). Chicago, IL: University of Chicago Press.

Charlés, L. L. (2007). *Intimate colonialism: Head, heart, and body in West African development work*. New York, NY: Routledge.

Charlés, L. L. (2008). *When the shooting stopped: Crisis negotiation at Jefferson High School*. Lanham, MD: Rowman & Littlefield.

Charlés, L. L. (2010). Family therapists as front line mental health providers: Using reflecting teams, scaling questions, & family members in a primary & secondary care hospital in a war-affected region of Central Africa. *Journal of Family Therapy, 32*, 27–42.

Erickson, M. H. (1980). Further clinical techniques of hypnosis: Utilization techniques. In E. L. Rossi (Ed.), *The collected papers of Milton H. Erickson* (Vol. 1, pp. 177–205). New York, NY: Irvington.

Erickson, M. H., & Rossi, E. L. (1980). Varieties of double bind. In E. L. Rossi (Ed.), *The collected papers of Milton H. Erickson* (Vol. 1, pp. 412–429). New York, NY: Irvington.

Flemons, D. (2002). *Of one mind: The logic of hypnosis, the practice of therapy*. New York, NY: W. W. Norton.

Flemons, D., & Gralnik, L. (2013). *Relational suicide assessment: Risks, resources, and possibilities for safety*. New York, NY: W. W. Norton.

Flemons, D., & Green, S. (2018). Therapeutic quickies: Brief relational therapy for sexual issues. In S. Green & D. Flemons (Eds.), *Quickies: The handbook of brief sex therapy* (3rd ed.). New York, NY: W. W. Norton.

von Clausewitz, C. (1989). *On war* (Indexed ed., M. Howard & P. Paret, Eds./Trans.). Princeton, NJ: Princeton University Press.

Whyte, D. (2012). No one told me. In *River flow: New and selected poems* (Rev. ed., p. 131). Langley, WA: Many Rivers Press.

World Bank Group. (2017). *The toll of war: The economic and social consequences of the conflict in Syria*. Washington, DC: Author.

Chapter 10
The Role of Family and Culture in Extreme Adversity: Psychosocial Response to the Ebola Virus Disease (EVD) Epidemic in Guinea, West Africa

Neda Faregh, Alexis Tounkara, and Kemo Soumaoro

Introduction

My, Neda's, first memory of Guinea is that the airport was mercifully clean and orderly when I arrived there. I did not yet know the contrast it represented to all that I would see and know in the months that followed. On that first meeting between me and all of Guinea, a uniformed official handed me a few custom forms and did not smile back. The wait line to the passport-control booth was a sleepy snake that coiled itself around the short length of a hallway with low ceiling. Once in a while, the tall man standing behind me crept closer by a few inches until I could hear his heavy breath and impatient mumbling. His every move sent a whiff that weaved into the stifling air and stung my nostrils. This odor continues to wrap all my memories of Guinea. It is unique in its unpleasantness and a nod to the country, its heat, its food and bottled-water, and the presence of men. The women never smelled in this way or at least they never stood quite so close.

On the other side of the snake, the single carriage belt creaked in front of an audience of hundreds waiting for their luggage. I stood back and let my eyes search for someone, or some sign, that might confirm I was expected and would be picked up. I heaved three larger-than-life suitcases to my trolley and pretended they were all full of books. They were full of books and food and clothes, medicine and first aid kits, disinfectants and bleach, and shampoos and shoes. In my mind, I had come prepared to work for a few months alongside the mysterious Ebola and its survivors.

N. Faregh (✉)
Carleton University, Montreal, QC, Canada

A. Tounkara
Independent Consultant, Conakry, Guinea

K. Soumaoro
Universite Gamal Abdel Nasser de Conakry, Conakry, Guinea

© Springer Nature Switzerland AG 2019
L. L. Charlés, G. Samarasinghe (eds.), *Family Systems and Global Humanitarian Mental Health*, https://doi.org/10.1007/978-3-030-03216-6_10

However, neither the content of my luggage nor the extensive pre-trip planning had equipped me for encountering the crises that my host country was undergoing. Despite previous experience working in the region, I was ill-informed of the lived historical and sociopolitical experiences of the communities and the more contemporary but intense transformations they were confronting.

After clearing security and exiting the airport, I spotted a truck marked with my organization's name waiting close by. Two prospective colleagues were already in the back seat, talking in French. The driver pushed their small suitcases around to make room for all of mine. I sat in the front, introduced myself, and asked the driver his name. His name was Keita. I asked him for the spelling and wrote it down in my notebook. I did not yet know that Keita, like his passengers, was highly privileged. He was a proper employee of an international organization and drove a car tattooed on the outside with a company logo. Although we did not work in the field together, he drove me on many occasions. I quickly learned that I could count on him to help me out where and when I got stranded and that he would go out of his way to make sure I arrived safely to places I thought I had to go, even after dark or when he was off duty. Everyone said his kind gestures were because I gave him money for his family, but I thought it was because I always called him "Monsieur Keita" and because he saw me cry when children with polio dragged their legs on the asphalt to come up against the car window and ask for food or money. In retrospective, I think it was because his name and his caste was Keita. Later in this chapter we will explore in detail the significance of the family name and the importance of the caste systems in Guinea as representations of the family system.

I was the last person to be dropped off at a hotel near the ocean. At the entrance of the hotel, two men stood up and pointed to a plastic water container and instructed me to wash my hands. I rinsed under the faucet as the water trickled out the smell of chlorine. I shook my hands dry while one of the men pointed a thermometer like a handgun at my temple and pronounced me fever-free. This was my first introduction to the hygiene rituals that played out at the entrance of each building, hospital, restaurant, office, and even town. My hotel room was dingy and drowned in an odd smell. Opening the window ushered in the reek of rotting fish, and I saw the night spreading over the stretch of Conakry visible from the hotel's side wall. I slept badly. In the morning I looked out the window and saw the murky haze that hanged over the Atlantic. I thought it was glorious and took a picture with my phone.

The project we three co-authors worked on was a Mental Health and Psychosocial Support (MHPSS) program and a component of the international response to the Ebola outbreak in West Africa. The objective of the project was to support the MHPSS program implementation in Guinea. The program implementation was overseen by the Ministry of Health. The main goal was to strengthen and develop capacity in the context of the outbreak so that frontline health workers could better provide psychosocial support to families affected by the epidemic. Risk communication in an atmosphere of uncertainty constituted a serious challenge to ongoing intervention efforts (Elliott & Greenberg, 2008; Bedrosian et al., 2016; Joffe & Haarhoff, 1982; Ki, 2014; Nuriddin et al., 2015; Schol et al., 2018; Semalulu, Wong, Kobinger, & Huston, 2014). Along with an ethical responsibility to be transparent about ambiguity of evidence, and dearth of information, in the context of the epidemic (Landry, Foreman, & Kekewich, 2015; Royo-Bordonada & García López, 2016), which is characteristic of EVD outbreaks (Smith & Silva, 2015), there was a need for cultural competence (Southall, DeYoung, & Harris, 2017) in designing mental health interventions that were responsive to the psychosocial context (Shrivastava, Shrivastava, & Ramasamy, 2015). Almost all components of the MHPSS program had to be culturally adapted (Abramowitz et al., 2015), consistent (Guidry, Jin, Orr, Messner, & Meganck, 2017), and focused on rebuilding trust[1] and community connections (Espinola et al., 2016).

In this chapter we will focus primarily on one aspect of the MHPSS program: the processes of family system therapeutic work and the adaptations it required. We will use a case study to illustrate the approaches, methods, and applications of family system therapy. Before delving further, a basic introduction to the country and the nature of the Ebola epidemic is warranted. We also include an elementary review of the political history of Guinea and selected cultural elements, though my understanding of them is necessarily rudimentary. These sections are included because of their significant impact on the implementation of the MHPSS program, the family system therapy work we will explore, and relevance to the themes examined in this chapter.

Background

Guinea is a coastal country located in the western part of the African continent, halfway between Ecuador and the Tropic of Cancer. It covers an area of 245,857 km². It is bordered by Guinea-Bissau and the Atlantic Ocean to the West, by Senegal and Mali to the North, by Côte d'Ivoire to the East, and by Sierra Leone and Liberia to the South. Guinea's geo-ecological diversity gives each of its four distinct regions (maritime, mountain, savanna, and forest) a unique climate, vegetation, and way of life of the populations. The socioeconomic context is marked by persistent poverty, with more than half of population living below the poverty line before the Ebola epidemic outbreak. In 2012, the economic growth was estimated at 3.9%, driven mainly by agriculture and bauxite mining industry. The country has a population of 11.5 million, made up of several ethnic groups and languages. The main ethnic groups and dialects are Soussou, Malinké, Peul, Kissi, Toma, and Guerzé. About two-thirds of the population is illiterate, especially in rural areas and especially the women. The majority of the population adheres to Wahhabiyya Islam (followers of seventeenth-century Sunni cleric from Saudi Arabia) or Christianity; some are animist. Although various population surveys provide no definition for the animist religion, Cherif suggests that irrespective of the adopted religion, the majority of

---

[1] Building Public Trust Is a Key Factor in Fighting West Africa's Worst Ebola Outbreak. Accessed at: http://www.ipsnews.net/2014/08/building-public-trust-is-a-key-factor-in-fighting-west-africas-worst-ebola-outbreak/

Guineans continue to practice the traditional religion: "the way of the ancestors" (Le Chemin des Ancêtres).

The Guinean population is young; about half are under 15 and fewer than 7% are over the age of 60. An average household has six or seven inhabitants, with 17% headed by women mostly because men leave home to work in rural agricultural sectors. Only a quarter of Guinean households have electricity. About three-quarters obtain their drinking water from a clean source, and one-third spend 30 min or more per day to stock up on drinking water. More than half of households have no or unimproved toilets. The UNDP ranks Guinea the 179th, among 187 countries in its Gender Equality Index. Nearly all girls and women (98%) have undergone female genital mutilation (FGM). The average age of marriage for girls is 14 and 25 for men. Among most ethnic groups, particularly the Malinké, consanguine marriages along the female line are common (first maternal cousins). Marrying outside of the family (exogamy) is considered cross-caste and frowned upon. Exogamy is further discouraged by a cultural conviction that caste-mixing will result in weakened blood and impurity and hereditary diseases.

Cultures of Guinea are rich in mythology, oral histories, connection to land, the supernatural, dreams, and contracts with ancestral spirits. Guineans rely on and trust their traditional healers, elders, and older brothers, as traditional custodians of culture, and the griot (storytellers), to make meaning and develop knowledge and rules to live by. The oral tradition is a sacred and important part of the Guinean ways of knowing. A Meding proverb asserts that "through Parole (dialogue) humanity was created and Parole assures humanity's maturation, initiation, education, healing, and death." Parole is represented and given by the griot. The griots are repositories of oral history and belong to a social caste invested in cultural continuity, truth-telling, and event censorship. Parole given by the griot is abided. The Guinean-French psychotherapist, Cherif, insists on the importance of using griot foundational parole even with Guinean diaspora, because parole provides cultural representations that help decode everyday difficulties and crises. The Guinean modern history has weakened these practices, and recent attempts at cultural re-invention were interrupted with the emergence of EVD epidemic.

The Family System and Its Enduring Legend

According to legend, Sunjata Keita, the first son of the King Naré and his ugly hunchback wife, Sogolon Condé, was born crippled. After the King's death, Sogolon Condé feared for Sunjata's life and took him and his sisters into exile, traveling from country to country in the Ghana Empire until she was given asylum by the king of Mema (the Inner Niger Delta, a region of current day Mali). When King Sumaoro of the Sosso conquered the Mading people, messengers were sent to find Sogolon Condé and her children and to return them home because a prophecy revealed that Sunjata was destined to become a great leader. Sunjata Keita who by then could speak all the languages of Africa defeated Sumaoro Kanté, the king of the Sosso, and become the emperor of the Mali Empire (includes current day Guinea). Under his competent reign, ancient slave trades ceased, the commerce of gold and cola flourished, and agriculture boomed. In his wisdom, he created social rules and attributes that divided his people into castes, according to their ancestral origins and family names. He made his descendants, the Keita family, the caste of the noblemen. He counseled them to become the defenders and protectors of the Mading people and to represent the empire. He made the Kanté family the second caste because they were the masters of fire. He counseled the Kanté to become ironsmiths and to provide weapons for the noblemen and iron plows and axes for agriculture. Because he had defeated Sumaoro, the king of the Sosso, he made the Sumaoro family the third caste and bade them to become blacksmiths even though the King had been a nobleman and fought against slavery. He made the Tounkara the shoemakers and counseled them to become leather tanners. He made the Somoni the fishermen. As to the Kouyate griots who were masters of the word and the Diabaté Djialo who were masters of music, they must be Keita's spokespersons and sing to the end of time Sunjata's praises and that of his ancestors and his generals, including the Traoré whose forefather conquered the Kingdom of Gambia, who were masters of the hunt, and older brothers to the Diabaté Djialo. After Sunjata's death, the griots took care to keep his story in the form of an epic tale, called the Sunjata Fassa: the praise song for Sunjata.

The Sunjata Epic is considered a masterpiece of African oral literature and continues to be recited and orally transmitted by Kouyaté, Diabaté, and Djialo griots in West Africa. The tale praises Sunjata's royal dynasty, the Keita, and the battles of the Traoré. It is a historical novel and a living tale in which Sunjata remains allegorical and his praises are always inferring and insinuating, as they teach the way of life.

Recital of the ultimate version of the Sunjata Epic is rare, its content is cautiously guarded, and recordings are prohibited. The tales are transmitted from father to son across generations of griot families whose function is to discern, censor, preserve, and chronicle history of their people and events as they see fit. The griots are considered masters of the word, trusted historians, and knowledge keepers and esteemed as the only ones to have the necessary words that have the power to order the affairs of life and to put society on the right track. Documentation of the Sunjata Epic requires competent translation with sensitivity toward the culture and regional variation and the collaboration of the griots who continue their family traditions of concealment to preserve the Epic and its mystery. Several transcriptions are available in written form. Their authenticity is verifiable by the conventions of authorship which must include the names of the editor(s), translator(s), and griots.

Today, the caste system among the Mading (the Malinke and several others) provides a social code and information on lineage. Family names indicate ancestral heritage, traditional philosophies, the shadow (Ja), the family's protection fetish (Boli), and the nature and the number of the secret initiation societies (Jo). The Ja, or the shadow, is the mask associated with the family name. The masks carry special meanings and are imbued with myth and magic. The Jo represents the traditional education and tutoring which, if attained, allow an individual to dispense with ignorance and access to divinities. The secret initiation societies, Jo, form the bases of an individual's existence, thought, and knowledge. They are a set of stepped sequences of tutored programs. They are responsible for and ensure correct transformation, or metamorphosis, of the individual from one stage of development to the next. Each secret society helps the individual to die in one form and be reborn into another, ready for the next initiation of another secret society.

Together, these name-driven codes provide the essentials of one's life philosophy. Today, when Guineans meet, the greeting ritual includes salutations, each addressing the other, each addressing the other's father, and both addressing their common ancestor. The greeting is followed by the question "What sweet praise of the Sunjata Epic do you respond to?" This question is asking "If a griot sang the praises of your ancestor by the intermediary of the family name, what emotion would you experience?" The question ultimately asks the other person "What is your last name?," but the greeting ritual invokes feelings of interconnectedness and belonging through ancestral roots going back to Sunjata. The family name itself, of divine origin, provides information about kinship, endogamy, occupations, and social roles.

Political History

Information presented in this section provide insight into the relationship between the political history of the country and its ramifications on the culture and the family system. The reader is invited to consider the implications for family system therapy delivered by humanitarian agents, within a government-sponsored program where the program implementation was overseen by the Ministry of Health. Public health communication and education was accomplished through one-way top-down mass communication in a context of uncertainty about the disease. Keep in mind also that public health initiatives necessitated swift and oftentimes forceful execution of health measures.

Guinea is somewhat unique in its postcolonial history having endured a jihadist campaign (1956–1958) led by the Muslim cleric Asekou Sayon and 30 years of President Sekou Touré's Independent Socialist Regime (1958–1984) which imposed a brutal "demystification program" on the country. The demystification program was part of the Guinean cultural revolution, modeled after the Maoist cultural revolution, and intended to replace existing traditions with a new modern national identity that would supplant ethnicity, class and caste systems, and religious identification.

Sekou Touré (1922–1984) was a Sunni Muslim and a Malinke. Like his grandfather, General Samory Touré, who assembled his own independent army to resist the French colonization of the Upper Guinea, Sekou Touré was charismatic and self-taught. He studied the works of Marx, Lenin, and Mao whose philosophies formed the foundations of his ideologies. He later wrote that Maoist philosophy, in particular, matched African cultures' community and collectivist orientation. He was further influenced by the post-World War II sociopolitical events in the Balkans and the struggle for independence from imperialism by India and Yugoslavia. Touré's revolutionary ideologies were expanded into his political philosophy for Guinea that included his models of (1) the "African personality," (2) non-capitalism, and (3) the party state (ref). Each of these is reviewed below with the goal of identifying the impact on the family system.

1. African Personality: Touré's definition of the African personality encompassed the psychological and intellectual characteristics unique to the "African man" and the associated social behaviors based on group interdependence and solidarity. He believed that the negative impacts of the colonial rule operated beyond cultural hegemony because it denigrated the African personality. The African personality could not coexist within the incompatible colonial structures that were based on European individualistic culture and egocentricity. His political philosophy was based on the premise that (a) Africa needed to rehabilitate itself after the injustices and humiliations it had suffered at the hands of the slave trade and colonialism and (b) the richness of the African collectivist culture, once regained and reaffirmed, would liberate the continent from Western domination.

   To revive the African personality, Touré wanted to reverse all negative images of the "African," demeaned by the colonists as superstitious and fetishistic. The cultural rehabilitation would therefore restore people's pride in their heritage so that they would never again succumb to external rule. The Guinea's socialist cultural revolution set out to raise the level of consciousness of Guineans to their unique "African personality." He saw tribalism, the caste system, and ethnic groups as the main threat to modernizing Guinea and set out to eliminate their leadership. These groups consisted of religious and traditional chiefs and the heads of secret societies.

   For generations, they had overseen the affairs of their communities, settled disputes, and ensured non-transgression of family and patrimonial values. They organized and headed age- and gender-segregated secret society events that ensured the rites of passage: the rituals of initiation, marriage, fecundity, protection of life force, agriculture, and more. They were also responsible for ensuring the ancestral spirits were respected and appeased who in turn communed with divinities and intervened on behalf of the people conferring protection. These rituals involved well-guarded secrets of the mystique represented by an array of wooden masks and multitudes of magic-infused artifacts.

   Sekou Touré's iconoclastic thrust used violence to arrive at systematic burning and destruction of arts representing ethnic groups, masks, and cultural artifacts. Sacred forests and mangroves were also destroyed. For full appreciation of the cultural significance of the environmental destruction of sacred forests and mangroves, see the work of Marcel Griaule (ref) and his description of the invisible "doubles." Briefly, to be complete there must be two of everything. Unless born with a twin, each human is given an invisible double. The invisible double lives in the form of an animal in the forest and hides in the mangroves. Without it no human can be whole. The conceptualization of the kola nut's twin seeds as the symbol of the union of two and a profound symbol of culture, affinity, friendship, and tribal knowingness is further evidence of the importance of the double.

These events were successful at interrupting intergenerational cultural acquisition and transfers and subduing a complex socioreligious system that relied on tradition to order and make sense of life affairs and the order of things.

2. Non-capitalism: This notion followed from Maoist collectivism and led to the development of policies for crop sharing and agricultural land use. These policies were incompatible with traditional chiefdom, secret society leadership, and caste systems that determined landownership.

3. The party state: He believed that Africa had to modernize in order to become an equal player in the world economy and that the modernization had to occur without westernization. This would require, he wrote, the total abandonment of the aspects of culture that inhibited or threatened modernity. He developed a series of policies that restricted peoples' alliances with any ideology or activity outside of the party state. Religious associations were forbidden, evening gatherings were restricted, group prayers were banned, and participation in any secret society initiation or ritual was punishable by law and resulted in imprisonment. Travel across the Guinea borders was severely restricted. State surveillance was omnipresent and harsh. These actions were accompanied by multiple campaigns that forced the population to mobilize into political parties and various campaigns including mass education (re-learning of African languages for children and adults) and state-sponsored sports and state-approved cultural events. With the help of party-sympathizer griots, music, and dance associations, political ideas were popularized via mass communication programs. Communication between party officials and the masses was a unidirectional top-down transmission of party messages. He built prisons, known as Guinean concentration camps, where thousands of opponents were imprisoned, tortured, or executed. Many died of systematic starvation inside camps. Note here that Ebola health facilities and quarantine zones were commonly referred to as Ebola camps. Most who entered died.

The end of Touré's violent regime ensued political uncertainties and a nascent democracy along with a legacy of fear and distrust. A renewed interest in ethnic kinship, cultural reclamation, and re-ethnicization was confounded by poverty of the fragile state and subsequently the devastations of the Ebola epidemic. The corollary of the EVD crisis in Guinea needs reframing to be understood within this sociopolitical landscape.

The Epidemic

The 2014–2016 West African epidemic is the largest in history. The epidemic resulted in more than 28,000 known cases of EVD transmission and 11,000 reported deaths. What started as a public health emergency morphed into a global threat to international security. The EVD epidemic was the second international health to prompt a response from the UN Security Council in September of 2014. The first health crisis with a passed UN Security Council resolution was the HIV. The EVD and HIV epidemics share many similarities including the unequal geographical spread and impact that disproportionately affected the African continent. Similar to the HIV epidemic, the EVD epidemic primarily unfolded in a fragile context where in addition to inequalities, inequity at all levels played a major role in the impact of the disease, exacerbated by historical, cultural, and contextual factors. Together, these factors increased the precariousness of the epidemic environment. The large majority of the international health investments in Ebola prevention was devoted to capacity building in surveillance and disease control and setting up of centers devoted to rapid response teams to be mobilized in the event of disease outbreaks. These efforts failed to consider the profound psychosocial and cultural upheavals that took place in these regions. There is evidence that failure to respond to the outbreak in a culturally sensitive manner significantly increased the likelihood of infection and death. Estimates suggest traditional belief systems and customs carried out by initiation societies and the mortuary practices were critical to the outbreaks and were responsible for 50% increase in the disease burden. It is estimated that traditional burial practices contributed 22% of the total number of infections.

The Ebola Virus Disease

EVD remains an understudied infection with uncertainty about many aspects of the disease and its transmission. Direct contact with bodily fluid is the primary mode of transmission with increasing evidence that other, including aerosol, modes of transmission are also possible. The more than 17,000 clinically recovered Ebola survivors in West Africa constitute a reservoir of the virus with unknown risk of disease recrudescence (reappearance of symptoms), resurgence (susceptibility to reinfection after recovery), and transmission to others.

Public Health Intervention Measures

During the epidemic, EVD transmission was mainly through contact with bodily fluids. The rate of transmission was exacerbated by traditional West African funeral practices that involved washing, touching, and kissing the body (Schol et al., 2018; Semalulu et al., 2014). Given the lack of effective therapeutic treatments or vaccines (Landry et al., 2015), other measures were necessary to curb the spread of the infection. These measures included quarantine of suspected cases, case isolation, contact precautions, sanitary burial practices, and a countrywide no touch policy. General population guidelines for prevention and risk reduction of EVD transmission included school closures (with many children not returning to school after re-opening), mandatory hand and feet washing with chlorinated water from tanks placed at all building and organization entrances, mandatory checking of body temperature before entering business or government buildings, avoidance of public events and mass gatherings, refraining from food sharing and communal breaking of kola (a common socially indicated means of connecting and relating), and touching dead bodies. The only form of allowable greeting was elbow handshakes when fully covered by clothes. While helping to curb the epidemic, these guidelines were isolating, fear-inducing, traumatizing, and culturally incongruent. They also represented an enormous logistical challenge and were difficult to implement.

Ebola Social Consequences

The high number of infections and deaths tore at the fabric of families, many of which rejected survivors and were left with major gaps in the structures of the community-oriented culture. Fear and resistance to public health efforts to contain the epidemic were common social reactions. Examples include aggression and violence against public and health officials. A monthly average of ten attacks was reported against Red Cross volunteers ranging from verbal to physical assaults (Shrivastava et al., 2015). Towns and cities barricaded themselves disallowing exits and entries. Road barricades remained active until the end of the epidemic, attracting markets and commercial activity at checkpoints where those needing to cross were subjected to mandatory body temperature checks and compulsory washing in chlorinated water. These events coupled with lack of information deepened the sense of isolation and distrust in a system that had only inadequately met the needs of the population prior to the EVD epidemic. Fear that quarantine procedures were intended to deliberately infect and fear of being cremated and not receiving a proper family burial led some infected individuals to escape isolation.

Culture and Community

To the uninitiated eye, Ebola killed and destroyed lives. To the Guineans, Ebola destroyed a culture and continues to maim those who survived it and their decedents and communities:

> A normal death needs Kola. When your brother dies, or your mother, or your neighbor, you bring 3 or 5 kilos of Kola and you bring money. Maybe they make rice and meat, the family comes, and they read the Koran. You shake hands, you rub each other, you hold each other tight. Someone reads the Koran, 9 maybe 11 people have to read it. You sit in a circle, you listen. Every time they open the koran, every time they close the Koran, you throw money in the circle, you take a Kola and you pray to it. You ask for your wish, for what you want, then you throw it in the circle. They will gather the money, they will gather the Kola, divide it between all the people who read the Koran and give it to them. Then you eat, shake hands, go home.

> On the last day of the funeral services, strangers will go to pay respect. Maybe the friend of a neighbor, or a friend not well known to the family. The stranger will bring money. The family will thank the stranger and give him a Kola. Kola is a symbol of respect, symbol of union, of putting back together, of uniting what's been broken. But with Ebola you don't bring Kola anymore. Kola carries contamination. It can carry disease, because you pass it from one person's hand to another's. When there is Ebola you can't pass food around. You can't sit together and crunch Kola. ~Mr. Diallo – Driver

Fears and uncertainties about the unknown in an atmosphere of instability and crisis can be deeply disorienting. The disorientation can be intensified when cultural practices, sociability, intimacy, and other shared rituals that support meaning-making must be abandoned or altered in favor of disease eradication. There is a need to fill the resulting vacuum through seeking and sharing of plausible information from available credible sources. It is not uncommon for misconceptions and misinformation to be integrated in this process of distressed knowledge creation. Lessons learned from the EVD epidemic include the need to prioritize and improve the cultural congruence of interventions and the importance of empowering the community for a participatory approach to co-creating and co-learning. During the EVD outbreak, these factors were shown to be critical for success:

> If there is Ebola, there is no body. They come and take it. They close the house. The family is quarantined. You don't bring Kola. You can't pray to the Kola. You don't know Ebola, you don't know the death. You don't know where your brother goes. You don't ask for anything from the Kola. Ebola is not normal death, you can't bring Kola. -Mr. Conde, Driver

Ebola Survivors

The Guinean "National Strategic Plan for Management of EVD and its Survivors" operationally defines Ebola survivors as persons directly and indirectly impacted by the virus. Categories include (a) persons recovered from the virus, (b) orphans, (c) widows and widowers, (d) family members of survivors, (e) family members of deceased Ebola victims, and (f) health workers who worked in Ebola prevention efforts and volunteers of the Red Cross who were responsible for removal of bodies. The designation also includes community members stigmatized through implication, such as burial workers.

Impact of EVD

Estimations of the secondary impact of EVD suggest the impact is multiplied by drivers of poorer human capital outcomes in future generations (Bava, Saul, Gow, & Celinski, 2013). By early 2015, the estimated number of orphaned children was about 10,000 and acknowledged as an underestimation. It was predicted that orphaned children would be absorbed into the extended family. The field experience, evidence from the literature, and lessons learned from other epidemics (HIV) suggest that disease stigma played a role in the quality of care for orphaned children. Children and adolescents orphaned by Ebola did not benefit from traditional mechanisms of orphan support; many were feared and rejected (Rosenfeld, Caye, Ayalon, & Lahad, 2005). With EVD, families were severely affected by multiple stressors. EVD rates of fatality were higher for adults than for children or elderly and for women. Often several adult members of the same family were infected. This left the family system highly vulnerable and burdened with orphan rates surpassing the capacity of remaining female family members to care for them. These factors lead to lower quality of fostering, lower likelihood of investing in the human capital of the orphans, and increased likelihood of involving school-aged orphans in domestic work or labor market (Bava et al., 2013; Saul, 2014; Erikson, 1976). As has been shown with HIV epidemics, it is anticipated that the most unmet needs of Ebola survivors will be mental health services.

Evidence from West Africa suggests that sharing of misinformation, as much as communication of indecipherable or culturally incoherent guidelines, was a contributing factor to misconceptions, high-risk behavior, and complacency (Kpanake, Gossou, Sorum, & Mullet, 2016; Winters et al., 2018) which were instrumental challenges in the outbreak management.

Case Study

In December of 2015, we and our colleagues were called on to evaluate a patient presenting with psychosocial problems and whose attending physicians required assistance in evaluation and treatment protocol. The consultation was requested by two hospital physicians. They had met a patient with psychological problems but had not yet been able to arrive at a diagnosis. The patient had consented to further consultation because he wanted to "feel less bad and more comfortable." The evaluation method was clinical interview. No patient file was available for review.

- Medical history: No medical problems were reported prior to Ebola infection.
- Current symptoms and complaints: Mr. T's symptoms were consistent with post-Ebola sequels and included persistent chronic pain in all joints (pain levels reported at 4/10, 4 days a week with no functional impediment). Insomnia, tinnitus, loss of appetite. Frequent headaches, feeling of itchiness inside the brain, burning sensation of the scalp. He reported repeated nightmares. Patient continued to work full time.
- Family psychological history: One brother may have undiagnosed psychological or psychiatric problems.
- Relevant history: Mr. T was a 31-year Ebola survivor and father of four children ages 5, 6, 7, and 8. He believes he was infected on December 24, 2014. His 26-year-old wife was subsequently infected and died in January 2015. Mr. T lost 15 members of his family in the course of the Ebola infection within the span of

a few short months. The deceased included his parents, brothers including the older brother, sisters, cousins, aunts, and uncles. It was not clear who in the family was the vector case and we did not pursue this line of questioning. Mr. T is the only remaining family member able to take care of his children, but he does not feel competent enough to do so. He is often assisted by two female neighbors especially for the care of the two younger children. He prefers not to spend time with his children because doing so gives him a great sense of inadequacy and guilt. He feels responsible for the death of their mother. He prefers not to see them or to be involved with them as they are a great cause of guilt, discomfort, and difficulty to him. He has a sister who lives near him but with whom he gets along badly, because "she talks too much" and proposes activities to him (e.g., to remarry) which would be frowned upon by their father, who is now deceased.

- Employment: Mr. T works full time as a survivor peer-support worker with a community outreach organization. He likes his work and feels appreciated by the community, his team, and especially his team leader.
- Current mental status and observations: Psychomotor delay, irritability, crying, feelings of guilt. Reported symptoms are agitation, hopelessness, suicidal ideation, and recent suicide attempt by hanging. During the attempt the rope broke and he survived. He reports his gallows remain in his bedroom and he plans to obtain new ropes; he is planning a new attempt. During the interview, he appeared determined and unwavering in his motive to kill himself. He stated he was waiting to find an appropriate rope to prevent another missed attempt.
- Main current complaints: Despair, loneliness, bad thoughts (referring to suicidal thoughts), financial problems which are especially distressing when he cannot meet his children's needs. He would prefer not to have the responsibility of looking after the children and their needs.
- Diagnosis: Major depressive disorder, possible PTSD. The patient is at imminent risk of suicide. Possible risk of harm to minor children.
- Recommendation: Immediate removal of the four minor children from the home. Admission to inpatient psychiatric ward. Initiate psychotropic medication.

Although these were our official recommendations, they could not be carried out without reference to social, cultural, contextual, and family factors surrounding the case of Mr. T. More importantly they could not be carried out without our personal involvement.

The contextual and cultural factors were as follows:

- No psychotropics were available in the region.
- No psychiatric services were available in the region.
- No means of transport were available for the patient to travel to the only psychiatric ward in the country.
- No community or social or child protection agency, including international aid agencies, was operating in the region.
- Mr. T's sister was unemployed and full-time caretaker for 14 minor nieces and nephews who had survived their parents Ebola deaths, as well as siblings and other family members who were Ebola survivors and too frail to be left alone.

- Patient could not be removed to a hospital without a culturally endorsed permission of an older brother.
- Mr. T's older brother was deceased due to Ebola – We learned that in the absence of "the" older brother, another older brother's permission could be sought.
- The only surviving brother was an Ebola survivor who had lost his wife and children and was suffering from either (a) developmental delays, (b) long-standing psychiatric problems, or (c) neuropsychological problems related to Ebola virus or its consequent hemorrhagic fevers. This permission, therefore, could not easily be obtained.

The Need for Cultural Congruence

When you want to get married, you buy a lot of kola. You take a few, maybe six, and package them together, add 10,000 FG, and you bring it with you to meet her parents. When the time is right, you prepare another bundle of Kola and bring to your second meeting. You say "I've seen something, maybe someone, around here, and I'd like to see her again. Is she single? Can I meet her?" If they agree you can meet with your beloved and make your plans. You wait until her parents invite you back. You make another bundle of kola, add a lot of money, maybe 100,000 FG and meet the whole family. You have to buy a suitcase and fill it with beautiful things, clothes, jewels. Your older brother and your sisters will help you fill the suitcase. When you go to meet the Imam you make the fourth bundle of Kola and give it to him. This is the best part because you are getting married. After the marriage, maybe you buy her a cow, and then you make a fifth bundle of Kola and bring it to her father, and you bring clothes for him. When your son is born, when you have trouble with your wife, your older brother decides for you. Everyone brings Kola and your older brother gives your son a name. And this is how it's done. You are never alone. You don't have to make decisions by yourself. That would be too difficult for life. You have to listen. Nothing good comes out of making up your own mind alone. Mr. Keita

The public health efforts, particularly those that interfered with funeral practices, were antagonizing to customs and tenets of people. The reasons had roots in the common prevalent beliefs about the nature and causation of illness:

- Ill health may be triggered by biological agents but is caused by individual short-coming, anger of ancestors, other spirits, curses, or sorcery.
- Sudden illness or death is due to supernatural forces brought on by transgression, curses, or jealousy.
- Such events necessitate ecological reparation through supernaturally conferred protection.
- Interfering with cultural practices can exacerbate problems and hinder convalescence.

Mr. T was a Traoré. The family system was a Traoré. The caste implication was that the family system was similar to that of the noblemen or the Keita. The family's identity and social role were determined by the characteristics of the family name. The lineage created the social identity, a feeling of place and position in society.

Mr. T's family system was fragmented by multitudes of losses. The distresses related to the multigenerational loss of parents, siblings/partner, and offspring were exacerbated by their unknowable position in the ancestral realms due to cause of death. The loss of a significant relationship (the older brother) obscured the family's solution-seeking pathways. The absence of funerary rites of passage for all the 15 family members represented a profound dishonoring of the deceased that left them unprotected in the ancestral and spirit worlds. This brought disgrace on the family system via social marginalization (external stigma), in addition to other forms of stigma related to the mysterious and contagious nature of EVD. It also implied potential repercussions from the spirit world whose displeasure could cause illness and death (internalized stigma). Each dishonored death galvanizing the circle of external and internalized stigma in the visible world, and inciting the wrath and furry of the spirit world, put in motion the undeniable chain of sickness and death that had by all measures unraveled the fabric of Mr. T's family system.

An analysis of the sociocultural ramifications of the characteristics of this family system was only feasible through working with Guinean colleagues. While the interpretation of this set of information was left to my Guinean counterparts, neither of us knew the impact of the family's status as Ebola survivors on their identity. The cascading pattern of crisis and marginalization was many levels deep. The Ebola and the survivor stigma barred any sense of inclusion in the sociocultural matrix. Surpassing the already convoluted matter of Ebola and bereavement, the family system was further affected by the corollary of mental illness and attempted suicide, deepening the isolation and stigma.

The Necessity of an Eclectic Approach to the Therapeutic Orientation

Our team's collective trainings in transcultural psychology, knowledge of cultural variation in help-seeking pathways, and cultural influences on psychological needs and well-being were only useful to the extent that they were reminders of all that we could not know.

Cultural competence refers to developing a meaningful and intimate knowledge of cultural, ethical, and systemic factors that affect both the therapist and the patient. Ebola survivors were undergoing what might be akin to acculturation. Acculturation is referred to as the process of adjusting to a new culture and eventual assimilation into the new society. In this context, the former culture was difficult to pinpoint given the political history of the region and its cultural impact; the new culture had yet to evolve; and the new society was morphing into a post-epidemic future.

What was clear however was the family system in its raw state. It was made up of an interconnected group of individuals with shared losses and mutual reliance. Whether positively or negatively, they self-defined in relation to each other and their common ground. They sought change and were searching for a joint solution. The only frame of reference for our therapeutic approach was the family system itself. The family members were the only experts of their own lives and their shifting culture.

Our Approach

The ultimate approach we took to the family system therapy was eclectic in nature. We borrowed the framework of discursive therapies, focusing more on solution-focused therapy (SFT). This orientation made allowances for our "not knowing." It also provided the needed platform to view the family as our expert collaborator and each member as a teacher who helped to construct and attempt a number of viable solutions. We needed to adapt some aspects of SFT framework. The component of the SFT which focuses on assisting the family system to identify and use personal strengths was not practical to our context. In humanitarian settings, a strength-based approach is shifted to focus more on coping and functioning and less on successful living and positive growth.

The intervention did not just employ the resilience lens; it had to actively search for and find "what works" and "where the strengths are" and leverage them to the maximum. In this way, the intervention may shift to adapt itself to ways that can maximally benefit from any and all existing resources. The definition of success is adjusted to focus on finding available means of adaptive coping. The goal formulation is necessarily short-term which excludes self-efficacy as an objective inside the crisis context. Pragmatism and flexibility are necessary where resources and competencies are scarce. While the Traoré family's internal resources were recognized and exploited to the extent possible, the objective was not to help the family system develop them.

The strength-based approach and the SFT focus on what is good and what is positive, advocating for an optimistic orientation toward life. This approach is pragmatic because it discourages an inefficient focus on the givens of life, but it can be imprudent where cultural dynamics are poorly understood and adversity is extreme. Nevertheless, this orientation can safeguard against inadvertent undertakings than could undermine empowerment and exacerbate the sense of victimhood. Short-term approaches carry the potential of unsustainability and increasing dependency (Greene et al., 2017), and as a systematic issue, there is ample room for development of new appropriate guidelines.

Revising the Recommendations

We adjusted the plan as follows:

- We recommend Dr. O to visit patient at his home on a daily basis and to cut down the gallows on his first visit. We recommended the prescription of strong but daily doses of benzodiazepines to allow Mr. T to rest and sleep while a solution was being sought.

- We recommend that Mr. T's best friend be persuaded to spend nights with him as his suicide watch.
- We visited Mr. T's sister to persuade her to take in the four children. We met a middle-aged woman who complained of her sense of overwhelm from being the only remaining caretaker in the family responsible for 14 minors, who were Ebola survivors and the children of deceased family members. She also looked after other family members who were Ebola survivors and no longer capable of self-care. She told us that her marriage suffered from the strain of caretaking
- We visited the local chapter of a national NGO to obtain food for the four children for the duration of Mr. T's absence from his children.
- We visited Mr. T's older brother to ask permission for his removal to Conakry.
- We will work with other international aid agencies to find an ambulance for Mr. T's transport to Conakry.

Follow-Up

Mr. T's four children were forcibly removed and left in the care of Mr. T's sister. We were able to engage a national NGO to provide bags of rice, clothes, and soap to the family for 6 months. We visited Mr. T's brother and, with some difficulty, were able to obtain permission to admit Mr. T to the hospital in Conakry. An aid agency provided an ambulance for transport. However, they had to know the reason for transport and it turned that Mr. T was one of their employees. Given the collectivist culture, it was seen appropriate for the national staff to request the psychological report of the patient, and under normal circumstances the ambulance could have received copy. But given the Ebola context and the employment relationship, we decided not to provide the report. This matter was taken up several levels until it was eventually resolved at the headquarters. Mr. T was to be transported by an ambulance provided by his employer without disclosing the cause. A member of our team accompanied Mr. T in the ambulance.

On the way to the Capital Conakry, the ambulance had an accident and a few motorists were severely injured. The injured and bleeding motorists could only be assisted by Mr. T who, as a survivor, was the only person immune to potential risk of Ebola infection from the bleeding victims. While the injured were being assisted by Mr. T, their ambulance which had a logo of the international aid agency, and their party, was attacked by the mob who were fearful of an "Ebola ambulance" and attempted to set it on fire. The police intervened and hid Mr. T and others while we appealed to yet another aid agency to send in an unidentified car to continue the trip to Conakry.

Mr. T was severally shaken and affected by these events. Upon arrival at the hospital, he presented in a state of high anxiety, fear, and low emotional control and what might have been fearful flashbacks from his recent stay in an Ebola treatment center. A sedative was offered by a nurse but Mr. T refused treatment and attempted to flee from the psychiatric ward. He was restrained by a dozen bystanders including nurses, orderly, and family members of other patients. He was tied to a bed and forcibly treated with tranquilizers and antipsychotic medication for the next 2 months, although he felt better within a week. After the first week, he called the first author on a daily basis and threatened to kill her upon his release.

We pleaded with the attending psychiatrist multiple times, and he eventually agreed to cease forced treatment with antipsychotics but continued to prescribe benzodiazepines in high doses. Mr. T collected the pills during the remainder of his stay at the hospital without taking them. Upon his return home, he swallowed them all at once. He survived the overdose. His attending physicians reported the incident was an accidental overdose, as per Mr. T's account. The following week, a large international aid agency visited the hometown of Mr. T, and the head of the agency along with cameramen and TV reporters visited the home of Mr. T as part of an awareness campaign aimed at fundraising for the agency. They shook hands with him and announced him not only an Ebola survivor, but the first mentally ill survivor of Guinea to have ever been diagnosed. We never learned how this information had leaked out but continued to be concerned for Mr. T's safety and well-being.

Sequel

Through the help of a number of aid agencies, we were able to procure appropriate medication for Mr. T, who traveled to Conakry on a regular basis to collect free medication from a central pharmacy. The pharmacy dispenses enough medication, including benzodiazepines for 1 month at a time. Our multiple interventions resulted in Mr. T traveling to Conakry with his sister who collected the medication on his behalf. Upon their return to their hometown, he reportedly leaves the benzodiazepines in the care of Dr. O who dispenses them a few at a time. Mr. T's children were returned to him. We visited Mr. T at his home in March of 2016. He offered us a thank you letter for having saved his life. We met with his children and observed typical post-Ebola inflammation in the left eye of the youngest child, pointing to a potential clinical manifestations of post-Ebola ocular complications and presence of viable Ebola virus in aqueous humor in the inflamed eye. The child was referred to the local hospital for routine care. As we said goodbye, Mr. T pointed to a series of small homes attached to his one room house and told us these were left to him from his father and other deceased relatives that he might consider renting them but that as a known Ebola survivor his chances of business success were low.

Epilogue

When everything he knew had fallen apart and when everything we knew was far away, what brought us together, all of us, his motherless children, his tired old sister, and the missing older brother who symbolized kinship in ways we could hardly grasp, in the shadows of the invisible ancestral spirits and faraway Canadian winters and Guinean rains, was this one element: empathy. This empathy was not based on mutual understanding or common grounds. Rather, it was empathy based on tacit acceptance of the vast differences that separated us. Each of us a product of the lottery of birth and fate, we acknowledged that we were shaped differently by our respective cultures and social contexts and the consequent dynamics of power and privilege. Furthermore, we were both inside the same circle of vulnerability, the epidemic. The empathic form of relating was about our willingness to engage and negotiate the therapeutic relationship just as it was: convoluted and ambiguous.

Circles of Vulnerability

In this section, we discuss the nearly indefinable but pervasive experience of participating in many circles of vulnerabilities as a systemic aspect of family therapy.

The concept of circles of vulnerability was developed in the context of collective trauma and posttraumatic reactions (Bava et al., 2013; Rosenfeld et al., 2005). It was expanded to identify vulnerability factors among the different types and targets of traumatic events. Parallel work has focused on collective resilience and recovery (Saul, 2014). Models of circles of vulnerability recognize current and historical contexts, including political contexts of affected communities (Bava et al., 2013; Erikson, 1976, 1994; Wessells & Strang, 2006). Ayalon extends this body of work with considerations of intercultural challenges in circles of vulnerability and, more importantly for our purpose here, the environments in which victims and helpers are similarly exposed (Ayalon, 2008). Basing the analysis on Winnicott's *Playing and Reality*, helpers from the "circles of support" are studied as they themselves become part of the "circles of vulnerability" through "shared fate" and "shared exposure." Both helpers and victims suffer losses and grief; both experience shock, confusion, and fear. The work briefly considers the possibility of enmeshment that occurs as a result of social and emotional proximity of the two groups.

The helper in the humanitarian context is impacted and must cope inside the crisis environment. Some factors are identical to those that impact the patient and the family; others may be unique to the individual therapist. The humanitarian crisis environment is a microcosm of the wider world, where men tend to hold positions of power, and abuses of this power remain prevalent. In addition to the objectification of women and gender-based power dynamics that are prevalent within a given environment and culture, women working in the humanitarian crisis contexts typically face additional challenges. They may be perceived as vulnerable and assailable and simultaneously seen as symbols of oppression and colonization. Minority and marginalized women are subjected to compounded inequities. The consequences for all women are witnessed in unfortunate incidents including unbridled harassment and rape.

Yet, the effects of women's presence as gendered expressions of agency are commonly perceived as nonthreatening. Women are able to draw on firsthand understanding of family needs and the gendered effects of humanitarian and development settings. They use communication strategies that easily bridge the gap between "feeling and knowing," and they are well equipped to identify the needs of families. Women are also able to build social capital with other women and children, gaining insight into otherwise inaccessible sources of information, hence building trust where misgivings may be prevalent among vulnerable populations. The safety of these spaces allows vocalization of oppression, encouraging women's engagement as agents of change.

The circumstances of oppression are not bounded by group identification. What impacts a Guinean woman also impacts the humanitarian worker. The fears associated with contracting the disease are shared. While one may be severely impacted after having survived the disease, the other is fearful of contracting it.

Conclusion

The mechanisms required to ensure rapid deployment of public health strategies in response to emerging infectious disease (Kudchodkar et al., 2018) are well established (Kudchodkar et al., 2018). However, lessons learned from the successes and failures of the public health initiatives in the course of the EVD outbreak in West Africa (Fidler, 2015; Dawson, 2015; Honigsbaum, 2017) provide compelling evidence that cultural and contextual adaptation of targeted public health strategies is essential to outbreak management and that of its immediate and future impact.

References

Abramowitz, S. A., McLean, K. E., McKune, S. L., Bardosh, K. L., Fallah, M., Monger, J., … Omidian, P. A. (2015). Community-centered responses to Ebola in urban Liberia: The view from below. *PLoS Neglected Tropical Diseases, 9*(4), e0003706.

Ayalon, O. (2008). Beyond words–trauma-healing experience & methods in the wake of the tsunami disaster. *Community Stress Prevention, 6*, 32–40.

Bava, S., Saul, J., Gow, K. M., & Celinski, M. J. (2013). Implementing collective approaches to massive trauma/loss in western contexts. In K. M. Gow & M. J. Celinski (Eds.), *Mass trauma: Impact and recovery issues*. New York, NY: Nova Science Publishers.

Bedrosian, S. R., Young, C. E., Smith, L. A., Cox, J. D., Manning, C., Pechta, L., … Daniel, K. L. (2016). Lessons of risk communication and health promotion – West Africa and United States. *Morbidity and Mortality Weekly Report, 65*(3), 68–74.

Dawson, A. J. (2015). Ebola: What it tells us about medical ethics. *Journal of Medical Ethics, 41*(1), 107–110.

Elliott, C., & Greenberg, J. (2008). *Communication in question: Competing perspectives on controversial issues in communication studies*. Toronto, ON: Thomson Nelson.

Erikson, K. (1976). *Everything in its path: Destruction of Buffalo Creek*. New York, NY: Simon and Schuster.

Erikson, K. T. (1994). *A new species of trouble: The human experience of modern disasters*. New York, NY: W. W. Norton.

Espinola, M., Shultz, J. M., Espinel, Z., Althouse, B. M., Cooper, J. L., Baingana, F., ... Rechkemmer, A. (2016). Fear-related behaviors in situations of mass threat. *Disaster Health, 3*(4), 102–111.

Fidler, D. P. (2015). Epic failure of Ebola and Global Health Security. *The Brown Journal of World Affairs, 21*(2), 180.

Greene, M. C., Jordans, M. J. D., Kohrt, B. A., Ventevogel, P., Kirmayer, L. J., Hassan, G., ... Tol, W. A. (2017). Addressing culture and context in humanitarian response: Preparing desk reviews to inform mental health and psychosocial support. *Conflict and Health, 11*, 21.

Guidry, J. P. D., Jin, Y., Orr, C. A., Messner, M., & Meganck, S. (2017). Ebola on Instagram and Twitter: How health organizations address the health crisis in their social media engagement. *Public Relations Review, 43*(3), 477–486.

Honigsbaum, M. (2017). Between securitisation and neglect: Managing Ebola at the borders of global health. *Medical History, 61*(2), 270–294.

Joffe, H., & Haarhoff, G. (1982). Representations of far-flung illnesses: The case of Ebola in Britain. *Social Science & Medicine, 54*(6), 955–969.

Ki, M. (2014). What do we really fear? The epidemiological characteristics of Ebola and our preparedness. *Epidemiology and Health, 36*, e2014014.

Kpanake, L., Gossou, K., Sorum, P. C., & Mullet, E. (2016). Misconceptions about Ebola virus disease among lay people in Guinea: Lessons for community education. *Journal of Public Health Policy, 37*(2), 160–172.

Kudchodkar, S. B., Choi, H., Reuschel, E. L., Esquivel, R., Jin-Ah Kwon, J., Jeong, M., ... Muthumani, K. (2018). Rapid response to an emerging infectious disease – lessons learned from development of a synthetic DNA vaccine targeting Zika virus. *Microbes and Infection.* https://doi.org/10.1016/j.micinf.2018.03.001

Landry, J. T., Foreman, T., & Kekewich, M. (2015). Reconsidering the ethical permissibility of the use of unregistered interventions against Ebola virus disease. *Cambridge Quarterly of Healthcare Ethics, 24*(3), 366–369.

Nuriddin, A., Jalloh, M. F., Meyer, E., Bunnell, R., Bio, F. A., Jalloh, M. B., ... Morgan, O. (2015). Trust, fear, stigma and disruptions: Community perceptions and experiences during periods of low but ongoing transmission of Ebola virus disease in Sierra Leone. *BMJ Globalization and Health, 3*(2), e000410.

Rosenfeld, L. B., Caye, J. S., Ayalon, O., & Lahad, M. (2005). *When their world falls apart: Helping families and children manage the effects of disasters.* Washington, DC: NASW Press.

Royo-Bordonada, M. Á., & García López, F. J. (2016). Ethical considerations surrounding the response to Ebola: The Spanish experience. *BMC Medical Ethics, 17*(1), 49.

Saul, J. (2014). *Collective trauma, collective healing: Promoting community resilience in the aftermath of a disaster.* New York, NY: Routledge.

Schol, L. G. C., Mollers, M., Swaan, C. M., Beaujean, D., Wong, A., & Timen, A. (2018). Knowledge, perceptions and media use of the Dutch general public and healthcare workers regarding Ebola, 2014. *BMC Infectious Diseases, 18*(1), 18.

Semalulu, T., Wong, G., Kobinger, G., & Huston, P. (2014). Why has the Ebola outbreak in West Africa been so challenging to control? *Canada Communicable Disease Report, 40*(14), 290–298.

Shrivastava, S. R., Shrivastava, P. S., & Ramasamy, J. (2015). Public health interventions to prevent the international spread of Ebola virus disease. *International Journal of Advanced Medical and Health Research, 2*(2), 142–143.

Smith, M. J., & Silva, D. S. (2015). Ethics for pandemics beyond influenza: Ebola, drug-resistant tuberculosis, and anticipating future ethical challenges in pandemic preparedness and response. *Monash Bioethics Review, 33*(2), 130–147.

Southall, H. G., DeYoung, S. E., & Harris, C. A. (2017). Lack of cultural competency in international aid responses: The Ebola outbreak in Liberia. *Frontiers in Public Health, 5*, 5.

Wessells, M., & Strang, A. (2006). Religion as resource and risk : the double-edged sword for children in situations of armed conflict. In N. Boothby, A. Strang, & M. Wessels (Eds.), *A world turned upside down: Social ecological approaches to children in war zones.* Bloomfield, CT: Kumarian Press.

Winters, M., Jalloh, M. F., Sengeh, P., Jalloh, M. B., Conteh, L., Bunnell, R., ... Nordenstedt, H. (2018). Risk communication and Ebola-specific knowledge and behavior during 2014–2015 outbreak, Sierra Leone. *Emerging Infectious Diseases, 24,* 336.

Index

A
African personality, 149
Amazing Mother Syndrome, 63
Americas region, 78
Animal Assisted Therapy Program, 20
Argentine Forensic Anthropology Team
    (EAAF), 37

B
Bateson, G., 123, 131, 132
Bellicose foreign policies, 83
Bioconstitutionalism
   absolute certainty, 38
   actors, 38
   analytics of raciality, 42
   DNA samples, 37
   EAAF, 37
   empowerment, 40
   experimentation, 40
   forensic anthropologists, 39
   forensic humanitarian professionals, 38
   global publics, 39
   ICRC principles, 41
   institutions and audiences, 41
   international workers, 40
   objective fact, 39
   populations, 37
   professionalism, 41
   public-private relations, 38
   scales, 37
   scientific and legal, 37
   scientific methods, 41
   scientific objectification, 39
   socio-technical configurations, 40
   SOP, 38, 39
   transitions, 38
   valuation, 40
Blake proclamation, 140

C
Canadian winters and Guinean rains, 161
Caribbean bear testimony, 79
Child marriage legislation, 83
CING's Laboratory of Forensic Genetics
    (LabFoG), 37
Circles of vulnerability, 161
Clinical skills training, 12
CNN Town Hall, 16, 17
Cognitive and behavioral therapy, 71
Cold War, 77
Collectivist culture, 159
Committee on Missing Persons (CMP), 37
Communication, 130
Communication information technologies, 24
Communities
  mapping risk and resilience
    cartographic conventions, 28
    citizen-based actions, 29
    countermapping, 29
    creating knowledge, 30
    geographical model, 28
    inhabitants, 30
    interdisciplinary team, 28
    interpretation, 27
    natural/anthropocentric hazard, 30
    radical geography, 27
    relational minds, 30, 31
    satellite images, 28

Communities (*cont.*)
    semi-professional and professional
      drone, 30
    socio-environmental conditions, 28
    tridimensional map, 29
Community-based mapping, 28
Community Counseling Service (CCS), 53
Community participation, 24
Complex emergencies, 1, 2
Consensus's structural adjustment
    mechanisms, 92
Contextual and cultural factors, 155
Convention on the Rights of the Child
    (CRC), 89
Couple and family therapy (CFT), 4
Courageous Conversations, 19
Cultural competence, 157
Cultural Congruence, 156–157
Cybernetic vocabulary, 132
Cyprus Institute of Neurology and Genetics
    (CING), 37

D
Department of Immigration and Customs
    Enforcement, 59
*Diagnostic and Statistical Manual of Mental
    Disorders*, 62, 64
Disasters
    discursive and narrative therapies, 26
    education, preparedness and mitigation, 25
    hierarchical approach, 25
    interventions, 25
    militaristic and bureaucratic approach, 25
    repair and rebuild approach, 25
    resilient approach, 25
    risk reduction strategy, 25
    social inequality, 25
    transdisciplinary approach, 25
    validating/challenging inequity, 26
Domestic worker, 81
Dominican Republic (DR), 87
Double bind, 131–134, 138
Drama therapy, 71
DroneLab, 29, 31

E
Ebola epidemic, 145, 150
Ebola epidemic outbreak, 145
Ebola infection, 154, 159
Ebola virus disease (EVD), 93, 127
    culture, 152
    epidemic, 153

    fatality, 154
    fears and uncertainties, 153
    infections and deaths, 152
    logistical challenge, 152
    prevention and risk reduction, 151
    secondary impact, 153
    transmission, 151
    West Africa, 151
Ein El Hilweh Palestine refugee camp
    (EHC), 70
Emerging media, 24, 26, 27
Emerging technologies, 23
Employment, 155
English-speaking Caribbean, 80
Euroamerican psychotherapeutic approach, 8
European colonial powers, 85
Evolutionary theory, 82
Exogamy, 146
Expert knowledge, 24

F
Face-to-face training, 124
Family and Human Systems Studies, 70–71
Family connection, 23
Family psychological history, 154
Family systems approaches (FSAs)
    client families and communities, 5
    client's appreciation, 4
    community workers, 111
    concept of family, 110
    concepts, 119
    counsellors, 6
    couple and family interventions, 4
    disruptors, 8, 9
    DNA testing, 8
    educative and entertaining, 107
    evidence, 4
    evidence-based approach, 5
    experimental research, 4
    facilitator, 104, 106
    female preschool teachers, 112
    foreign expats, 7
    geopolitical differences, 7
    geopolitical locations, 6
    LGBT, 111
    MHPSS, 119
    multi-, trans-, and interdisciplinary
      innovation, 5
    observers, 106
    policy level, 8
    portfolio of approaches, 5
    practitioners and reviewers, 120
    principles, 120

process, 110
psychotherapeutic intervention, 3
    challenges, 2
    clinical session, 2
    family psychosocial health and state
        policy, 3
    family therapist, 2
    global cross-, trans-, and
        interdisciplinary collaboration, 3
    global mental health practice, 3
    HICs, 2
    humanitarian settings, 3
    psychosocial health, 2
    refugees, 3
    resources, 3
    substantial unlearning and relearning, 3
    systemic intervention, 3
pure brand version therapy, 5
qualitative evidence, 5
qualitative meta-synthesis, 4
reflection groups, 110
social inequality, 8
socio-cultural, political and historical
        factors, 7
spatial migratory issue, 7
stigma, 7
systemic approaches, 4, 5
theories and principles, 120
tools and strategies, 105
transdisciplinary professionals, 6
transportability, 1, 2
unconventional sensibility, 6
volunteers, 104
Family systems therapy (FST), 99
Family therapy, 75, 76
Family-therapy trained practitioners, 137
Female genital mutilation (FGM), 146
Foreign policy failure, 86
Fragile, conflict and violence-affected states
        (FCVs), 2

G
Gender-based inequities, 85
Gender inequity, 82
Geohistorical situation, 70
Global mental health practice, 3
Global South humanitarian project, 37
Government control agencies, 24
Gross domestic product (GDP), 125
Guinea's socialist cultural revolution, 149
Guinean concentration camps, 150
Guinean counterparts, 157
Guinean-French psychotherapist, 146

Guinean population, 146
Gun control, 17, 20, 21

H
High-income country (HIC), 2
Hindu Marriage Act of 1945, 89
Homines oeconomici, 40
Hopes Chart, 116
Human Development Report (HDR), 79
Human rights, 92
Human rights and gender, 90
Human security, 79
    cultural violence, 84
    elements, 80
    evolution, 81
    gender-based violence, 84
    gender-status beliefs, 82
    HIV and AIDS, 81
    principles, 80
    violence, 84
Human security framework, 90
Humane Society of Broward County, 20
Humanitarian crisis, 3
Humanitarian deployment, 24
Humanitarian projects, DNA identification
    bioconstitutionalism
        (*see* Bioconstitutionalism)
    forensics, 35–37
    mediators, 42–44
    stutters, ruptures and healing
        anti-memories, 50
        biotechnological response, 49
        capital's limitations, 46
        cognitive dissonance, 47
        commemorative ceremony and physical
            interment, 47
        decolonization, 48
        enslavement and colonization, 45, 46
        governance process, 48
        grappling, 48
        Greek Cypriot, 48
        guarantors, 46
        historico-epistemological production, 46
        innovations, 47
        interlocutors, 45, 50
        lamentation, 50
        liberal imperialist epistemology and
            ontology, 47
        minority and majority racialized
            populations, 49
        nation, 44
        palimpsest, 45
        paralysis, 47

Humanitarian projects, DNA
        identification (*cont.*)
    personhood and physical-moral
        aspects, 45
    transgressions, 45
    transitional sites, 46
    transnational player, 47
    violence, 35
Humanitarian settings, 2
Humanitarianism, 36
Hurricanes, 11, 13–15, 21
Hypnotherapy, 129

I
Intense national media coverage, 11
International aid agency, 160
International Committee of the Red Cross
        (ICRC), 37
International humanitarian law (IHL), 36
International Labour Organization (ILO), 78

L
Latin American immigrants, 53
Legitimacy, 131
Lesbian-gay-bi-transgender (LGBT)
        groups, 99
Low and middle income countries
        (LMIC), 2

M
Maoist cultural revolution, 148
Marriage and Family Therapy Club, 13
Master's in marriage and family therapy
        program (MS in MFT), 12
McKinsey Global Institute, 79
Mental health and psycho-social support
        (MHPSS), 144
    counselling and broader, 101
    family problems, 102
    implementation, 145
    professionals, 103
    resources, 103
    socio-political and economical changes, 101
    Sri Lanka, 102
    WHO, 102
Meta-communication, 132
Meta-conversation, 123
Meta-humility, 132
Metaphors, 69, 71, 75, 76
    application, 69
    EHC, 70

    proverbs, 69
    psychotherapist, 71
    refugees, 70
Military violence and economic hardships, 86
Ministry of Health, 144, 148
Mourning process and commemoration, 42, 43
Multiculturalism, 89
Muslim Marriage and Divorce Act of 1961, 89

N
National Child Traumatic Stress Network
        (NCTSN), 19
National Rifle Association, 17
National Union of Domestic Employees
        (NUDE), 82
National Weather Service, 13
Natural events, 23
Naturalisation Law, 87
Neurology Center in Cyprus, 40
Non-communicable diseases (NCDs), 93
Nova Southeastern University (NSU), 12, 14

O
Of One Mind, 127
Oppression and colonization, 161
Organization of American States (OAS), 87

P
Palestine refugees from Syria (PRS), 70
Palestine refugees in Lebanon (PRL), 70
Palestinian political universe, 70
Palestinian refugees, 69
Pan American Health Organization (PAHO), 78
Parkland school shooting
    allegations, 18
    campus-based family therapy clinic, 16
    connectedness, 17
    couple therapy class, 15
    faith-based work, 16
    licensed professionals, 16
    media coverage, 16
    online support group, 18
    PFA, 17
    political turmoil, 17
    students and faculty, 16
Participatory mapping, 28
People-centered foreign policy, 93
Poblaciones, 27
Post-conflict zones, 40
Post-Ebola inflammation, 160
Pragmatism, 158

PROMISE program, 12, 13, 16, 18–20
Psychological first aid (PFA), 16, 17, 19
Psychological functioning, 17
Psychosocial practitioners, 111
Psychosocial problems, 154
Psychotherapy studies, 70
Public health communication and education, 148
Public-health efforts, 156

Q
Qualitative evidence, 5

R
Raciality, 42
Red Cross volunteers, 152
Reflection team, 106
Relational Suicide Assessment, 138
Research Center for Integrated Disaster
    Risk Management in Chile
    (CIGIDEN), 28
Resilience Center, 20, 21

S
School shooting, 11
Sex/gender-based violence (SGBV), 94
Shared community, 11
Sidon-Lebanon refugee camp, 72
Single-session letter
    biopsychosocial evaluation, 61
    implications
        advocating for change, 65
        global experience, 63
        power of hope, 64
        strengths-based therapy, 64
        tearing down walls, 64
    mentorship, 65
    motherhood, 62
    physical violence, 61
    posttraumatic growth, 63
    psychological diagnoses, 63
    T-VISA, 61
    undocumented applicants, 61
Skype, 124, 128, 138
Slave-descended communities, 85
Slavery and colonialism, 85
Small Island Developing States (SIDS), 8
Social justice, 11, 12
Social media, 14, 19
Social networks, 24
Societal context, 13
Socioreligious system, 150

Solution-focused therapy (SFT), 158
Sri Lanka Medical Council (SLMC), 102
Sri Lankan society, 99
Standard operating procedures (SOPs), 38
Statelessness, 88
Strength-based approach, 158
Strengths-based counseling
    biopsychosocial evaluation, 56
    co-constructed list, 58
    distress, 57
    emotional and psychological distress, 56
    family's collective distress, 56
    fighting, 57
    historical and legal context, 58, 59
    immigration policy and reform, 58
    mental health workers, 59–61
    session transcription, 56
    undocumented families, 55
    vocational calling, 57
Stress management, 12, 17
Sunjata Epic, 147, 148
Supervisory consultation, 7
Sustainable Development Goal 3 (SDG 3), 78
Syria, 123–125, 127–129, 138
Syrian Arab regime, 70
Syrian civil war, 70
Syrian refugees, 69
Syrian training, 124
Syrian war, 124
Systemic family therapy, 8, 9

T
Tale of Cinderella, 74
Touré's revolutionary ideologies, 149
Toward a Theory of Schizophrenia, 131
Trafficking visa (T-VISA), 61
Trance, 136
Trauma
    administrative and accreditation, 21
    cohesive community, 19
    community services, 20
    culturally sensitive family therapists, 19
    direct and vicarious symptoms, 20
    dissertation group, 18
    microaggression, 18
    national media, 20
    PFA, 19
    physical and social landscape, 21
    political landscape, 21
    school shootings, 18
    self-care, 20
    social media, 19
    survivors, 19

Trauma-based services, 12
Traumatic event, 124
Turkish Cypriot community, 36

U
U.N. High Commissioner for Refugees
        (UNHCR), 86
U.N. Human Rights Council, 87
Undocumented immigration
    biopsychosocial evaluations, 54
    co-creation, 55
    co-responsibility, 55
    culture and personal beliefs, 55
    and deportation, 53
    individual and group therapy, 54
    magical realism, 55
    master's and doctoral training stems, 54

shared family history, 54
single-session mindset, 54, 55
strengths-based counseling, 55–58
trauma, 54
United Nations specialised agency, 78

V
Vicarious trauma, 135

W
Whats App program, 14
Whole-of-government approach, 90
Wordlessness and breathlessness, 124
World Health Organization (WHO),
        4, 123
World War II, 148

Printed by Printforce, the Netherlands